The Deregulation
of the World Financial Markets

THE Deregulation OF THE
World Financial Markets

MYTHS, REALITIES, AND IMPACT

Sarkis J. Khoury

Q
Quorum Books

NEW YORK · WESTPORT, CONNECTICUT · LONDON

Library of Congress Cataloging-in-Publication Data

Khoury, Sarkis J.
    The deregulation of the world financial markets : myths,
realities, and impact / Sarkis J. Khoury.
        p.   cm.
    Includes bibliographical references (p.).
    ISBN 0–89930–455–9 (lib. bdg. : alk. paper)
    1. Financial institutions—Deregulation.   I. Title.
HG174.K47   1990
332.1—dc20   89–27238

British Library Cataloguing in Publication Data is available.

Library of Congress Catalog Card Number: 89–27238
ISBN: 0–89930–455–9

First published in 1990 by Quorum Books

Greenwood Press, Inc.
88 Post Road West, Westport, Connecticut 06881

Printed in the United States of America

The paper used in this book complies with the
Permanent Paper Standard issued by the National
Information Standards Organization (Z39.48–1984).

10 9 8 7 6 5 4 3 2

To: Mona for her touch
Leila for her intellect
Natalie for her charm
Alexandra for her madness

Contents

Exhibits

Preface

The deregulation of financial markets began in the mid-1960s, accelerated in the 1970s, and exploded in the 1980s. It cut across national borders, cultures, and government strategies and philosophies. Even the insular Chinese have felt its effects. This deregulation represents the most dramatic revolution of the twentieth century, with soldiers in glass towers wearing ties and not military uniforms.

This book examines in great detail the deregulatory steps taken in major financial markets, their impetus, their potency, and their effects on the operational, promotional, and allocational efficiencies of financial markets; the effects of deregulation on the riskiness/stability and the integration of financial markets and the movement toward political and economic integration are also reviewed.

Deregulatory developments in three major financial markets—the United States, Britain, Japan—and in a few other representative markets—Australia, Hong Kong, and Canada—are examined. The nature of the developments in these markets and the relationship among them are scrutinized, as is the impact of deregulation therein. Of particular concern are the dynamics of the deregulation process and the forces that generated it in each market.

This book represents the continuation of a commitment to the study of the inner workings of the international financial markets and the relationships among them. This commitment began with my Ph.D. thesis and has been demonstrated in recent years in the continuing symposium I organize with Alo Ghosh on "Recent Developments in International Banking and Finance." This symposium started in 1986 and has thus far produced three volumes (one per symposium), dealing with the major aspects of international banking and finance.

Bankers should find this book as useful as academicians and regulators will. It could serve as supplementary reading for an introductory international finance course or as the main reading for an advanced international finance/banking course. Bankers would benefit from the review of the developments and opportunities in each financial market and the implications of these factors for the banking industry and the economy as a whole. Regulators would benefit from the analysis of the interrelationships among various policy options/initiatives and from the impact studies of regulation, deregulation, and reregulation.

This study turned out to be much more difficult than originally anticipated. It seemed that no matter how hard I worked and how many individuals I involved in the research, I never had the feeling that the entire information set was accounted for. The literature on deregulation and the developments in the international financial markets in terms of products and strategies are so dynamic that unexpected major events appear to take place every day, with wide-ranging implications for the financial markets. I have decided, therefore, to concentrate on the major trends and products and leave the rest to another book, perhaps.

The enormity of the task was made bearable through the assistance of many outstanding individuals. I benefited considerably from discussions with Maurice Levi, Ron Giammarino, and Moshe Kim of the University of British Columbia (UBC). The research assistance provided by Suherman Sentosa, William Daniel, Yo Soo Yong, Bahman Soltani, Ted Johnson, and others too numerous to count has been excellent, and I feel a deep sense of gratitude to these individuals. The financial support arranged by Ilan Vertinsky of UBC is gratefully acknowledged. Joyce Khoury and Lynn Scheltens helped considerably in the editing and typing of the manuscript, and I owe them many thanks for their work and patience.

The above named individuals, while extremely helpful, do not bear the burden of the errors, if any, in the manuscript. These, unfortunately, are mine, and mine alone, to bear.

1

The Evolution of Worldwide Deregulation of Financial Markets: New Concepts, Strategies, and Products

It began as a trickle, and it turned into a tidal wave. It overwhelmed laid-back investment managers, slow-to-react regulators, protected markets, and archaic ideologies that insisted that dirigisme is inherently superior to and more stable than a free market in which participants use their talents and unconstrained imaginations to maximize portfolio returns while keeping risk in check.

The transformation of the financial markets since the mid-1960s has gone beyond anyone's expectations. What used to be seen as fiction, that only the likes of Isaac Asimov could conceive, became a stunning reality, leading investment managers and bankers to reexamine the very foundation of their ideas and strategies. Much of the transformation, interestingly, was neither planned nor predicted. No one we are aware of predicted that the Dow Jones Industrial Average would surpass the 2,700 mark; that the cumulative federal deficit could mushroom from $1 trillion to $2.6 trillion in less than eight years; that technology would make the execution of transactions all over the world virtually instantaneous; that the largest bank (in terms of assets), the largest exchange (in terms of total valuation), and the largest trading room would be Japanese; or that the largest creditor nation and the nation with the highest nonmilitary foreign aid would be Japan. Also, no one predicted that the U.S. dollar would depreciate by more than 60 percent against the Japanese yen in a period of less than four years, or that the stock market would lose 508 points (as measured by the Dow) in a single day—a 22.61 percent drop that was far greater than the 12.82 percent drop on October 28, 1929, that preceded the Great Depression. This wrenching experience did not help the market gurus to predict another huge drop, one of 190 points, on October 13, 1989. No one predicted that the debt crisis would be so severe, especially in terms of the timing of its occurrence and the inability of the financial system to provide a real and effective solution to it, or that hundreds of U.S. banks and savings institutions would collapse, leaving the Federal Deposit Insurance Corporation (FDIC) more vulnerable than ever in terms of its ability to contain the problem and reassure the public. Also, no one predicted the emergence of the junk bond market and its growth to $180 billion, or the size of the fines ($650 million) imposed by the Securities and Exchange Commission (SEC) on Drexel Burnham for federal securities laws violations, or the leveraged buyouts (LBOs)—a Wall Street term for taking a company private—that would amount to over $42 billion by the end of 1988. Most dramatically, no one anticipated that the cultural revolution of China would evaporate and be replaced by a system that partially endorses the free market concept, that Eastern Europe would confirm the bankruptcy of communism and the value of the democratic process, and that perestroika would be the modus operandi of the Soviet Union, making Orwell's prediction in *1984* that the world would ultimately evolve into three blocks (American, European, and Asian) an almost complete reality.

These dramatic changes left many mesmerized and scurrying to catch up with the events and their implications. It is no wonder, therefore, that over 300 seminars are successfully organized each year to help practitioners and academics stay in tune with market developments. The educational system was also restructured, often unwittingly, to train a new breed of money managers (mostly quantitative in their skills and orientation) and to give existing managers the necessary flexibility and information to cope. Those holding doctorates in finance, mathematics, computer science, and even physics were suddenly in great demand on Wall Street. Professors, initially disdained for their preoccupation with "academic" arguments, found themselves being offered huge salaries by investment banking and banking firms. The result is that the largest, and perhaps the best, finance departments may not be housed in academic institutions, but rather in investment banking firms.

The changes in the financial markets are not only wide and deep, but also truly international. Some dreams were broken, and new opportunities began to unfold, creating untold fortunes for some, losses for others, and penalties and growth opportunities in the process.

Abundant evidence of the international character of the revolution in the financial markets can be found in the banking industry, the investment banking industry, the money markets, and the capital markets. It is also found in the intensive and extensive use of technology and in the educational system as MBA programs proliferate throughout Europe and even in China.

THE BANKING INDUSTRY

The banking industry has become truly international. In fact, one can argue that in 1988, purely domestic banks became extinct, especially as the interbank market continued to mushroom. The national barriers to foreign banks have crumbled, and the signs of Tokai, Sanwa, and other Japanese banks dot the

California landscape. These institutions compete with their American counter-parts on every level and operate under the same rules and conditions since the passage of the International Banking Act of 1978. Exhibit 1.1 shows the level of involvement of foreign banks in the U.S. banking industry. This involvement is even greater if the data are broken up on a regional basis. As indicated in Exhibit 1.1, the total assets of large, weekly reporting U.S. branches and agencies of foreign banks in the United States amounted to $171.9 billion at the end of November 1988. This represented 12.49 percent of the total assets ($1,376 billion) of large, weekly reporting commercial banks in the United States. Over 260 foreign banks were operating in the United States during 1989 with assets equal to 21 percent of the total U.S. domestic banking industry.

The U.S. banking industry was no less aggressive internationally. In fact, U.S. banks, led by Citicorp and Chase Manhattan, were the first truly international banks. The total assets of foreign branches of U.S. banks amounted to $493.7 billion at the end of October 1988 (Exhibit 1.2), almost three times the size of foreign bank assets in the United States. Over two-thirds of these assets are denominated in U.S. dollars. The currency distribution of the liabilities is prac-tically the same.

The geographical distribution of the assets and liabilities of foreign branches of U.S. banks is concentrated in a few countries. In October 1988, the assets in the London branches alone accounted for 31.5 percent of all assets in foreign branches. The assets booked in the Bahamas and the Cayman Islands accounted for 31.45 percent of all such assets. The rest of these assets are distributed around the world, with increasing emphasis on the Far East, especially Japan. The geographic distribution of the liabilities was similar to that of the assets. The reasons for these distributions are quite well known. London is the hub of international activities for Europe and the world, and the home of the Eurocur-rency markets. The Bahamas and the Cayman Islands are most attractive because of their favorable tax laws.

Exhibit 1.2 tells only part of the story. U.S. banks are involved even more extensively in international activities through loans to home and foreign multina-tional corporations through their Edge Act subsidiaries and through their interna-tional banking facilities (IBFs).

The fact that U.S. or British banks are international is neither new, nor dramat-ic. What is dramatic, however, is the multinationalization of the Japanese bank-ing and investment banking industries and the penetration of the Japanese bank-ing industry by foreign banks. In 1988, 6,988 foreign bank employees worked in Japan, looking after the assets of 79 foreign banks totaling ¥16,599,021 mil-lion, up from only ¥7,777 million in 1979. Foreign bank assets in Japan ac-counted for only 2.56 percent of total Japanese banking assets in December 1987. Foreign assets of Japanese banks, however, accounted for 22.05 percent of their total assets in December 1987. Therefore, the door to the Japanese banking market is only ajar. It is a long way from being wide open, but the trends are in that direction.

The international expansion of Japanese banks is another remarkable trend of

Exhibit 1.1

Large, Weekly Reporting U.S. Branches and Agencies of Foreign Banks:[1] Assets and Liabilities, 1988

(Millions of dollars, Wednesday figures)

Account		1988								
		Oct. 5	Oct. 12	Oct. 19	Oct. 26	Nov. 2	Nov. 9	Nov. 16	Nov. 23	Nov. 30
1	Cash and due from depository institutions	10,810	10,389	11,434	10,286	11,233	12,579	11,887	11,126	10,817
2	Total loans and securities	111,005	109,214	111,938	109,648	111,506	111,583	112,279	110,161	112,853
3	U.S. Treasury and government agency securities	7,978	8,035	7,756	7,760	7,885	7,751	7,834	7,546	7,651
4	Other securities	7,178	7,186	7,320	7,315	7,288	7,237	7,242	7,202	7,259
5	Federal funds sold[2]	8,064	7,583	10,198	9,290	8,489	9,036	10,864	7,293	10,173
6	To commercial banks in the United States	5,690	5,201	7,972	6,852	5,823	6,729	8,861	5,465	7,878
7	To others	2,374	2,382	2,226	2,437	2,666	2,307	2,003	1,828	2,294
8	Other loans, gross	87,785	86,410	86,663	85,283	87,843	87,558	86,340	88,120	87,771
9	Commercial and industrial	56,508ʳ	55,974ʳ	55,384ʳ	55,229ʳ	56,483	55,888	55,485	55,635	56,064
10	Bankers acceptances and commercial paper	1,679	1,595	1,617	1,630	1,555	1,604	1,689	1,736	1,554
11	All other	54,829ʳ	54,378ʳ	53,767ʳ	53,599ʳ	54,928	54,283	53,797	53,899	54,511
12	U.S. addressees	53,093ʳ	52,758ʳ	52,185ʳ	51,931ʳ	53,223	52,608	52,224	52,279	52,871
13	Non-U.S. addressees	1,736	1,620	1,582	1,668	1,704	1,675	1,573	1,620	1,640
14	To financial institutions	17,212	16,615	17,759	16,460	17,062	17,078	16,136	17,424	16,307
15	Commercial banks in the United States	13,114	12,330	13,462	12,372	12,648	12,773	11,902	13,038	12,018
16	Banks in foreign countries	1,025	974	1,247	1,133	1,350	1,174	1,157	1,221	1,220
17	Nonbank financial institutions	3,074	3,311	3,050	2,955	3,065	3,130	3,076	3,166	3,070
18	To foreign governments and official institutions	639	642	637	548	621	743	820	801	830
19	For purchasing and carrying securities	1,647	1,432	1,238	1,235	1,611	1,467	1,449	1,805	1,761
20	All other	11,779ʳ	11,748ʳ	11,645ʳ	11,810ʳ	12,066	12,382	12,448	12,455	12,808
21	Other assets (claims on nonrelated parties)	30,253	30,248	30,166	30,442	30,628	31,572	32,296	32,715	33,025
22	Net due from related institutions	17,264	16,149	17,907	18,220	17,526	16,796	14,936	18,101	15,233
23	Total assets	169,331	166,000	171,546	168,596	170,893	172,529	171,399	172,104	171,928
24	Deposits or credit balances due to other than directly related institutions	44,095	44,238ʳ	43,954	44,232	43,758	43,029	43,390	43,941	44,179

25 Transaction accounts and credit balances[3]	3,785	3,820	3,836	4,393	4,549	3,642	4,301	3,888	3,954
26 Individuals, partnerships, and corporations	2,459	2,471	2,486	2,613	2,655	2,350	2,882	2,497	2,451
27 Other	1,326	1,349	1,350	1,780	1,894	1,292	1,418	1,391	1,503
28 Nontransaction accounts[4]	40,310	40,417ʳ	40,118	39,838	39,209	39,387	39,089	40,053	40,225
29 Individuals, partnerships, and corporations	33,344	33,443ʳ	33,308	33,030	32,723	32,891	32,634	33,630	33,713
30 Other	6,966	6,974	6,809	6,808	6,486	6,496	6,455	6,423	6,512
31 Borrowings from other than directly related institutions	69,346	67,445	72,608	69,962	69,132	70,561	68,504	67,646	68,197
32 Federal funds purchased[5]	34,338	33,094	35,647	35,242	33,914	33,385	31,479	24,603	31,021
33 From commercial banks in the United States	19,425	16,299	18,337	19,373	17,088	17,674	16,307	12,087	16,454
34 From others	14,914	16,795	17,309	15,869	16,826	15,712	15,172	12,516	14,567
35 Other liabilities for borrowed money	35,007	34,351	36,961	34,720	35,218	37,176	37,024	43,043	37,176
36 To commercial banks in the United States	24,526	23,776	26,219	23,552	23,628	25,763	25,668	28,072	25,744
37 To others	10,481	10,575	10,742	11,168	11,590	11,413	11,356	14,971	11,432
38 Other liabilities to nonrelated parties	31,423	31,387	31,439	31,354	31,582	32,911	33,837	33,964	34,168
39 Net due to related institutions	24,468	22,931ʳ	23,546	23,048	26,420	26,028	25,668	26,552	25,383
40 Total liabilities	169,331	166,000	171,546	168,596	170,893	172,529	171,399	172,104	171,928
MEMO									
41 Total loans (gross) and securities adjusted[6]	92,202	91,683	90,504	90,424	93,035	92,081	91,516	91,659	92,957
42 Total loans (gross) adjusted[6]	77,045	76,462	75,427	75,348	77,862	77,092	76,440	76,910	78,048

1. Effective Jan. 1, 1986, the reporting panel includes 65 U.S. branches and agencies of foreign banks that include those branches and agencies with assets of $750 million or more on June 30, 1980, plus those branches and agencies that had reached the $750 million asset level on Dec. 31, 1984. These data also appear in the Board's H.4.2 (504) release.

2. Includes securities purchased under agreements to resell.

3. Includes credit balances, demand deposits, and other checkable deposits.

4. Includes savings deposits, money market deposit accounts, and time deposits.

5. Includes securities sold under agreements to repurchase.

6. Exclusive of loans to and federal funds sold to commercial banks in the United States.

Source: Federal Reserve Bulletin (February 1989): A21.

Exhibit 1.2
Foreign Branches of U.S. Banks: Balance Sheet Data,[1] 1985–1988 (Millions of dollars, end of period)

All foreign countries

Asset account	1985	1986	1987	1988 Apr.	May	June	July	Aug.	Sept.	Oct.[p]
1 Total, all currencies	458,012	456,628	518,618	488,939	492,844	487,677	488,283	487,895	490,582	493,728
2 Claims on United States	119,706	114,563	138,034	139,176	141,790	140,932	147,662	157,021	155,386	155,281
3 Parent bank	87,201	83,492	105,845	102,957	104,299	104,405	109,929	117,525	115,286	115,954
4 Other banks in United States	13,057	13,685	16,416	13,332	14,625	14,424	15,954	16,176	16,121	14,593
5 Nonbanks	19,448	17,386	15,773	22,887	22,866	22,103	21,779	23,320	23,979	24,734
6 Claims on foreigners	315,676	312,955	342,520	314,348	315,302	311,308	305,556	295,270	298,466	301,105
7 Other branches of parent bank	91,399	96,281	122,155	103,090	102,931	106,722	103,646	98,299	102,355	100,609
8 Banks	102,960	105,237	108,859	101,233	103,427	100,669	99,660	98,982	98,563	102,208
9 Public borrowers	23,478	23,706	21,832	20,827	20,991	20,438	19,276	18,709	18,444	18,205
10 Nonbank foreigners	97,839	87,731	89,674	89,198	87,953	83,479	82,974	79,280	79,104	80,083
11 Other assets	22,630	29,110	38,064	35,415	35,752	35,437	35,065	35,604	36,730	37,342
12 Total payable in U.S. dollars	336,520	317,487	350,107	327,736	334,112	334,990	336,233	342,906	340,901	337,346
13 Claims on United States	116,638	110,620	132,023	133,289	136,078	135,348	141,415	151,581	149,764	149,562
14 Parent bank	85,971	82,082	103,251	100,320	101,578	101,422	106,792	114,943	112,621	113,569
15 Other banks in United States	12,454	12,830	14,657	12,318	13,600	13,661	14,434	14,901	14,687	13,114
16 Nonbanks	18,213	15,708	14,115	20,651	20,900	20,265	20,189	21,737	22,456	22,879
17 Claims on foreigners	210,129	195,063	202,428	179,722	182,980	183,568	179,076	174,433	174,271	171,717
18 Other branches of parent bank	72,727	72,197	88,284	75,654	76,136	79,774	78,071	73,792	76,506	73,508
19 Banks	71,868	66,421	63,707	54,588	57,102	55,234	54,189	54,839	52,503	54,793
20 Public borrowers	17,260	16,708	14,730	14,407	14,342	13,851	13,247	12,933	12,770	12,616
21 Nonbank foreigners	48,274	39,737	35,707	35,073	35,400	34,709	33,569	32,869	32,492	30,800
22 Other assets	9,753	11,804	15,656	14,725	15,054	16,074	15,742	16,892	16,866	16,067

6

United Kingdom

23 Total, all currencies	148,599	140,917	158,695	152,592	156,184	151,835	151,017	149,646	147,329	155,580
24 Claims on United States	33,157	24,599	32,518	31,618	32,832	33,852	35,708	36,307	32,048	36,210
25 Parent bank	26,970	19,085	27,350	26,155	27,506	28,535	30,615	30,767	26,661	30,569
26 Other banks in United States	1,106	1,612	1,259	1,013	1,360	1,322	1,064	1,197	1,238	994
27 Nonbanks	5,081	3,902	3,909	4,450	3,966	3,995	4,029	4,343	4,149	4,647
28 Claims on foreigners	110,217	109,508	115,700	112,261	114,452	107,856	105,594	103,527	105,824	109,793
29 Other branches of parent bank	31,576	33,422	39,903	33,019	33,849	32,446	30,228	29,656	31,758	33,103
30 Banks	39,250	39,468	36,735	38,790	39,883	37,108	37,805	38,259	38,848	40,236
31 Public borrowers	5,644	4,990	4,752	4,914	4,987	4,742	4,665	4,543	4,250	4,190
32 Nonbank foreigners	33,747	31,628	34,310	35,538	35,733	33,560	32,896	31,069	30,968	32,264
33 Other assets	5,225	6,810	10,477	8,713	8,900	10,127	9,715	9,812	9,457	9,577
34 Total payable in U.S. dollars	108,626	95,028	100,574	93,214	97,188	95,326	94,492	96,767	93,790	99,868
35 Claims on United States	32,092	23,193	30,439	29,555	30,736	31,855	33,795	34,535	30,116	34,134
36 Parent bank	26,568	18,526	26,304	25,137	26,608	27,672	29,706	29,837	25,692	29,667
37 Other banks in United States	1,005	1,475	1,044	781	1,068	1,069	870	1,039	910	606
38 Nonbanks	4,519	3,192	3,091	3,637	3,060	3,114	3,219	3,659	3,514	3,861
39 Claims on foreigners	73,475	68,138	64,560	59,434	62,018	57,969	55,832	57,037	58,474	61,034
40 Other branches of parent bank	26,011	26,361	28,635	24,867	25,448	23,843	22,549	22,465	24,472	25,703
41 Banks	26,139	23,251	19,188	18,065	19,555	17,477	18,025	19,165	19,066	20,488
42 Public borrowers	3,999	3,677	3,313	3,412	3,252	3,188	3,133	3,105	3,022	2,984
43 Nonbank foreigners	17,326	14,849	13,424	13,090	13,763	13,461	12,125	12,302	11,914	11,859
44 Other assets	3,059	3,697	5,575	4,225	4,434	5,502	4,865	5,195	5,200	4,700

Bahamas and Caymans

45 Total, all currencies	142,055	142,592	160,321	152,930	156,353	159,718	160,516	165,771	164,313	155,265
46 Claims on United States	74,864	78,048	85,318	88,283	90,896	88,116	92,308	99,090	99,541	94,301
47 Parent bank	50,553	54,575	60,048	59,240	60,419	58,579	61,397	67,034	66,607	62,709
48 Other banks in United States	11,204	11,156	14,277	11,470	12,489	12,236	13,863	13,967	13,878	12,353
49 Nonbanks	13,107	12,317	10,993	17,573	17,988	17,301	17,048	18,149	19,056	19,239
50 Claims on foreigners	63,882	60,005	70,162	58,818	59,374	65,855	62,508	60,822	57,887	54,630
51 Other branches of parent bank	19,042	17,296	21,277	17,790	18,463	24,745	22,797	20,789	20,320	17,331
52 Banks	28,192	27,476	33,751	26,700	27,019	27,650	26,120	26,866	24,545	25,463
53 Public borrowers	6,458	7,051	7,428	6,849	6,955	6,835	6,457	6,185	6,219	6,045
54 Nonbank foreigners	10,190	8,182	7,706	7,479	6,937	6,625	7,134	6,982	6,803	5,791
55 Other assets	3,309	4,539	4,841	5,829	6,083	5,747	5,700	5,859	6,885	6,334
56 Total payable in U.S. dollars	136,794	136,813	151,434	145,398	148,545	152,219	152,685	157,975	156,409	147,481

1. Beginning with June 1984 data, reported claims held by foreign branches have been reduced by an increase in the reporting threshold for "shell" branches from $50 million to $150 million equivalent in total assets, the threshold now applicable to all reporting branches.

Source: Federal Reserve Bulletin (February 1989), 57.

7

the 1980s. By the end of 1988, the international assets of Japanese banks had reached $129 billion.

THE EQUITY MARKETS

The transformation of the character of every equity market is historic. Today one can speak of raising funds internationally and be assured of real access to accumulated savings throughout the world. Trading in equities is truly a 24-hour market—reserved for well-established firms, however.

A report by Salomon Brothers, shown in Exhibit 1.3, clearly illustrates the enormous flow of equity funds across the major markets, including the size of the flows and the roles played by Japan and the United States. The inflows and outflows are not symmetric for many reasons, one of which is the barriers set up by some countries against a free flow of capital from foreign sources. Investors trading on exchanges other than their home exchanges have been very active. In 1987, foreigners accounted for 27.6 percent of total turnover on the Canadian exchanges, 24.2 percent on the Australian exchanges, 23.3 percent on the Spanish exchanges, and 22.8 percent on the U.K. exchanges.

The cross-listing of securities across national borders is now pervasive. At the end of 1987, 67 foreign companies, 28 of which were European, were listed on the New York Stock Exchange (NYSE) (Exhibit 1.4). The total market value of the securities was $84,153 million or 3.8 percent of the value of all equities listed on the New York Stock Exchange. The number of these companies had increased to 71 at the end of 1988.

The number of foreign companies trading in the over-the-counter NASDAQ system is much higher. The number of companies trading through American depository receipts (ADRs) on NASDAQ amounted to 95. And the number of companies trading as foreign common shares totaled 181 as of October 31, 1988. The overwhelming number (115) of these companies were Canadian.

The Tokyo Stock Exchange (TSE), the largest in the world in terms of valuation, has more foreign securities listed than the NYSE does. As of December 8, 1988, 109 foreign companies were trading on the TSE; of these, 68 were American, 16 British, 3 Dutch, 4 German, 5 Australian, and 6 Canadian. The American companies were almost universally large multinationals such as Citicorp, ITT, Proctor and Gamble, and Eastman Kodak.

The most international exchanges are the European, especially that in London (Exhibit 1.5). The international stock exchange in London consists of four markets: U.K. equities, international equities, gilts, and traded options. More than one-third (120) of its corporate membership is made up of non-U.K. securities houses. Of the 523 foreign securities traded in London, only 74 are from continental Europe. The remainder are largely U.S., Canadian, and Japanese.

The attraction of London stems from a long tradition of high standards of disclosure and excellent financial analysis, the strong reputation the city has acquired as a result of the incredible expansion in the Euromarket, and the competitive rates for listing and trading, especially after the Big Bang. Also

Exhibit 1.3
International Equity Flows

International Equity Flows — Gross Transactions, 1986
(US Dollars in Billions)

Investor from:

Market to:	United States	United Kingdom	Continental Europe	Japan	Rest of World[a]	Market Total
United States	—	$64.61	$78.27	$26.90	$107.73	**$277.51**
United Kingdom	$32.59	—	27.69	2.50	21.53	**84.31**
Continental Europe	22.27	44.03	73.86	3.86	44.45	**188.46**
Japan	25.62	50.00	59.52	—	54.43	**189.57**
Rest of World	21.06	15.00	18.94	1.52	4.42	**60.93**
Investor Total	**$101.53**	**$173.63**	**$258.26**	**$34.79**	**$232.57**	**$800.78**

[a] Includes "offshore" fund managers.

International Equity Flows — Net Transactions, First-Quarter 1988
(US Dollars in Billions)

Investor from:

Market to:	United States	United Kingdom	Continental Europe	Japan	Rest of World[a]	Market Total
United States	—	$(0.60)	$(0.31)	$1.07	$(0.92)	**$(0.75)**
United Kingdom	$(0.48)	—	0.01	(1.53)	2.01	**0.00**
Continental Europe	0.57	(0.78)	1.27	(0.01)	(1.68)	**(0.63)**
Japan	(1.01)	0.75	1.69	—	3.12	**6.57**
Rest of World	(0.21)	(0.39)	0.54	(0.10)	0.04	**(0.12)**
Investor Total	**$0.88**	**$(1.01)**	**$3.20**	**$(0.57)**	**$2.58**	**$5.08**

[a] Includes "offshore" fund managers.

Major World Equity Markets — Measures of Trading Activity, 1986-87
(US Dollars in Billions)

Market	Turnover		Foreigners As a Pct. of Total Turnover		Trading Ratio[a] by Nationals in:	
	Total	By Foreigners	1986	1987	Domestic Equities	Foreign Equities
Canada	$165.3	$45.7	23.9%	27.6%	16.0	38.5
United States	4,297.3	481.9	7.8	11.2	168.4	84.0
France	169.2	28.4	26.3	16.8	6.2	37.0
Netherlands	155.5	27.8	20.6	17.9	28.0	24.1
Spain	72.2	16.8	19.2	23.3	8.9	13.3
Switzerland[b]	441.2	32.7	7.4	7.4	219.3	70.8
United Kingdom	632.0	144.1	25.0	22.8	41.1	41.4
West Germany	405.6	76.8	25.6	18.9	45.2	41.4
Japan	4,067.9	354.5	8.5	8.7	48.3	6.7
Australia	106.4	25.8	24.8	24.2	7.9	17.6

[a] Ratio of turnover (purchases plus sales) to new money inflows.   [b] Excludes Zurich.

Source: Salomon Brothers, *International Equity Flows, 1988* (September 1988), 5.

Exhibit 1.4
Cross-listing of Securities

LISTED SECURITIES

Stocks Listed at the End of 1987 (shares and value in millions)

		Common Stocks			All Stocks		
Industry	No. Cos.	No. Issues	No. Shares	Market Value	No. Issues	No. Shares	Market Value
Industrials	1,055	1,052	46,978	$1,591,925	1,239	47,793	$1,616,702
Transportation	50	46	1,990	53,273	62	2,028	53,961
Utilities	203	174	11,685	322,646	506	11,973	333,070
Finance, R.E.	339	334	9,642	203,714	437	10,009	212,578
Grand Total	1,647	1,606	70,295	$2,171,557	2,244	71,802	$2,216,311

Historical data on p.81.

WARRANTS LISTED AT THE END OF 1987 (warrants and value in millions)

	No.of Cos.	No.of Issues	No. of Warrants	Value
Warrants	16	19	172	$867

STOCKS OF FOREIGN CORPORATE ISSUERS LISTED BY GEOGRAPHIC REGION AT THE END OF 1987
(Shares and value in millions)

		Common Stocks			All Stocks		
Region	No. Cos.	No. Issues	No. Shares	Market Value	No. Issues	No. Shares	Market Value
Asia	10	10	46	$1,957	10	46	$1,957
Australia	2	2	7	128	2	7	128
Caribbean & other	3	3	361	9,715	3	361	9,715
Europe	28	28	612	27,116	30	680	28,158
Middle East	1	1	16	16	1	16	16
North America	22	22	2,409	43,474	23	2,422	43,703
South Africa	1	1	10	476	1	10	476
Total	67	67	3,461	$82,882	70	3,542	$84,153

Source: New York Stock Exchange, *Fact Book 1988* (New York: NYSE, 1989), 25.

Note: The NYSE reported share volume in these 70 foreign issues amounted to 1,988.2 million shares in 1987.

adding to London's reputation as a hub for international equity trading is the Stock Exchange Automated Quotations (SEAQ) system, introduced in 1986. This system is similar to its U.S. counterpart (NASDAQ) and reports prices on "over 67 securities." Also noteworthy is the value of international equities ($853 billion) versus that of U.K. equities ($412.8 billion). This is the only major market where domestic equities represent only one-third of the total market value of all equities traded.

All these developments have helped create a truly international market for equity offerings. Exhibit 1.6 shows the top 10 lead managers for international equity offerings in 1987 and 1988. Noteworthy is the incredible improvement in the rankings of the two Japanese investment banking firms—Yamaichi Securities and Nomura Securities—in just one year. The first improved its position from 41

Exhibit 1.5
Stock Exchange Listed Companies (End Dec. 1987)

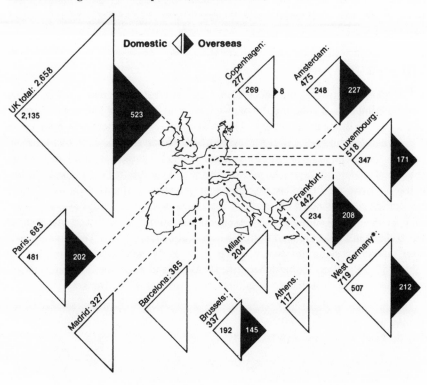

Source: "Toward a Single Market 1992," *Supplement to Euromoney* (September 1988): 70. Reprinted with permission.

Exhibit 1.6
Top 10 Lead Managers: International Equity Offerings, 1987–1988 (Unsyndicated offerings excluded)

Rank 1988	Rank 1987		Amount ($m)	1988 No. of Issues (1st half)	Share (%)	1987 Amount ($m)	No. of Issues	Share (%)
1	1	Goldman Sachs International	547.92	10	25.67	4,127.82	14	21.92
2	32	Drexel Burnham Lambert	265.00	1	12.42	92.88	3	0.49
3	10	Shearson Lehman Brothers Int'l	147.90	9	6.93	593.60	15	3.15
4	41	Yamaichi Securities	144.68	3	6.78	27.39	2	0.15
5	12	Deutsche Bank	130.71	1	6.12	522.74	4	2.78
6	19	Nomura Securities	126.43	3	5.92	286.16	4	1.52
7	14	Dresdner Bank	108.40	2	5.08	484.77	4	2.57
8	13	Salomon Brothers	95.94	4	4.50	509.06	9	2.70
9	3	Merrill Lynch Capital Markets	93.78	5	4.39	1,093.67	17	5.81
10	8	Woody Gundy	67.65	1	3.17	692.93	5	3.68

Source: "A Long, Tough Road to Recovery," *Euromoney* (September 1988): 176. Reprinted with permission.

to 4, and the second from 19 to 6. It would not surprise market observers if the Japanese should capture the first position as they have in other markets. As documented below, as markets become international, so does the investment banking function.

THE DEBT MARKETS

The most interesting, the deepest, and the broadest of the debt markets is the Eurobond market. By the middle of 1988, Nomura Securities held a comfortable lead over the other underwriters. This remarkable achievement was realized in 1987 when Nomura Securities surpassed CSFB/Credit Suisse, up to that time the premier Eurobond underwriter. In fact, as Exhibit 1.7 shows, three of the top five Eurobond underwriters are Japanese. Their hold on the market is likely to become firmer in the future because they appear to have a superior ability to place the underwritten bonds as a result of their high domestic savings rate and their high trade surplus with attending excess dollar holdings. For fixed rate issues, Deutsche Bank held the lead with 9.81 percent of the market. The floating rate note market was dominated by CSFB with 25.53 percent of the market by mid-1988. However, Nomura Securities was far and away the dominant underwriter for bonds with warrants, taking 36.96 percent of the market.

Exhibit 1.7
Top 30 Lead Managers—All Issues, 1987–1988

Rank 1988	Rank 1987	Bank	Amount ($m)	1988 No. of issues	Shares (%)	Amount ($m)	1987 No. of issues	Shares (%)
1	1	Nomura Securities	10,486.60	76	10.72	18,285.90	115	13.52
2	2	CSFB/Credit Suisse	8,799.73	54	9.00	10,391.00	79	7.68
3	3	Deutsche Bank	6,886.79	47	7.04	7,831.23	67	5.79
4	5	Dawa Securities	5,781.51	52	5.91	6,748.24	68	4.99
5	4	Nikko Securities	4,757.64	36	4.86	7,100.56	52	5.25
6	11	SG Warburg	3,828.84	17	3.91	4,007.56	36	2.9
7	12	Banque Paribas	3,725.22	26	3.81	3,588.78	38	2.6
8	6	Yamachi Securities	3,520.90	30	3.60	6,517.17	65	4.8
9	8	JP Morgan Securities	3,373.03	22	3.45	4,428.23	40	4.2
10	13	Union Bank of Switzerland	3,279.07	26	3.35	3,094.84	26	2.2
11	40	Bankers Trust International	3,029.49	26	3.10	647.12	10	0.4
12	21	Merrill Lynch Capital Markets	2,890.99	18	2.96	1,518.40	15	1.1
13	10	Industrial Bank of Japan	2,354.24	25	2.41	4,100.22	37	3.0
14	14	Commerzbank	2,101.47	18	2.15	2,561.96	27	1.8
15	9	Salomon Brothers	2,076.59	13	2.12	4,386.10	35	3.2
16	7	Morgan Stanley International	1,982.32	17	2.03	4,998.39	34	3.6
17	16	Swiss Bank Corp Investment Banking	1,982.16	17	2.03	2,368.51	25	1.7
18	17	Goldman Sachs International	1,748.01	14	1.79	2,112.25	19	1.5
19	22	Hambros Bank	1,720.47	26	1.76	1,456.11	37	1.0
20	15	Dresdner Bank	1,379.87	12	1.41	2,436.47	21	1.8
21	18	Baring Brothers	1,251.74	11	1.28	2,052.71	17	1.5
22	19	Long-Term Credit Bank of Japan	1,203.80	10	1.23	2,008.63	16	1.4
23	27	Credit Commercial de France	988.44	9	1.01	1,066.70	12	0.7
24	35	Barclay's Bank Group	975.01	5	1.00	841.71	5	0.6
25	30	Klenwort Benson	974.77	7	1.00	999.67	11	0.7
26	28	Societe Generale	964.34	8	0.99	1,043.20	11	0.7
27	32	Amro	864.33	11	0.88	910.87	15	0.6
28	24	Westdeutsche Landebank Girozentrale	847.44	13	0.87	1,136.95	15	0.8
29	46	Credit Lyonnais	697.50	5	0.71	512.43	5	0.3
30	31	Wood Gundy	688.45	10	0.70	972.38	14	0.7

Source: "Eurobond Nomura Holds on to Pole Position," *Euromoney* (September 1988): 136. Reprinted with permission.

As to currency denomination, the Japanese firms, awash with dollar holdings and riding the strength of the equity warrants market as a result of their experience and tough competitive posture, captured four of the top five positions in the underwriting of U.S. dollar issues. These four firms, led by Nomura Securities, captured 48.6 percent of the market, while Merrill Lynch managed only 5.15 percent. The yen-denominated issues were predictably dominated by the Japanese despite the deregulation of the yen Eurobond market in 1986. Only one non-Japanese firm, Bankers Trust International, appeared among the top 10 underwriters, with only 4 percent of the yen issues.

The European Currency Unit (ECU) denominated issues were even stronger in 1988 than in 1987. The Japanese had basically no stake in this two billion ECU market, and the top 10 firms were almost all European.

The quantum jump achieved by ECU bonds in 1988 was truly phenomenal.

In the first half of 1988, ECU bond issues totalled $5.5 billion, as compared with $1.9 billion in the second half of 1987. In the third quarter of 1988 issues rose to $10.7 billion—surpassing the 1985 record of $10 billion. According to Bank of England figures, it now accounts for 2.5% of bank international lending, and 4% of all international bond issues.[1]

Euromoney speculated that the reasons for the ECU market success are the improving swap opportunities for ECU-denominated bonds; the issuance of ECU-denominated bonds by the Italian and British treasuries in 1988, which improved the acceptance of this type of bond and the liquidity of its market; and the increased versatility of the issues (equity features attached and so on). Add to this the traditional reason for ECUs—reduction of currency risk through diversification—and the growth of the market is better justified.

Nomura Securities, however, held the lead underwriter position for issues by the private or public sector in 1988. Japanese issuers of Eurobonds of all types and currency denominations have a distinct, almost exclusive preference for Japanese underwriters. Nomura Securities handled 33 percent of the market by Japanese issuers.

The one area where American firms held on dearly to their position of leadership was in Eurobonds. The basis for the boom and the large American share is the takeover mania among American and British firms. According to *Euromoney*, Citicorp was in the lead with $17 billion in loans or 9.47 percent of the market, followed very closely by J.P. Morgan with 9.28 percent of the market. The American banks predictably, and perhaps wisely, stayed away from syndicated loans to Eastern European countries. This $1.5 billion market was dominated by European and Japanese firms.

The short-term Euro CP and Euro CD markets were dominated by American banks and investment banks, followed by European firms. This market is large: the value of all issues for the first half of 1988 was $2 billion.

On the United States' level, the size of the Yankee bond market (foreign debt issues sold in the United States) was $4.3 billion in 1987. The market was split among Goldman Sachs, Merrill Lynch Capital Markets, Salomon Brothers, Shearson Lehman Brothers, and First Boston. Foreigners also had a great appetite for U.S. securities issued by U.S. firms and by the U.S. government. Foreigners, especially the Japanese, accounted for 18.6 percent of all holdings of U.S. government securities in 1988. This is largely how the United States financed its infamous twin towers: the budget and trade deficits of the 1980s. The Japanese alone accounted for 35.9 percent of gross purchases of marketable Treasury bonds and notes in the second quarter of 1988.

On the London bond markets, the level of foreign interest in the gilts market has been strong. In 1988, foreign purchases of gilts accounted for 10.3 percent of the total U.K. government debt outstanding. In this market, the number of market makers went from 8 to 25, 3 of which are continental European houses, since the Big Bang.

In Japan, the share of foreign bidding on new issues by the Japanese government was allowed to increase from 1 to 3 percent. This percentage is bound to grow as more pressures are applied on the Japanese to further open their financial markets.

Even the German bond market was not spared the effects of international activity and pressures. Indeed, several financial writers have argued that the entire change in the archaic German capital market was foreign driven. CSFB, Morgan Stanley, and the Japanese newcomers made major inroads in the $17.5 billion German bond market during the first nine months of 1988. The large German banks, led by Deutsche Bank, were lead managers for 88 percent of the issues in the first nine months of 1988, however.[2]

FOREIGN DIRECT INVESTMENT

Foreign direct investment is another medium for increasing the integration of the world economies. The difference between this form of investment and the portfolio investment discussed earlier lies in control. In a portfolio investment, the investor is concerned only with the risk/return tradeoff in absolute and relative terms. In direct investment, the investor is interested in control over the firm's operations and the results.

Direct investment in the United States and by the United States is an excellent example of the secular trend in this sector. Some major exceptions have been observed recently in Europe, however, because of the economic integration of Europe expected in 1992. Several European multinationals are on an acquisition binge in each other's home turf in order to position themselves for an integrated Europe in 1992, representing a combined market comparable to that of the United States. In 1992, "the European market will consist of 320 million people, with an annual gross domestic product (GDP) of $2.7 trillion, exports of $680 billion and imports of $708 billion."[3] The Cecchini Report on European integration prepared under the aegis of the European Commission, projects the economic consequences reported in Exhibit 1.8 as direct results of the integration of

Exhibit 1.8
Economic Consequences of EC Market Integration

Four scenarios	GDP (in %)	Consumer Prices (in %)	Employ-ment(in millions)	Public budget balance (% GDP)	External balance (% GDP)
Central scenario-No policy changes	4.5	-6.1	1.8	2.2	1.0
Option A-Fiscal Stimulus	7.5	-4.3	5.7	0	-0.5
Option B-Fiscal Stimulus but balanced external accounts	6.5	-4.9	4.4	0.7	0
Option C-Combination of Options A and B	7.0	-4.5	5.0	0.4	-0.2

Source: Cecchini Report
NOTE: The Cecchini Report examines four scenarios for the economic
consequences of market integration. The so-called Central scenario
envisages that governments follow the single market directives, but
otherwise do not alter their fiscal policies.
   Option A is a variation in which governments plough the entirety of
what they save back into the member states' economies in the form of tax
cuts. Option B is along the same lines, but governments ensure that
their external accounts remain balanced and therefore the fiscal
stimulus is slightly reduced. Option C is a combination of Options A
and B.

Source: "A New Chapter for Europe," *Supplement to Euromoney* (September 1988): 4. Reprinted with permission.

Europe. These rosy results have stimulated intra-European interest and American interest in Europe.

The U.S. direct investment position of the United States rose from $259,562 million in 1985 to $308,793 million in 1987, an increase of 19 percent despite a falling dollar against all major currencies. The direct investment in Europe increased from $122,165 million in 1986 to $148,954 million in 1987, an increase of 22 percent. Much of this increase was in the form of new acquisitions. The biggest beneficiary of the heightened American interest in Europe was, as has traditionally been the case, the United Kingdom, which accounted for $44,673 million of the $148,954 million (30 percent) the Americans had committed to Europe by the end of 1987. A check with the U.S. Department of Commerce suggests that the trend continued in 1988 despite further weakness of the U.S. dollar against all major European currencies.

The interest by Americans in foreign companies was significant in the manufacturing sector, where the direct investment position of the United States increased from $104,877 million in 1986 to $126,640 in 1987, a 21 percent increase in one year. The largest increase in the U.S. direct investment position overseas was in the finance sector (banking, insurance, real estate), however. That investment rose from $34,413 million in 1986 to $49,097 in 1987, a 43 percent increase.

The interest of foreigners in the United States was also intensive during 1987. Exhibit 1.9 shows that the size of the direct investment position of foreigners in the United States rose from $220,414 million in 1986 to $261,927 million in 1987, an increase of 19 percent in one year. Over two-thirds of this investment came from Europe, with the largest European share going to the British ($74,941 million) or 42 percent of the European investment and 28.6 percent of world investment in 1987). The British interest was largely in the manufacturing sector.

The Dutch were the second largest investors in the United States in 1987, well ahead of the Japanese. Many Americans find this surprising, given the extensive news reports about the Japanese presence on the West Coast and especially in Hawaii. However, it is only a matter of time before the Japanese become the

Exhibit 1.9
Foreign Direct Investment Position in the United States, 1985–1987

	Direct investment position			Change			
	Millions of dollars			Millions of dollars		Percent	
	1985	1986	1987	1986	1987	1986	1987
All areas	**184,615**	**220,414**	**261,927**	**35,799**	**41,513**	**19.4**	**18.8**
Petroleum	28,270	29,094	35,395	824	6,301	2.9	21.7
Manufacturing	59,584	71,963	91,025	12,379	19,063	20.8	26.5
Wholesale trade	29,051	33,997	37,580	4,946	3,583	17.0	10.5
Other	67,711	85,360	97,927	17,649	12,567	26.1	14.7
Canada	**17,131**	**20,318**	**21,732**	**3,187**	**1,414**	**18.6**	**7.0**
Petroleum	1,589	1,432	1,433	−157	1	−9.9	.1
Manufacturing	4,607	6,108	7,478	1,502	1,370	32.6	22.4
Wholesale trade	1,532	1,496	2,393	−36	897	−2.4	60.0
Other	9,403	11,282	10,427	1,878	−854	20.0	−7.6
Europe	**121,413**	**144,181**	**177,963**	**22,768**	**33,782**	**18.8**	**23.4**
Petroleum	25,636	26,139	32,787	503	6,648	2.0	25.4
Manufacturing	45,841	56,016	70,598	10,175	14,582	22.2	26.0
Wholesale trade	13,778	16,430	18,391	2,652	1,960	19.3	11.9
Other	36,158	45,596	56,188	9,438	10,592	26.1	23.2
Of which:							
Netherlands	37,056	40,717	47,048	3,661	6,331	9.9	15.5
Petroleum	11,481	(D)	(D)	(D)	(D)	(D)	(D)
Manufacturing	13,351	13,293	16,120	−58	2,826	−.4	21.3
Wholesale trade	2,158	2,621	2,205	463	−416	21.4	−15.9
Other	10,066	(D)	(D)	(D)	(D)	(D)	(D)
United Kingdom	43,555	55,935	74,941	12,380	19,006	28.4	34.0
Petroleum	12,155	11,758	(D)	−397	(D)	−3.3	(D)
Manufacturing	11,687	16,500	23,510	4,813	7,010	41.2	42.5
Wholesale trade	4,044	5,676	6,958	1,632	1,282	40.4	22.6
Other	15,670	22,001	(D)	6,332	(D)	40.4	(D)
Japan	**19,313**	**26,824**	**33,361**	**7,511**	**6,537**	**38.9**	**24.4**
Petroleum	31	−34	30	−65	64	(1)	(1)
Manufacturing	2,738	3,578	5,232	840	1,654	30.7	46.2
Wholesale trade	11,796	13,687	14,667	1,891	980	16.0	7.2
Other	4,748	9,593	13,432	4,844	3,840	102.0	40.0
Other	**26,758**	**29,091**	**28,871**	**2,333**	**−220**	**8.7**	**−.8**
Petroleum	1,014	1,556	1,145	543	−411	53.5	−26.4
Manufacturing	6,398	6,261	7,718	−137	1,458	−2.1	23.3
Wholesale trade	1,945	2,384	2,128	439	−255	22.6	−10.7
Other	17,401	18,890	17,880	1,489	−1,011	8.6	−5.4

D Suppressed to avoid disclosure of data of individual companies.
1. Percent change is not defined because the position is negative in 1 of the 2 years.

Source: Survey of Current Business (August 1988): 69.

dominant investors in the United States, considering the rate at which their investments in the United States have been growing. The growth rate in 1987 alone was 24 percent. This projection assumes, of course, that the Japanese have continued access to the U.S. market—that is, that no new restrictions, general or Japanese-specific, are placed on foreign direct investment in the United States.

The statistics cited above reflect a world economy in which corporate executives are shedding ethnocentricity in strong favor of a geocentric approach. This shift appears to be permanent. The motivation for this phenomenon has been explained by various theories and empirical studies on foreign direct investment. The most accepted of the theories are the risk diversification theory, the oligopoly model, the internalization model, and the eclectic model. All these models have been discussed extensively in the literature and are beyond the scope of this chapter.

STOCK MARKET BEHAVIOR

The October 19, 1987, market crash illustrated in a dramatic fashion how a bust, like a boom, is transmitted across all national markets throughout the financial landscape. Having surpassed the 2,400 mark in April 1987, the Dow Jones Industrial Average began to weaken. Then, after a significant and persistent increase in the volatility of stock rates of return and a progression of economic bad news, the market collapsed on October 19, 1987, falling 508 points (a 22.6 percent drop) in one day. The reverberations of this collapse were felt immediately throughout the world. Stocks on London, Toyko, Hong Kong, and other exchanges followed New York's lead. The fall of share prices in London was 10.8 percent in one day. Also of interest is the instantaneousness of the reaction of the other markets. This fact has been confirmed repeatedly, even during normal periods.

Two 1987 studies—the first by Hans Schollhamuer and Ole Christian Sand, the second by Sarkis J. Khoury, Bajis Dodin, and Hirozaku Takada—confirmed that the U.S. stock market leads the other stock markets of the world and that the lead time is less than one day.[4] Both studies used several European countries and Japan to conduct the test. The authors of the second study concluded, based on the evidence, that the U.S. stock market would constitute an excellent proxy for the performance of the world financial market because it consistently led the other financial markets during the sample period. These studies, followed by other types of studies, show that international diversification is highly desirable as its efficiency frontier dominates that of a purely domestic portfolio.[5] Other studies show that international diversification is realized better through a multinational corporation than through homemade diversification.[6]

All this evidence, in addition to the rising correlations among equity markets (increased interdependence), serves to further accentuate the point that financial markets are more integrated today than ever before. This trend will continue and is extremely unlikely to be reversed.

The increased openness of financial markets and their acquisition of an international character brought about an avalanche of new products and new portfolio management strategies, which had considerable positive and occasional negative impacts on the market. A discussion of a few of these new products follows.

NEW FINANCIAL INSTRUMENTS

The integration and deregulation of financial markets brought about an avalanche of new financial instruments. The most important of these are option contracts and futures contracts, and in fact many of the other instruments are derivatives of these two products. The modern origin of these instruments is decidedly American. The first option contracts were on common stock and began trading on the Chicago Board Option Exchange on April 26, 1973. The first financial futures contracts covered foreign exchange and were introduced in the international monetary market on May 16, 1972. The explosion since then in these types of contracts, the instruments they cover, the uses they are put to, the market efficiency considerations they evoke, and other factors has been phenomenal.

Today there are about 60 major futures and options markets, covering mostly stocks, bonds, and currencies. These markets are not independent, but rather are interconnected (e.g., Singapore and Chicago, and London and Chicago) with sophisticated electronic networks allowing traders in one country to trade on the other's exchange with the right of offset. This privilege allows one trader to buy (sell) on one exchange and sell (buy)—offset—on the other exchange. Considering the time differences among Europe, the Far East, and the United States, these linkages between the exchanges allow for a continuous market where trading can effectively take place around the clock. This development is similar to that in the spot market for currencies, for example; here trading takes place 24 hours a day and is similar to the interlisting of common stocks on the various exchanges in the world.

One exchange has taken the lead in extending trading hours on the road to 24-hour trading. On September 16, 1987, the Philadelphia Stock Exchange became the first U.S. securities exchange to initiate evening trading sessions in foreign currency options. By April 1988, the evening session accounted for "more than $20 billion in underlying trading value." On January 20, 1989, the Philadelphia Stock Exchange also introduced the early morning trading session. Trading now begins at 4:30 A.M. and continues until 2:30 P.M. Evening trading then commences at 6:00 P.M. and ends at 10:00 P.M. The exchange, as a result, is now open for 14 hours of trading—the longest of any exchange.

The other innovations deal not only with new instruments but also with new ways to underwrite them (e.g., shelf registration) and with new ways to unbundle traditional services, allowing for greater flexibility in producing better profit figures and for further blurring of the investment banking/banking function. One of the more interesting new innovations was proposed to the SEC in late 1988. It involved the unbundling of a stock unit into a 30-year bond paying interest equal to the current stock dividend, a share of preferred stock entitling the holder to any dividends declared by the company in excess of the current dividend, and a stock appreciation certificate giving the holder the right to purchase the company's stock for cash in 30 years for the principal amount of the bond and the preferred stock. This unbundling provides a good defense against hostile takeover and has wide-ranging implications, the full nature of which has yet to be fully examined and understood. The unbundled stock unit is, however, a hedging tool against takeover risk and is not unlike the other instruments or structures that fundamentally hedge against other risks, such as foreign exchange risk, interest rate risk, portfolio risk, etc.

We can see, therefore, that the presence of risk is an inducement to innovation in order to shift the burden of risk. The other forces motivating the changes in the marketplace are the increased competition in the financial market, the desire and need to circumvent regulatory constraints (as is demonstrated in the chapters to follow), the shifting patterns of net flows of international savings and investments, the emergence of new countries and currencies to compete effectively with the United States, the need to create a massive pool of funds to finance huge projects with increasing diversity and complexity, and the shifting preferences of borrowers and lenders. All these factors and others make for a very dynamic market where staying on the top is becoming increasingly more difficult.

Coverage of all the innovations in products and techniques in an introductory chapter is simply impossible, and perhaps unnecessary. We shall focus on only a few major innovations.

Note Issuance Facilities

Note issuance facilities (NIFs) effectively change the banking function into an underwriting function by unbundling the lending function of the bank. Here the issuing company is provided with a borrowing mechanism instead of just a loan, which allows it to issue a stream of short-term notes called Euronotes. Should the notes not be fully subscribed, the bank becomes the buyer of last resort, thus underwriting part of the credit risk (the other portion is assumed by the other buyers of the notes). NIFs therefore allow the bank to earn fees without assuming the full credit risk for the funding. In the process, the bank has shifted an on-balance-sheet asset to an off-balance-sheet item requiring no immediate utilization of liquid assets. The attractiveness of NIFs is evidenced by their huge success. The market increased tenfold between 1984 and 1986, rising to $75 billion.

Currency and Interest Rate Swaps

The simplicity and the usefulness of swaps make any observer wonder why they were not utilized until 1979. A swap is a transaction in which two counterparties agree to exchange cash flow streams consisting of interest (typically) and amortized principal (rarely) over the life of the swap. The exchange could be a fixed cash flow for a floating cash flow, one cash flow stream indexed to the

London Interbank Offer Rate (LIBOR) for another indexed to prime, or one cash flow stream in one currency for one in another. Currency swaps involve the exchange of principal at the time of origination, while interest rate swaps do not.

Swaps are of two basic types: asset-based swaps and liability-based swaps. The former fixes a rate of return on an asset and the latter raises the cost of the liability to the counterparty.[7]

The swap market exploded from $25 million in 1979 to an estimated $250 billion in 1988. The major players therein are banks and investment banks. A bank in this market can act as a dealer (who warehouses the swap) or as a broker. When acting as a principal, a bank assumes the credit risk of the counterparty, not unlike the case in the commercial loan. The popularity of a swap lies in its multiple uses for hedging and speculative purposes. Swaps have been used to provide below-market financing, improve yield on assets, hedge interest and currency exposure, and speculate on the changes in the yield curve.

The September 1988 issue of *Euromoney* reported that big money-center banks have been assuming an increasingly conservative posture toward swaps by pulling back from currency swaps and by "cutting back" on dealing limits with other financial institutions. Yet, in the October 1988 issue, *Euromoney* argued, in a special section on swaps, that the recent trends in the swap market are bullish indeed:

- New Cooke Committee rules on capital adequacy may not cut into commercial banking swap returns as severely as imagined.
- A concern over capital efficiency has driven one commercial bank to try to rally its peers around a mark-to-market swap.
- More and more big regional banks in the United States are getting into the swaps act.
- A huge and relatively untapped market sector, big institutional investors, is now moving into more complicated structures.
- Swaps are increasingly being used to solve tax problems.
- Swap options, a huge and growing market, continue to find new applications and new players.[8]

No matter what the argument, it appears the swap market still has much room to grow, provided that the regulators do not suffocate it with undue constraints and that better risk management models are developed and applied.

THE OTHER INDICATORS OF THE NEW INTERNATIONALISM

Never in the recorded history of the stock market that we were able to uncover have stocks been so sensitive to announcements about trade balance or the strength, or lack thereof, of the U.S. dollar. It has been noted by market analysts that the final push toward the market crash of October 19, 1987, came with the announcement by Treasury Secretary James Baker of U.S. policy vis-à-vis the dollar and the larger-than-expected trade deficit. The weakness of the dollar, it is reasoned, can lead to an increase in interest rates and/or price levels, both of which are bearish signs for the stock market. Exhibit 1.10 shows the dramatic changes in the trade-weighted value of the U.S. dollar and the U.S. nominal internal balances during the period of 1978–1988. The increased importance of the exchange rate is not a complete surprise, however. Economic theory tells us that exchange rates become the channel through which monetary policy has its effect on the economy in a world of almost perfect capital mobility and highly coordinated national monetary policies. In this regard, the exchange rate replaces the interest rate as a policy variable.

The full analysis of this and other effects is reserved for Chapter 4. The intent at this juncture is to call attention to one of the major international economic issues which was covered intensively in the professional and popular press.

Another major international finance news item is the sovereign debt crisis[9] and the appropriate methods for dealing with it. The recent sovereign debt crisis began with the declaration by Poland in 1980 that it would not be able to meet its debt obligations. Despite the default by Poland and the subsequent difficulties of most Latin American countries (not all of them independent as the problem is transmitted through the interbank market), outstanding sovereign debt continued to grow. It almost doubled in two years (Exhibit 1.11).

This crisis produced an avalanche of suggestions and policy changes for public and private banking. The story was told and the effects were felt in the board rooms of New York and the barrios of São Paolo. The headlines were read in the sad eyes of the hungry and barefoot children of Mexico and in the newspapers of every city. The new policy of banks and developed countries and the implications were discussed from every perspective in hundreds of forums. The final solution remains elusive despite successful experiments by Chile and Mexico with debt/equity swaps.

The most promising "new" proposal is that of an international debt facility whereby the debt of sovereign countries would be purchased in the open market and debt relief is provided to the countries involved. The funds to purchase the outstanding debt would be borrowed in the capital markets and/or supplied by developed countries. This facility would transfer risk from private banks to governments or multinational institutions and ultimately either to those buying the bonds to fund the purchases of outstanding debt or to the citizens of those countries bailing out the commercial banks.

Another proposal with considerable international support is debt relief, or rather debt forgiveness to the poorest of the debtor countries. While politically attractive, it sets a dangerous precedent and is badly reasoned from an economic perspective. The issues here appear to be easy and clear-cut but are in fact much more complex, as the author has demonstrated in an independent study on debt forgiveness.[10] Debt rescheduling, as of now, remains the preferred method for easing the pressures on less-developed countries. The terms are more concessionary to the poorer countries, however.

Exhibit 1.10

Changes in the Trade Weighted Value of the U.S. Dollar and the U.S. Nominal External Balances, 1978–1988

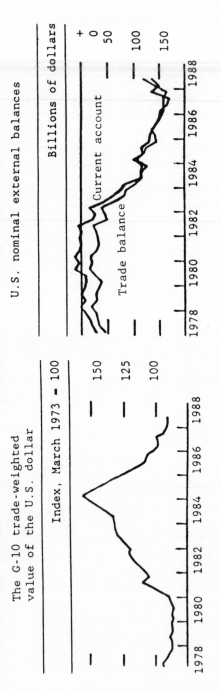

Exhibit 1.11

World Debt Figures: World Bank 111 Reporting Countries, 1984–1988 (Billions of U.S. dollars)

	1988	1987	1986	1985	1984
All developing countries	1200	1170	1053	962	579
to official Institutions with Govt Guarantees		436			165.4
to private Institutions with Govt Guarantees		469			196.7
to private Institutions without Govt Guarantees		90			75.6
Mexico	105.5*	107.8	101.7	97.1	57.4
Brazil	125.7*	123.9	110.6	106.7	70

Source: World Bank, privately released, 26 November 1988.

The pressures for a dramatic move on the sovereign debt front have abated recently. The danger lies in the fragility of the international economic conditions. An International Monetary Fund review published in September 1988 found the world economy "resilient in 1988." The prognosis for 1989 and beyond is not as optimistic, however. A major downturn in economic activity could unravel all the patches and create a crisis of major proportions.

In anticipation of the worst scenarios, U.S. commercial banks with less developed country (LDC) exposure set up large reserves in 1987. Citicorp took the lead by adding $3 billion to its bad debt reserves (about 25 percent of its third world debt), and Chase Manhattan followed suit with $1.6 billion (25 percent of its troubled foreign debt), as did other New York and regional banks. This experience is bound to have an effect on the lending behavior and the risk aversion of U.S. commercial banks.

We now look at another major event of international significance: U.S. bank failures.

U.S. BANK FAILURES

The stories about bank failures were thought to be relived from the depression era. In fact, since 1933 the challenge to the system of deposit insurance has never been greater than it is now. Of the 3,000 thrift institutions in the United States, half are considered insolvent by the FSLIC. These institutions were caught in a classic squeeze between the rising costs of funds and a long-term portfolio of assets (60 percent of assets) unable to yield returns high enough to offset the increased costs. Add to this woefully mismatched and inflexible portfolio the incompetent and in some cases corrupt management found in many problem institutions, and you get a prescription for a crisis.

The preferred means by which to dispose of a troubled thrift institution is the merger, whereby healthy thrifts or banks acquire ailing institutions. The second option is the management consignment program, which provides an injection of new supervision and active management. The third option is recapitalization, and the fourth is liquidation.

The number of institutions placed in these programs by the FSLIC during the 1986–1988 period is shown in Exhibit 1.12. The cost of liquidation to the FSLIC in 1988 alone amounted to $2.2 billion. The size of the FSLIC investment portfolio—one major source of funds to support liquidation losses—was between $1.5 and $2 billion toward the end of 1988. McKinsey & Co. estimates that "the amount by which liabilities exceed earning assets in America's unhealthy thrifts has grown from $39 billion in 1987 to $59 billion in 1988. It predicted that by the end of 1989 the figure will have grown to $109 billion."[11]

In fact, on December 28, 1988, the Federal Home Loan Bank Board (FHLBB) agreed to provide $5.1 billion in government funds over the next 10 years to assist in the takeover of five problem thrift institutions in Texas. These thrifts were being taken over by the investment group of MacAndrews and Forbes. This follows an ever larger assistance package of $5.5 billion provided in the merger of Sunbelt Savings Association and seven other Texas institutions in August 1988. These and other packages bring the total pledged by the FHLBB to $30 billion in 1988. The FHLBB has, obviously, deeper pockets than those of state thrift insurance funds. Two of these funds, Ohio and Maryland, were bankrupted by their troubled thrifts.

This financial time bomb will be hard to disarm in an era when the first priority of the Bush administration is to balance the U.S. budget. Yet, with surprising swiftness, the Bush administration moved to quell, if not solve, the problem. On February 6, 1989, it submitted a $90 billion plan to bail out savings and loans (S&Ls) by covering their expected losses. The elements of this plan are as follows:

• The U.S. government would issue $50 billion in bonds over a three-year period to cover the cost of failed institutions. Part of the interest on the bonds would be paid by the higher FDIC insurance premiums charged to banks and thrifts.

• The FDIC would have, henceforth, oversight over S&Ls' insurance funds. These funds would not be commingled with those of banks.

• A new agency—the Resolution Trust Corporation—would be created with the charge of isolating the problem thrifts and resolving their affairs within five years.

• The Justice Department would get $50 million to investigate and prosecute fraud in financial institutions.

This proposal goes a long way toward reassuring depositors. The taxpayers, however, will pay for the industry's problems. The original estimated cost to taxpayers was $39.9 billion over 10 years. The final total estimated cost after lengthy negotiations during 1989 came to $150 billion.

The picture on the commercial banking side is not very comforting, despite the fact that U.S. commercial banks earned $5 billion in the first quarter of 1988.

Exhibit 1.12
Solutions to Problem Banks Provided by FDIC, 1986–1988

	1988	1987	1986
Resolved by Merger	117	31	28
Put in management			
Consignment Program	10	25	29
Recapitalized	1	--	--
Liquidated	25	17	21

Source: FDIC, private releases.

The history of bank failures has been quite cyclical. It is evident from Exhibit 1.13 that bank failures are at an all-time high. The 10 largest bank failures in the United States have occurred, interestingly, during the 1970s and 1980s, as Exhibit 1.14 shows. Geographically, the troubled banks are located largely in the Southwest (Texas and Oklahoma) and in the West (Exhibit 1.15). The southwestern problems are related to the drop in oil prices and the poor real estate market. The sovereign debt crisis did contribute to the problem, but only marginally.

These problems appear to have been effectively handled by the FDIC. Its chairman, L. William Seidman, opined in a 1988 news release that "After handling all of the major problems in Texas, and over 200 failures and assistance transactions for the year, the FDIC should end 1988 with a net worth between $15 billion and $16 billion." The total disbursements (losses) by the FDIC amounted to $4.6 billion in 1987 and to $8.07 billion by November 20, 1988.

It is clear that the banking industry is wounded. However, it showed considerable resiliency in 1988, which is likely to continue unless the economy turns downward.

THE NEW TRENDS ON THE EDUCATIONAL SIDE

The revolution in the financial markets brought about dramatic changes in the fields of education and research. Foreigners, more than ever before, have been flocking into U.S. universities to study at all levels, especially the advanced levels. Some U.S. universities award as many as 75 percent of their technical Ph.D.s to foreign students. Fortunately, about half of these foreign graduates stay in the United States. During the 1987–1988 academic year, 356,187 foreign students were studying in the United States. Of these students, 73,880 (20.7%) were in engineering, and 66,990 (18.8%) were in business and management.

Leading professors in America's business schools have set up consulting or investment management firms or have been consulting with banks and investment banks on a frequent and consistent basis. Some have even decided to leave academia for careers that are more rewarding (at least financially) in the investment world.

Exhibit 1.13
Number and Deposits of Banks Closed Because of Financial Difficulties, 1934–1987

| | Number | | | | | Deposits (in thousands of dollars) | | | | | Assets[4] |
| | | | | Insured | | | | | Insured | | |
Year	Total	Non-Insured[1]	Total	Without disbursements by FDIC[2]	With disbursements by FDIC[3]	Total	Non-Insured[1]	Total	Without disbursements by FDIC[2]	With disbursements by FDIC[3]	(in Thousands Dollars)
Total	**1,333**	**136**	**1,197**	**8**	**1,189**	**49,280,025**	**143,501**	**49,136,524**	**41,147**	**49,095,377**	**58,850,328**
1934	61	52	9	…	9	37,333	35,365	1,968	…	1,968	2,661
1935	32	6	26	1	25	13,988	583	13,405	85	13,320	17,242
1936	72	3	69	…	69	28,100	592	27,508	…	27,508	31,941
1937	84	7	77	2	75	34,205	528	33,677	328	33,349	40,370
1938	81	7	74	…	74	60,722	1,038	59,684	…	59,684	69,513
1939	72	12	60	…	60	160,211	2,439	157,772	…	157,772	181,514
1940	48	5	43	…	43	142,788	358	142,430	…	142,430	161,898
1941	17	2	15	…	15	29,796	79	29,717	…	29,717	34,804
1942	23	3	20	…	20	19,540	355	19,185	…	19,185	22,254
1943	5	…	5	…	5	12,525	…	12,525	…	12,525	14,058
1944	2	…	2	…	2	1,915	…	1,915	…	1,915	2,098
1945	1	…	1	…	1	5,695	…	5,695	…	5,695	6,392
1946	2	1	1	…	1	494	147	347	…	347	351
1947	6	1	5	…	5	7,207	167	7,040	…	7,040	6,798
1948	3	…	3	…	3	10,674	…	10,674	…	10,674	10,360
1949	9	4	5	1	4	9,217	2,552	6,665	1,190	5,475	4,886
1950	5	1	4	…	4	5,555	42	5,513	…	5,513	4,005
1951	5	3	2	…	2	6,464	3,056	3,408	…	3,408	3,050
1952	4	1	3	…	3	3,313	143	3,170	…	3,170	2,388
1953	5	…	4	2	2	45,101	390	44,711	26,449	18,262	18,811
1954	4	2	2	…	2	2,948	1,950	998	…	998	1,138
1955	5	…	5	…	5	11,953	…	11,953	…	11,953	11,985
1956	3	1	2	…	2	11,690	360	11,330	…	11,330	12,914
1957	3	1	2	1	1	12,502	1,255	11,247	10,084	1,163	1,253
1958	9	5	4	…	4	10,413	2,173	8,240	…	8,240	8,905
1959	3	…	3	…	3	2,593	…	2,593	…	2,593	2,858
1960	2	1	1	…	1	7,965	1,035	6,930	…	6,930	7,506
1961	9	4	5	…	5	10,611	1,675	8,936	…	8,936	9,820

Year	No.	No.	No.	No.	Deposits	Deposits	Deposits	Deposits[5]
1962	3	2			4,231	1,220	3,011	
1963	2		1	2	23,444		23,444	26,179
1964	8	1		7	23,867	429	23,438	25,849
1965	9	4		5	45,256	1,395	43,861	58,750
1966	8	1		7	106,171	2,648	103,523	120,647
1967	4			4	10,878		10,878	11,993
1968	3			3	22,524		22,524	25,154
1969	9	1		9	40,134		40,134	43,572
1970	8			7	55,229	423	54,806	62,147
1971	6			6	132,058		132,058	196,520
1972	3	2		1	99,784	79,304	20,480	22,054
1973	6			6	971,296		971,296	1,309,675
1974	4	1		4	1,575,832		1,575,832	3,822,596
1975	14	1		13	340,574	1,000	339,574	419,950
1976	17	1		16	865,659	800	864,859	1,039,293
1977	6			6	205,208		205,208	232,612
1978	7			7	854,154		854,154	994,035
1979	10			10	110,696		110,696	132,988
1980	10			10	216,300		216,300	236,164
1981	10			10	3,826,022		3,826,022	4,859,060
1982	42			42	9,908,379		9,908,379	11,632,415
1983	48			48	5,441,608		5,441,608	7,026,923
1984	79			79	2,883,162		2,883,162	3,276,411
1985[6]	120			120	8,059,441		8,059,441	8,741,268
1986[7]	138			138	6,471,100		6,471,100	6,991,600
1987[7]	184			184	6,281,500		6,281,500	6,850,700

[1] For information regarding each of these banks, see table 22 in the 1963 Annual Report (1963 and prior years), and explanatory notes to tables regarding banks closed because of financial difficulties in subsequent annual reports. One noninsured bank placed in receivership in 1934, with no deposits at time of closing, is omitted (see table 22 note 9). Deposits are unavailable for seven banks.

[2] For information regarding these cases, see table 23 of the Annual Report for 1963.

[3] For information regarding each bank, see the Annual Report for 1958, pp. 48-83 and pp. 98-127, and tables regarding deposit insurance disbursements in subsequent annual reports. Deposits are adjusted as of December 31, 1982.

[4] Insured banks only.

[5] Not available.

[6] Includes data for one bank granted financial assistance although no disbursement was required until January, 1986.

[7] Excludes data for banks granted financial assistance under Section 13(c)(1) of the Federal Deposit Insurance Act to prevent failure. Data for these banks are included in table 123.

Source: 1987 Annual Report (Washington, D.C.: Federal Deposit Insurance Corp., 1988), 49.

Exhibit 1.14
Ten Largest Bank Failures (By asset size)

	Assets	Deposits	Date
Franklin National Bank New York, New York	$3,655,662,000	$1,444,981,606	October 8, 1974
First National Bank and Trust Company, Oklahoma City, Oklahoma	1,419,445,375	1,006,657,507	July 14, 1986
The First National Bank of Midland, Midland, Texas	1,404,092,000	1,076,217,000	October 14, 1983
United States National Bank San Diego, California	1,265,868,099	931,954,458	October 18, 1973
United American Bank in Knoxville, Knoxville, Tennessee	778,434,000	584,619,000	February 14, 1983
Banco Credito y Ahorro Ponceno, Ponce, Puerto Rico	712,540,000	607,610,000	March 31, 1978
Park Bank of Florida St. Petersburg, Florida	592,900,000	543,900,000	February 14, 1986
Yankee Bank for Finance and Savings, FSB, Boston, Massachusetts	521,700,000	474,800,000	October 16, 1987
Penn Square Bank, N.A. Oklahoma City, Oklahoma	516,799,000	470,445,000	July 6, 1982
The Hamilton National Bank of Chattanooga, Chattanooga, Tennessee	412,107,000	336,292,000	February 16, 1974

Source: 1987 Annual Report (Washington, D.C.: Federal Deposit Insurance Corp.,
          1988), 11.

Several universities have built large new facilities for executive education to keep executives on top of developments in the financial markets and in the technology that impacts on these markets. The seminar business is very lucrative, and it seems that everyone with some ability is involved. Several banks and investment banks have in-house training programs that are more rigorous than the equivalent university courses are, and some of these courses are computer and mathematics intensive. The whole research design for the analysis of financial markets has also shifted. The trends in the theoretical framework go from descriptive economics to prescriptive finance along the following outline.

I. The Microeconomic Modeling of the Banking Firm
   A. Why banks exist
      1. The asset transformation function
      2. The role of the bank's liabilities
      3. The two-sided nature of the financial firm

    B. Overall optimization models of the banking firm
    C. Asset allocation models
       1. Reserve management modeling
       2. Portfolio choice models
    D. Liability choice models
       1. Deposit modeling
       2. The capital decision
       3. Two-sided modeling
    E. Modeling off-balance-sheet credit
    F. Credit rationing models
  II. The Microeconomic Modeling of International Banking
    A. International financial intermediation issues
    B. International industrial economics issues
    C. International macroeconomic transmission issues
 III. Financial Models of Risk Management
    A. Interest rate risk management
    B. Foreign exchange rate risk management
    C. Credit risk management
    D. Stock market risk management
    E. Toward a general model of risk management

Exhibit ·1.15
Percentage of Banks in Each Region on the "Problem Bank" List, 1987–1988

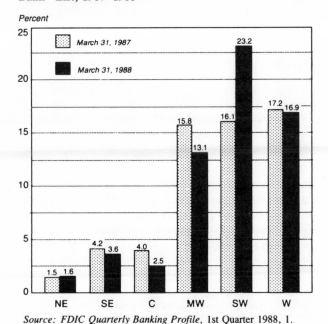

Source: FDIC Quarterly Banking Profile, 1st Quarter 1988, 1.

IV. The Change Agents: Some Details Regarding Trends
   A. Innovation
   B. Deregulation
   C. Technology
V. The Change Process: Some Details Regarding Processes
   A. Securitization
   B. Unbundling—repackaging
   C. Institutionalization
   D. Globalization
VI. The Industrial Economic Intermediation
   A. The structure-conduct-performance model in banking
   B. The five forces of Porter in the banking industry
   C. Cost economics in depository institutions
   D. Cost economics in insurance companies
   E. Cost economics in securities firms
   F. Technology and cost economics
   G. Internationalization and cost economics
VII. The Financial Management of Asset-Liability Risks
   A. Asset-liability management in theory and practice
   B. The simultaneous management of
      1. Portfolio risks
      2. Market risks
      3. Rate risks
      4. Credit risks
      5. Liquidity risks
      6. Underwriting risks

One can be certain that the evolution will continue, hopefully at the same pace as that of the dynamic market itself.

CONCLUSIONS

This chapter has shown the extent of internationalism at the banking, commercial, capital market, and educational levels. Some of the major events affecting the stability of the international financial system have also been discussed. It is hard, based on the discussion thus far, to draw firm conclusions or to suggest strong hypotheses. That is left for the chapters that follow.

The internationalization of the financial markets was realized as the financial markets were being deregulated. Whether internationalism caused deregulation or vice versa is not easy to ascertain. The weight of the evidence suggests, as presented in the chapters to follow, that the attempts to internationalize, due largely to the need to circumvent existing regulations, produced the deregulatory process that cut across all countries.

NOTES

1. Paul Keller, "The Market Approaches Critical Mass," *Euromoney* (January 1989):67–73.

2. *Euromoney* (September 1988):134–75.

3. Matthew Barrett, "A New Chapter for Europe" *Euromoney* (September 1988):2.

4. Hans Schollhamuer and Ole Christian Sand, "Lead-Lag Relationships among National Equity Markets: An Empirical Investigation," and Sarkis J. Khoury, Bajis Dodin, and Hirokazu Takada, "Multiple Time Series Analysis of National Stock Markets and Their Structure: Some Implications," in *Recent Developments in International Banking and Finance,* ed. Sarkis J. Khoury and Alo Ghosh (Lexington, Mass.: D.C. Heath, 1987).

5. See, for example, Bruno Solnik, "Why Not Diversify Internationally Rather Than Domestically," *Financial Analyst Journal* (July–August 1974):54–58.

6. See, for example, Vihang R. Errunza and Lemma W. Senbet, "The Effects of International Operations on the Market Value of the Firm: Theory and Evidence," *Journal of Finance* 36, no. 2 (May 1981):401–17.

7. For a detailed discussion, see Sarkis J. Khoury, "Interest Rate Swaps: Nature, Scope, and Risk Development," *Journal of Accounting and Finance* (forthcoming).

8. Ron Cooper, "Still Plenty of Room to Grow," *Euromoney* (October 1988):35.

9. For a comprehensive analysis, see Sarkis J. Khoury, "Sovereign Debt: A Critical Look at the Causes and the Nature of the Problem," in *Essays in International Business* (Columbia: University of South Carolina, 1985).

10. Sarkis J. Khoury, "Sovereign Debt Forgiveness: Political Expediency or Economic Rationality?" *Banker International* (forthcoming).

11. "A Big Event for American Bonds," *Economist* (29 October 1988):82.

2

The Economics and Nature
of Financial (De)Regulation

The regulation of financial institutions is an integral part of every national financial market—even that of Hong Kong. The most recent discussions in the financial literature have centered on regulatory reforms. No one, to our knowledge, has advocated lifting all regulations on all financial institutions and markets, however. Therefore, the issues relevant to economists are the following:

- The economic rationale for regulating the financial sector
- The degree of uniformity of regulation across product, type of institution, nationality of the institution, type of liability, size of institution, etc.
- The optimal level of regulation
- The effects of regulation on innovation, competitive structure, and stability of the financial system
- The effectiveness—absence of leakages—of regulation
- The nature of the regulatory cycle: absence of regulation—regulation—deregulation—reregulation
- The effects of regulation on macroeconomic variables, the conduct of monetary policy, and the pricing behavior of the firm
- The effects of regulation on the efficiency—allocational, promotional, and operational—of the financial markets
- The consistency with and impact of regulation on the economic system within which the nation conducts its business
- The dynamic nature of regulation and the optimum time for review of existing regulations
- The effects of regulation on the very character of banks as financial intermediaries

A detailed discussion of all these issues requires a book, if not several books. Only those issues that are most compelling will be considered here in order to dispel a few myths about regulation.

TO REGULATE OR NOT TO REGULATE

The U.S. regulatory system is based on an archaic collection of laws and regulations formulated in reaction to financial, economic, and political crises. It is not a system designed by a master financial planner, nor is it a system that emanated from one source: the federal government, or the banking industry, or an enlightened group of citizens. It is an amalgam that has been streamlined and is reasonably effective, at least in balancing the interests of all the contending parties.

The fundamental reasons for regulating the banking industry lie in the key role banks play in the efficient functioning of the economic system and in the conduct of an effective monetary policy. The regulation we speak of is that which influences the pricing of the assets and liabilities of banking institutions as well as the nature of the business they conduct and the mixture of assets and liabilities they hold.

Banks are not the only institutions subject to regulation. The airline industry, the steel industry, and every other industry in the United States are subject to direct and indirect regulation. Regulations dealing with the environment, work safety, product quality, truth in advertising, and similar issues affect all firms. The focus here, however, is on those regulations that are specific to the banking industry and their economic rationale.

The banking industry is primarily involved in providing liquidity to the economy by transforming nonliquid assets to liquid assets. This transformation allows banks to play a critical role in the allocation of resources from surplus units to deficit units within a free market economy. In so doing, banks provide a medium of exchange and become an integral part of the payment system.

The allocative function of banks is the collection of evaluations of credit risk and loan and investment decisions which are neither mandated by nor centralized in the office of a regulator or bureaucrat of any type. These decisions are guided by the "invisible hand" of the free market. The allocational efficiency of the financial market is therefore measured against this background. The standards applied by banks in assessing credit risk depend on credit availability, which is a function of monetary policy. An easy monetary policy places considerable pressure on banks to lend more money and consequently to lower lending standards. This, of course, has macroeconomic implications, especially in terms of interest rates and inflation.

The banking system is also a conduit to monetary policy, and the question that remains unresolved is whether increased regulation of banks, or any regulation of banks, is necessary for the effective conduct of monetary and fiscal policy. Is the Federal Reserve System (the Fed) less able to conduct monetary policy today than it was 10 years ago when banks were more heavily regulated? This question will be answered later.

The theoretical foundations for banking regulation are formed primarily in the theory of market failure stemming from asymmetric information. The traditional "economic" justifications are discussed below.

Protection of Depositors

Depositors are creditors to the banking system and are therefore subject to all the risks assumed by the bank. They, like stockholders, finance the asset side of the balance sheet. The security of their financial commitment depends on the quality of the asset underwritten and the capital of the bank. Because required capital funds only 5.5 percent of the asset side, the banking industry is highly leveraged. This is of particular concern, considering that many of the assets are interest rate sensitive. Three other risks are also borne by the depositor: (1) portfolio risk resulting from inadequate diversification of assets, (2) balance sheet risk resulting from duration mismatches of assets and liabilities, and (3) contingent liability risk, which is becoming increasingly significant as banks venture into new territories such as swaps, options, and underwriting agreements. These and other risks have been monitored by regulators, but insufficiently. E. J. Kane expressed the concerns best:

Examiners typically conceive a problem institution as one whose capital is low relative to potential default losses on outstanding loans. Because it ignores several important sources of risk . . . this conception of deposit risk is dangerously outmoded. Like the institution of federal deposit insurance itself, examination procedures are rooted in a 1930's concept of what causes bank failures. They implicitly embody the view that because loans are the chief asset of deposit institutions, and except for losses due to theft and embezzlement, institutions find themselves in irremedial trouble only when borrowers prove unable to service outstanding loan agreements. Besides risk from crime and default, examiners today must confront the possibility of losses caused by interest volatility, movement in exchange rates, political developments in foreign countries, and technological obsolescence.[1]

The concern of the depositor is therefore with the adequate assessment of these risks, especially in a free market, unregulated banking system. The difficulty in achieving this objective lies in the asymmetry of information between banks and their customers (depositors) and in the exposure of a major portion of bank liabilities to the possibility of sudden withdrawal. The information asymmetry is very difficult, if not impossible, to correct and is the main justification for regulation. Well-trained, experienced, and sophisticated regulators gave positive reports on Continental Illinois only a few months before it had to be taken over by the FDIC. This shows that even those with access to "full information" could err in a major way. Furthermore, the riskiness of a bank can dramatically shift immediately after any review (examination): a bank may shift, for example, from zero exposure in foreign exchange risk to exposure up to the limit, if not beyond. A bank may also decide to add a whole new class of borrowers whose credit worthiness is suspect and/or whose credit risk adds to the riskiness of the loan portfolios.

The small investor (depositor) whose life savings, minuscule as they may be, are on deposit with a bank may find the task of assessing the risk profile of that bank to be difficult, if not impossible. This task is not made much easier even if depositors decided to band together to share the responsibility of the valuation task. The Great Depression may have sensitized depositors to the risks involved in bank deposits. The history of "free market" banking that preceded the Federal Reserve Act of 1913 is not reassuring, either. The Federal Reserve System is, in fact, a byproduct of the panicky run on banks in 1907.

The above line of argument, some contend, can be applied to the small investor in the stock market. The valuation of industrial and commercial firms is not much easier than that of banks. Stock investments and bank deposits are not perfect substitutes. The holding of transaction balances in the form of cash or demand deposits is necessary to maintain solvency and liquidity. The liquidation of a stock portfolio on a periodic basis may be a very expensive way to maintain adequate cash flow. Additionally, the soundness of the banking system is necessary, as was pointed out earlier, to maintain the liquidity of the financial system and to conduct monetary policy. This takes the argument well beyond the realm of a single institution. Therefore, it is our conclusion that regulation is warranted if the policy objective is the protection of the small depositor.

Monetary Stability

The commercial banking system in the United States is the major issuer of money in the economy and acts as a clearing system for transactions among economic agents. This has been especially true since 1934:

The Gold Reserve Act replaced the gold standard with a system of credit money, most of which takes the form of checking deposits issued by private banks in the wake of credit extension to their debtors. This money form has the advantage (over the earlier commodity money) of creating an "elastic" currency, a money supply that responds endogenously to the liquidity and borrowing needs of the public. But this issue, through which private banks transform their no yield cash reserves into income earning loan assets, also poses a fundamental dilemma. It means that the creation of money, whose peculiar social functions make it a public good par excellence, is determined by the private profit motive of its issuers. Linked to bank lending, it is thus also subjected to the fluctuations of the credit cycle.[2]

The stability of this system requires the prevention of financial panic and the provision of a safety net in the event of a serious economic downturn or shock (e.g., the sovereign debt crisis).

Based on the above, some economists have argued that this constitutes a sufficient condition for regulation. This is illogical at best and dangerous at worst. The stability of the financial system is dependent on fiscal policy and especially monetary policy as conducted by the Federal Reserve System and not on the level of regulation. Otherwise, one could argue that the stability concern necessitates maximal regulation, the extreme form of which is government ownership of all financial institutions. The empirical evidence shows clearly that heavily regulated systems are not necessarily more stable than less-regulated systems are and that monetary policy is not necessarily more effective in regulated financial markets than it is in unregulated markets. Indeed, the deregulation of the Japanese financial markets, for example, was necessitated by the 1973–1974 recession caused by rising oil prices. The Japanese financial system needed more flexibility in order to cope with mounting budget deficits and changing corporate balance sheets.

Furthermore, stability is often confused with the absence of bank failure. This "myth" has led to dangerous results whereby regulators keep insolvent banks with negative equity open, well beyond redemption, and in the process increase the social cost of bank failure.[3] There is no reason why a bank should not be allowed to fail in a competitive environment—and this should be true for large as well as small banks. The counterargument to this proposition has been the "bank run" argument, which is another myth we discuss later in this chapter.

The above, however, is not an argument in favor of complete deregulation because compelling arguments exist for some forms and certain levels of regulation. The experience of Hong Kong, which moved its financial system from an open system to a regulated system, speaks forcefully to the benefits of some regulation. The Hong Kong experience is discussed in detail in Chapter 6. More convincing, however, is the fact that the empowerment of the Fed to regulate the creation of credit money by private banks makes certain regulatory controls indispensable in the management of economic activity: "the Fed has to define precisely which institutions to give the privilege of creating money, since it needs to control their reserves and lending. This is done by balance sheet restrictions on their sources and uses of funds (e.g. reserve requirements, types of deposits, types of loans.)"[4]

Efficiency of the Banking System

The economist's view of efficiency deals with the optimum allocation of resources in order to minimize the waste of finite resources and to produce at the lowest cost. Efficient resource distribution in a two-input (a,b), two-output (x,y) case requires that

$$\frac{MPP_{ax}}{MPP_{bx}} = \frac{MPP_{ay}}{MPP_{by}}$$

The ratio of the marginal physical product (MPP) of input a to that of input b in the production of output x should equal that in the production of output y. These conditions obtain in a purely competitive structure in the factors markets. Under such a system, the production process is at maximum efficiency.

In the output market, efficiency is achieved when the marginal rate substitution of one product for another (MRS_{xy}^{c1}) of one consumer is equal to that of another consumer (MRS_{xy}^{c2}). This condition is pareto optimal and is achieved in a purely competitive market system.

It can be argued that banks are in the "trust" business and in the information transformation and transmission business. Their output is a collection of banking services that are driven by publicly available and internalized information sets. The production of this output allocates resources from surplus economic units to deficit economic units. Efficiency is therefore measured by how much output is generated, given the labor, capital, and information available to the bank. This efficiency is reflected in the price of banking products, assuming a competitive market structure.

The other concern of economists is how regulation impacts on efficiency. The objective of bank regulation is to provide a framework in which competition can be enhanced. The method of achieving this is based on the myths that smaller is better and that accumulation of financial power in a few banks is per se anticompetitive and, consequently, efficiency reducing. Interstate branching was prohibited (McFadden Act of 1927), nonbank entities were barred from the banking business (Glass–Steagall Act of 1933), rate ceilings were set for deposits (Regulation Q), and balance sheet restrictions (minimum capital requirements, limits on specific assets and liabilities, etc.) were implemented with the idea of making banking a "safer" and more efficient industry. The results belie the expectations. These and other regulations helped create regional monopolies and did not promote efficiency. Furthermore, they prevented certain banks from achieving their optimum size at which bank products are produced at the lowest point of the total cost curve. The special subsidies and restrictions in terms, for example, of the composition of the loan portfolio placed on the S&L industry may have been responsible for most of the industry problems in the 1980s. This industry became a burden on the financial system and will cost over $100 billion before it is rescued.

It is reassuring, however, that the restrictions are being loosened. Yet the old philosophy still receives greater attention than it deserves, despite the fact that there is no basis "to believe that a structure of fewer and larger banks (or financial institutions) creates additional problems with respect to conflicts of interest, the allocation of credit, or the exercise of political influence."[5] Furthermore, the evidence from overseas indicates clearly that the Japanese, the Germans, the French, and even the Swiss have managed well, if not admirably, with a much smaller set of banking institutions than their American counterparts have.

It can be said in conclusion that regulation does not necessarily increase economic efficiency. Those regulations intended to prevent unscrupulous behavior, to keep criminals from owning and operating banks, etc., are clearly in the public interest, however, and should be continued. The question, once again, deals with the nature and the level of regulation, issues that will be examined further in Chapter 3.

Consumer Protection

Regulations intended to protect the consumer go well beyond the banking industry and have been accepted as a necessary part of a market economy. The banking laws in this regard require full disclosure of all information to borrowers, so they may make enlightened decisions, and equal treatment of everyone applying for a loan or making a deposit. An example of antidiscrimination regulation is that forbidding banks from redlining an area of a city.

In conclusion, to regulate is neither bad nor good per se. There are justifiable regulations, and there are bad regulations. Conversely, deregulation is not a panacea either. The reregulation of certain markets, products or financial, may be all the proof required to show that deregulation does not necessarily produce the desired results. Also, what is desired at one point in time is not necessarily desirable at another.

George J. Stigler, in a classic article on economic regulation, argues that there is a market for regulation.[6] How much regulation the system ends up with depends on the bidding power of the particular groups involved. The winning group effectively receives the right to tax the wealth of everyone else. That is, in a regulatory game, the outcome involves the transfer of wealth among the various groups contending for control.

Each group in the Stigler conception undertakes its own cost-benefit analysis for a regulation or a set of regulations. The cost is in the collection of information about the wealth implications of the regulation to the group and the attitude of the politicians involved in the issue. The gain is the tax the group will be able to impose on the rest of society. The group will bid if the net benefits are positive.

Stigler, however, sees shifting coalitions and diminishing marginal returns to group size in politics. As the group grows, the net benefits per member diminish because the size of the pie is fixed. It is perhaps these phenomena that keep the regulatory cycle alive.

THE REGULATORY EQUATION

The premise for regulatory intervention is information asymmetry or incomplete information. The bank and the bank customer (lender and borrower) are making decisions based on different information sets. The result of this is a market failure or an unusual market equilibrium as depositors discover that while they are aware of the possibility of bank failure, they are unable to decide which bank will fail and which will survive. In addition, depositors are unable to decide on whether the failure of a bank is specific to the bank or a reflection of problems in the banking industry—that is, whether the failure of a bank will lead to a run on all banks. This fear of a run may actually produce a run independent of whether one is warranted or not.[7] A run, should it occur, disrupts the payment system and the ability of the banking system to allocate resources efficiently. The quality of the investment decision is consequently diminished, and the economy will operate below optimal levels. This scenario underlies regulatory intervention.

Bank runs occurred in the United States in 1907 and during the Great Depression. These are different times—but few regulators and economists have understood the transformation in the financial markets and the resulting maturity of bankers and investment bankers. James Tobin pointed out the fallacy of relying on the lessons of the depression:

The memory of the Depression was a big reason for the policy of rescue, but in my opinion not a good reason. The analogy is misplaced. Bank runs in the Depression were an economywide catastrophe because they became a general run of depositors to currency. The banking system was drained of reserves, and the Federal Reserve was unable or unwilling to expand the supply of base money enough to offset the drain. The shift from bank money (requiring only fractional reserves) to 100 percent currency money cut down the total money supply—that's the monetarist way to look at it—and reduced the supply of loanable funds from banks—that's the eclectic way to put it.

In the 1980's runs to currency are not the problem. The deposit shifts we have seen have been from threatened institutions or particular types of institutions in particular jurisdictions, to similar deposits elsewhere. Such shifts do not destroy bank reserves in aggregate. Indeed central bank lending to the reserve losers . . . actually increased total reserves.[8]

The empirical evidence on the contagion effect—the failure of one bank leads to the failure of the banking system—is quite reassuring, as Anthony Saunders pointed out:

The body of empirical evidence discussed above appears to suggest that except for major crises contagion effects measured through spreads, deposit/loan flows or equity values have been relatively small. Indeed, if anything, the degree of contagion appears to have fallen since the early 1970's (the oil shock—Franklin National—Herstatt period). One possibility is that this has resulted from the more interventionist stance taken by bank regulators since 1974, as they become more aware of the social costs/externalities that could result from a major crisis in confidence in the international banking system. The massive financial support guarantees provided by the FED and the FDIC to Continental Illinois, and the more closely defined global responsibilities of central banks when overseas branches and subsidiaries of domestic parent banks are in trouble (following the Cooke Committee recommendations) have probably served to signal to the market that large bank failures will not be allowed to occur, or if they are they will not be allowed to adversely impact large depositors.[9]

Saunders' conclusions are fundamentally correct. A notable exception was registered, however, in the early 1980s as a result of the sovereign debt crisis—and its nature and effects were not altogether negative. This contagion effect was the result of the institutional structure of the market. The interbank market through which the pyramiding of banking transactions is effected (intentionally or not) was the contagion channel. As the seriousness of the debt crisis became acute, the aversion of banks, especially American banks, to commit new funds to troubled countries or even to other sovereign borrowers not yet on the critical list became practically universal. In March 1983, Citibank and Morgan Guaranty decided not to lend a mere $7.8 million each to a state agency in France. This all happened just when France was trying to make itself more acceptable to creditors by adopting an austerity program. The reason for declining to make the loan was the agency's refusal to include a cross-default clause in the loan agreement.

Furthermore, the moment a country experienced debt repayment difficulties, its risk became its region's risk, and credit limits were set across the region. Lending to third world countries in the first six months of 1983, for example, fell to $10 billion from $22 billion during the preceding six months.[10]

This across-the-board cut has mixed blessings. By cutting back credit lines, the banks limited their exposure nominally but may have increased the riskiness of the existing sovereign debt portfolio as liquidity was cut to the debtor countries, sinking them into a recession. The banks, after a hiatus, realized this and began lending again. Now, as documented in Chapter 1, the exposure increased because the sovereign loan portfolio was larger.

The critical point here is that this form of "contagion" did not threaten the banking system, and it was not likely to cause a run on banks or create settlement risk. The affected parties were the stockholders of the banks and not the depositors, although the tax-paying public did bear some of the costs of nonperforming loans through the large tax writeoffs taken by the banking sector. The short-run effects distorted the allocational efficiency of the financial markets and reduced their liquidity. The hedging function of the interbank market was not affected, however.

We can conclude, based on the discussion thus far, that there is not a compelling argument for the government to guarantee any bank, regardless of size, against failure. Also, the prevention of bank runs as a premise for banking regulation is a weak one indeed. The remaining justifications are the ones discussed earlier in this chapter.

The regulatory measures adopted by the United States and other countries can be broken down into two categories: preventive measures and prudential measures.

Preventive Measures

There are three major preventive regulatory measures: deposit insurance, bank closing, and lender of last resort.

Deposit Insurance

Deposit insurance is provided, in the case of commercial banks, by the Federal Deposit Insurance Corporation (FDIC), established in 1933. All banks that are members of the Federal Reserve System must buy insurance coverage. The premium paid is fixed, regardless of the size of the bank, its geographic location, or the distribution of its portfolio. The insurance coverage is limited to $100,000 of deposits per depositor. However, as the Continental Illinois case points out, the coverage for the larger bank is unlimited.

The insurance provided by the FDIC is not similar to conventional insurance. It does not pool or eliminate risk. Rather, it insures against systematic risk which cannot be eliminated by portfolio diversification. Without this insurance, the risk would be borne by the stockholders and depositors. The protection of depositors through FDIC insurance transfers that risk to the public. Thus, the ultimate guarantors to the system become the taxpayers. This insurance blanket is provided regardless of the causes of the bank troubles, whether they are due to pilferage, incompetent management, mismatched assets and liabilities, or any other cause. The cost of bank failure is ultimately reflected in higher direct taxes (rising personal income tax rates) or indirect taxes (inflation).

The economic justification for this insurance scheme is that the social costs of bank runs far exceed the cost of bailing out insolvent banks. The loopholes in this argument have already been discussed without ruling out the need for some insurance to the system, especially for the protection of small depositors.

The presence of FDIC insurance has produced a moral hazard problem. The insured bank is encouraged to assume a higher risk profile than would be the case without insurance. Indeed, the increase in insurance coverage over time has been accompanied by a precipitous decline in the capital/asset ratio. This ratio had to be boosted recently to 5.5 percent because it had become dangerously low. The lower the capital ratio, the higher the portion of the bank's systematic risk borne by depositors and ultimately taxpayers.

The problem is aggravated by the ignorance of the public. Banks A and B, paying equal rates on deposits, one solvent and the other insolvent, would be seen as equivalent banks by depositors. Consequently, no funds would be withdrawn from Bank B, the insolvent bank. Even the FDIC is unable, at a given point in time, to establish firmly which bank is solvent and which is not because insolvency could be strictly a temporary problem. Placing such banks on the insolvent list could present a serious problem. The management of these institutions, in a desperate attempt to reestablish solvency, could take on new gambles with payoffs so risky as to increase the expected loss from the bank to the FDIC in the event of an FDIC-arranged merger or a bank closing. Once again, the insurance policy would necessitate greater sacrifices by the taxpayers. Those who argue that bank supervision is the complete answer to this dilemma are naive at best. The entire risk profile of a bank can be changed radically the minute the bank examiners leave (assuming they have correctly assessed the riskiness of the bank in the first place).

The system of deposit insurance eliminates, for all practical purposes, the concerns of depositors about the safety of their deposits—and with it, the discipline of the market. Depositors need not demand higher returns from higher-risk banks. "Managers acting in the best interest of their shareholders would have the incentive to increase risk so that the insurance is essentially underpriced. This is referred to as a 'moral hazard' problem."[11] The logical consequence of this is a financial system with a lower allocational efficiency.

The insurance of deposits can be viewed as a put option[12] sold by the FDIC to the depositor. This view of deposit insurance allows for the use of a standard tool, option pricing models, to assess the risk of insurance. The option gives the long (the insurance buyer) the right to exercise at the face value of the deposit anytime during the life of the deposit. Therefore, while the market value of the bank assets exceeds the face value of the deposits, the short (the insurance seller) loses nothing. A loss is realized if the opposite holds and is equal to the difference between the face value of the deposits and the market value of bank assets. Therefore, the value of the option is a function of this difference, which is roughly equal to the value of the bank equity. Additionally, as with all put options, the value is a fraction of the variability of the underlying assets. This variability is always harmful to the short (the insurance seller). If assets exceed deposits, the insurer pays out nothing and collects the premium. If the value of the deposits exceeds that of the assets, the insurer pays the difference, and the sky is the limit unless the situation is carefully monitored and the portfolio adjusted or the bank closed. No matter what the expected payout, the premium per dollar issued is constant.

This view of insurance dramatically illustrates the need to supervise insured banks and the inadequacy of a flat insurance rate on deposits even if blanket insurance coverage is considered reasonable. The sale of insurance by the FDIC can only be justified through the "consumer protection of *small* depositors." The prevention of runs on banks can be more effectively handled by the Fed as lender of last resort, which would not necessarily require insurance coverage for large deposits.

Bank Closing

The closing of banks by the FDIC is an effective measure to stop contagion, if any, and minimize the loss to the FDIC. The problem, however, lies in political courage and timing. Using the S&L industry as an example, the inevitable kept being postponed until the industry began to sink of its wanton inefficiency. Had the FDIC placed the S&Ls on a full-market-value basis, about one-half of all of them would have shown negative equity. The decision to close these institutions or have them acquired by others was not made on a timely basis. The bureaucratic process was poignantly slow. The hemorrhaging continued while everyone knew the problem and the most effective solution. Interestingly, all the insolvent S&Ls kept on paying the same insurance premium as they did prior to the discovery of their problems, the same premium as any solvent institution.

The end of 1988 saw a tremendous rush to acquire some of these institutions. The acquirers, however, were not in the game for benevolent reasons—the salvation of an industry—but purely for tax advantages and short-run profits. Many of the acquirers knew little about the S&L industry. The 1990 Reagan budget (the last of his presidency) contained a bail-out budget for the S&Ls, and the government will be acquiring or liquidating many of the S&Ls that were thought to have been salvaged through the acquisitions of late 1988. The Bush plan of February 1989, discussed in Chapter 1, is a reasonable solution to the problem.

The federal government has thus far avoided a run on the S&Ls like the ones on the Ohio and Maryland state systems. The reason must be that the behavior of the Federal Home Loan Bank Board and the U.S. Treasury has produced, thus far, the needed comfort for depositors.

Lender of Last Resort

The third leg in the preventive measures triad is lender of last resort facilities. The fundamental justification for this measure is the fear that some market failure will turn a liquidity problem of a banking institution into a solvency problem. The social cost of such an event is deemed higher than the cost of providing the facility. The safety net appears to have performed well. The discount window was not systematically the target of abuse by the banks. There exists ample economic justification for this facility, especially after October 19, 1987, and October 13, 1989.

Prudential Measures

The prudential measures consist of capital adequacy, liquidity requirements, diversification rules, interest regulations, restrictions on permissible business activities, restrictions on market entry, and general banking supervision and inspection. Measures such as interest regulations and restrictions on permissible business activities shield existing banks from competition and allow certain forms of monopolies to perpetrate themselves under the banner of bank stability. The regulation of interest rates has been discontinued.

Capital Adequacy

Capital is the third line of defense against problem loans. The first is regulatory oversight, the second is bank profits, and then comes capital adequacy. The size of the bank capital is also important because it determines the maximum loan per customer.

Capital adequacy regulation deals with the capital/asset ratio, but problems have arisen in defining the numerator and the denominator. The numerator (capital) is the easier of the two; yet it has become more complex recently. Central banks such as the Bank of England allow their banks to count perpetual bonds as capital, while other central banks do not. On the asset side, the problem is whether to include off-balance-sheet items. Banks, for reasons discussed later, have managed to avoid the capital rules through the expansion of their off-balance-sheet activities. Central banks, realizing the increased risk to the banking industry as a result of this strategy, proposed a new way to deal with it. This proposal was advanced by the Federal Reserve System: 12 C.F.R. Part 225, Appendix A to Regulation Q (The Proposal).

The purpose of The Proposal is to provide for capital/total assets ratios that are explicitly and systematically sensitive to the risk profiles of individual banking organizations. The Proposal, circulated in 1987, is the product of a joint effort by the Federal Reserve Board, the Office of the Comptroller of the Currency, the Federal Deposit Insurance Corporation, and, interestingly, the Bank of England.

Under The Proposal, the capital position of a bank is assessed by taking into account both the volume of its assets at risk and the volume and nature of its off-balance-sheet risks. The objective with regard to swap transactions and other off-balance-sheet transactions is to convert off-balance-sheet items into balance-sheet credit equivalent amounts.

The proposed risk-based measure (RBM) is

$$\text{RBM} = \frac{\text{Primary capital}}{\text{Weighted risky assets}}$$

The weights are assigned to on- and some off-balance-sheet items. The risk weight for off-balance-sheet items is determined in two steps:

- Determine the credit equivalent amount of an off-balance-sheet item.
- Assign the credit equivalent amount to one of the five risk categories used for on-balance-sheet assets.

In the specific case of swaps, the credit equivalent amount is the sum of the current replacement cost plus a measure of potential future increases in the replacement costs.

The current replacement costs will be marked to market, which requires taking the present value of the net payment stream specified by the contract using current exchange and interest rates and the addition of accrued interest. Current replacement costs are calculated using credit conversion factors derived by estimating the volatility of exchange and interest rates and its impact on relevant contracts. Therefore,

Potential exposure = Notional principal × Proposed credit conversion factor

The use of credit conversion factors and their values for certain maturities are shown in Exhibits 2.1 and 2.2.

For swap transactions, the instruments included are simple currency interest rate swaps, forward rate agreements, over-the-counter interest rate options purchased, cross-currency swaps (including cross-currency interest rate swaps), forward foreign exchange contracts, over-the-counter foreign currency options purchased, and other instruments of a similar nature that give rise to similar credit risks.

The Proposal had been criticized. Some observers have argued that most U.S. banks are already overcapitalized relative to the risk assumed. Lumping the low-risk exposure banks with the largest U.S. banks is said to be neither necessary nor desirable. Also, the proposed guidelines related to swaps discourage "other types of off-balance-sheet risk spreading—may discourage some banks from using swaps to neutralize their exposure to interest rate risk."[13]

The Proposal is a step in the right direction, provided it is enforced with fairness and vigor. It can only reduce the burden on the insurance system.

Liquidity Requirements

The liquidity of the banking system is assured by the Federal Reserve System as a lender of last resort. Under the Monetary Control Act of 1980, the Fed provides liquidity after all other sources of funds have been exhausted in the form

Exhibit 2.1
Calculation of Credit Equivalent Amounts for Interest Rate–Related and Foreign Exchange Rate–Related Transactions

Type of Contract (remaining maturity)	(1) Notional Principal (dollars) ×	(2) Potential Exposure Conversion Factor [1/]	(3) Potential Exposure (dollars) +	(4) Current Exposure (dollars) [2/] =	(5) Credit Equivalent (dollars)
(1) 120-day forward foreign exchange	5,000,000	.04	200,000	100,000	300,000
(2) 120-day forward foreign exchange	6,000,000	.04	240,000	-120,000	120,000
(3) 3-year single-currency fixed/floating interest rate swap	10,000,000	.015	150,000	200,000	350,000
(4) 3-year single-currency fixed/floating interest rate swap	10,000,000	.015	150,000	-250,000	0
(5) 7-year cross-currency floating/floating interest rate swap	20,000,000	.12	2,400,000	-1,300,000	1,100,000
TOTAL	51,000,000				1,870,000

1/ For illustrative purposes only, these examples use credit conversion factors at the lower end of the ranges shown in Table 1.
2/ These numbers are purely illustrative.

Exhibit 2.2
**Potential Credit Exposure: Proposed Conversion Factors for Interest Rate
and Foreign Exchange Rate Contracts (Percentage of national principal amount)**

Remaining Maturity	Interest Rate Contracts	Exchange Rate Contracts
Less than one year:		
Less than three days	0	0
Three days to one month	0	1 to 2%
One month to three months	0	2 to 4%
Three months to one year	0	4 to 8%
One year or longer	$\frac{1}{2}$ to 1% per complete year remaining to maturity	(5 to 10%) + (1 to 2%) per complete year remaining to maturity

of short-term adjustment credit, seasonal credit, or extended credit. The latter credit requires collateral or the discount of eligible paper.

The system of required reserves provides minimal liquidity assurances because the banking institution with liquidity problems may not be able to tap any of its reserves when it needs them the most. In this regard, the reserve requirements become largely, if not exclusively, an instrument of monetary policy.

The reserve requirements are slated to become uniform across all depository institutions. Reserves may be in the form of vault cash, balances with the Federal Reserve System, or pass-through accounts at the Federal Home Loan Bank (for S&Ls), the Central Liquidity Facility (for credit unions), or a correspondent bank (for commercial banks). The reserve requirements are 0 percent for the first $2.4 million, 3 percent for deposits between $2.4 and $29.8 million, and 12 percent for deposits exceeding $29.8 million. All the reserves are noninterest-bearing.

The liquidity risk to banking institutions has been aggravated by the sharp increase in their contingent liabilities, as discussed in Chapter 1. These liabilities include repurchase agreements, notes issuance facilities, swap agreements, options contracts, letters of credit, and other similar commitments.

The reserve requirements may well be a mirage when banks are most in need of liquidity. They simply may not be usable. The Fed's discount window will be the only recourse, assuming the interbank market has already been exhausted. Thus, the justification of reserves on liquidity grounds is dubious at best.

Diversification Rules

The diversification rules are intended to reduce, if not eliminate, unsystematic risk in the bank portfolio of assets (loans and securities) and to ensure that the prudent man rule is observed in the selection of assets.

National banking institutions in the United States are restricted in terms of the ratio of total real estate loans to bank capital and time deposits, and state banking institutions are subject to various restrictions on their real estate portfolios. Commercial banks are also required to limit their loan commitment to a single borrower to 15 percent of the bank's unimpaired capital and surplus. An additional 10 percent is allowed if the loan is secured by readily marketable securities. The sovereign debt crisis made a mockery of this limit. It turned out that Citibank's exposure to Brazil alone was 73.5 percent of its capital as early as 1982.[14] The limit was circumvented by allowing government agencies in debtor countries to borrow under their own names, given their "independent" sources of income. It turned out, of course, that the independence was imaginary.

Banking institutions are also required to purchase only certain types of securities. The purchase of the securities of any one debt issuer is limited to 10 percent of its total equity capital. Banks are required to diversify by maturity across debt securities and are expected to maintain a balanced portfolio in terms of assets and liabilities' duration structure. In addition, banks are barred from holding an equity ownership except in subsidiary service companies.

The economic rationale for these regulations is to reduce the asset concentration risk and consequently the risk of bankruptcy assumed by the deposit insurance corporation. The monitoring of the system is not well developed. The Fed uses the ratio of commercial and industrial loans to total loans as one indicator of concentration because it has been shown to have high predictive power in bankruptcy models.[15]

The best lesson on the value of a diversified portfolio lies in the fate of the savings and loan industry documented in Chapter 1. The lack of diversification, it must be noted, is due to regulation in the first instance.

Restriction on Permissible Business Activities

The restrictions on nonbanking activities by banking institutions are contained in the Banking Act of 1933, otherwise referred to as the Glass–Steagall Act. The merits of this act and all the changes in it will be discussed in a separate section below. The currently permissible nonbanking activities are listed in Exhibit 2.3.

Restrictions on Market Entry

These restrictions are economically valid only so long as they prevent unsavory characters from entering the banking industry. Commercial and industrial companies in the United States, unlike in some European countries, are prevented from owning banking institutions. The merit of these restrictions is discussed below. Furthermore, many restrictions still exist on intrastate and interstate branching, although banks have found several effective ways to circumvent these restrictions. The economic benefits of these circumventions are significant and positive. They have served to break down many regional monopolies, improve the quality of service, and reduce the cost of banking services.

General Banking Supervision and Inspection

The present bank regulatory structure is shown in Exhibit 2.4. The Comptroller of the Currency charters, supervises, and examines all national banks. Member banks are supervised by the Federal Reserve System, as are all bank holding companies. The Federal Deposit Insurance Corporation directly super-

Exhibit 2.3
Currently Permissible Nonbanking Activities

1. Making, acquiring, or servicing loans or other extensions of credit such as made by a mortgage, finance, credit card, or factoring company
2. Operating as an industrial bank in a manner authorized by state law
3. Performing certain trust company activities
4. Acting as investment or financial advisor
5. Leasing personal property where the lease is functionally equivalent to an extension of credit and the lessor is fully compensated for the property investment and the estimated total cost of financing the property over the term of the lease
6. Making equity or debt investments in community welfare projects
7. Providing data processing services for others where the data is of a financial, banking, or economic nature
8. Acting as insurance agent or broker with respect to any insurance related to extensions of credit by a bank or bank-related firm, or any insurance sold in a community with a population of 5,000 or less, provided the holding company's principal banking business is also in a community with population of 5,000 or less
9. Acting as underwriter for credit life insurance and credit accident and health insurance directly related to credit extensions by the bank holding company system
10. Providing courier services for financially related data
11. Providing management consulting advice to nonaffiliated depository institutions
12. Selling at retail money orders having a face value of not more than $1,000, selling travelers checks, and selling U.S. savings bonds
13. Performing appraisals of real estate
14. Arranging commercial real estate equity financing
15. Providing securities brokerage services and related credit activities where brokerage services are restricted to buying and selling securities solely as an agent for customers
16. Underwriting and dealing in government obligations and money market instruments
17. Providing foreign exchange advisory and transaction services
18. Acting as a futures commission merchant on futures contracts for bullion, foreign exchange, government securities, certificates of deposit, and other money market instruments

Note: For a more detailed description of some of these activities, see Section 225.25(b) of Federal Reserve Regulation Y.

Source: Kenneth Spong, *Banking Regulation: Its Purposes, Implementations and Effects,* 2d ed. (Kansas City, Mo.: Federal Reserve Bank of Kansas City, 1985), 98.

Exhibit 2.4
Bank Regulatory Structure

	NATIONAL BANKS	STATE BANKS		
		MEMBERS OF THE FEDERAL RESERVE SYSTEM	INSURED NONMEMBERS	UNINSURED
CHARTERING AUTHORITY	Comptroller of the Currency	State Banking Department		
SUPERVISORY AND EXAMINING AUTHORITY	Comptroller of the Currency	State Banking Department and Federal Reserve System	State Banking Department and FDIC	
FDIC INSURANCE	Automatic with Charter	Automatic with Membership	Upon FDIC Approval	
FEDERAL RESERVE MEMBERSHIP	Automatic with Charter	Upon Federal Reserve Approval		
APPROVAL FOR BRANCH APPLICATIONS	Comptroller of the Currency	State Banking Department and Federal Reserve System	State Banking Department and FDIC	
APPROVAL FOR *† BANK MERGERS	Comptroller of the Currency	State Banking Department and Federal Reserve System	State Banking Department and FDIC	
APPROVAL OF BANK†‡ HOLDING COMPANY FORMATIONS AND ACQUISITIONS	Federal Reserve System			

*If the bank resulting from a merger is insured, the responsible federal agency also requests reports on the competitive effects from the Department of Justice and the other two federal banking agencies.

†Between the approval and consummation dates of a bank merger or a bank holding company acquisition involving a bank, the Department of Justice may bring action under the antitrust laws.

‡The Federal Reserve Board is required to notify and solicit the views of the Comptroller of the Currency on proposed holding company acquisitions of national banks and the appropriate state banking department on the proposed acquisition of a state bank. When the Federal Reserve sends the notification letters, a copy also is commonly sent to the FDIC.

Any uninsured bank becoming a subsidiary of a holding company must obtain federal deposit insurance.

Source: Kenneth Spong, Banking Regulation: Its Purposes, Implementations and Effects, 2d ed. (Kansas City, Mo.: Federal Reserve Bank of Kansas City, 1985), 39.

vises state-chartered banks that are not members of the Federal Reserve System. All these agencies use a monitoring system for banks that has two components: an inspection examination system and an early warning system. The examination takes place at least once every 18 months. The process was streamlined and made quite uniform in 1979 under what is being referred to as the Camel Approach.[16] The components of Camel are capital adequacy, asset quality, management quality and depth, earnings, and liquidity. Banks are scored on each component of Camel, with 1 being the highest score and 5 the lowest. An overall rating is then assigned as part of the bank examination. The rating, specific or overall, is arrived at using multifactor models.

The early warning system uses standard bankruptcy models to identify those banks likely to fail in the near future. The typical predictive model is one of the multiple discriminant analysis type using a series of financial ratios as predictive variables.[17] Banks are then given a clean bill of health, classified as closure or merger candidates, or categorized as requiring liquidity loans or closer supervision.

Supervision and examination are justifiable and rational. They allow the system considerable and necessary breathing space before drastic action is taken. The problem, however, lies in three major areas:

- The quality of the examination process
- The resolve of regulators to take strong and effective action when the situation calls for it
- The dynamic nature of any bank portfolio

No one is ever certain that the results of any test are 100 percent conclusive. The grey area leaves considerable discretion to the regulator who has to struggle with his will and conscience. The record of regulators on the savings and loan front is poor, leaving the taxpayers with a larger burden than would have resulted if political courage had not been in short supply.

The dynamic nature of the bank portfolio and its quality could transform a bank from one grade to another almost overnight. An excellent example of this is the sovereign debt crisis, which broke out in the early 1980s. Banks that were very healthy, or so they seemed, suddenly were faced with huge potential losses. The stock market immediately recognized this as the prices of shares of major money-center banks dropped, in some cases precipitously.

The reaction of the Fed, it must be noted, was neither swift nor comprehensive. Nonperforming loans were allowed to be carried at face value on the bank books for too long a period. The problem, while currently manageable, is far from resolved. The January 17, 1989, issue of *The Wall Street Journal* reported on the sudden re-emergence of Brazil as a debtor country with severe economic problems and a very low probability of resolving them anytime soon:

Brazil, embarking on a new attempt to beat inflation, suspended debt for equity swaps, postponed planned relending programs, centralized control of foreign exchange operations and said it doesn't rule out a new moratorium on foreign debt payments.

The firm stance toward foreign-creditor banks, announced by Finance Minister Mailson Ferreira de Nobrega, amounts to a political message that the government is not demanding sacrifices of Brazilians alone. It also appeared designed to win over foreign banks and the U.S. Government to Brazilian demands for a bridge loan and the immediate release of $1.2 billion in new foreign bank loans.[18]

Inflation in Brazil was running at 935 percent annually in early 1989. This is what prompted the government action. However, the restructuring of Brazil's $62 billion debt in 1988 did not appear to solve any of the fundamental problems. It simply postponed the day of reckoning.

These drawbacks should not, however, lead the reader to conclude that supervision is undesirable. On the contrary, they argue for a more vigilant system and for better and more continuous communication between bank and regulator. This will improve the flow and quality of information and consequently improve market efficiency. There is overwhelming evidence, for example, that the SEC has enhanced the efficiency of the stock and bond markets.

The G–10 Regulatory Environments

The regulatory environments across G–10 countries contain as many similarities as dissimilarities. Although the separation of banking and commerce is generally upheld (Exhibit 2.5), the glaring exception is West Germany.

Exhibit 2.5
Predominant Forms of Banking-Commerce Integration in the G–10 Countries

	Commercial Ownership of Banks	Bank Ownership of Commerce	Common Holding Company*	Generally Limited Integration+
Universal Systems				
France			X	
Germany		X		
Italy				X
Netherlands				X
Switzerland				X
Blended Systems				
Belgium			X	
Canada				X
Japan				X
Sweden				X
United Kingdom				X
United States				X

*The typical form of integration is for a single holding company to have significant ownership interests in both banks and commerce.
+In general, there are no controlling ownership affiliations between individual banks and commercial firms.

Source: Christine M. Cumming and Lawrence M. Sweet, "Financial Structure of the G–10 Countries: How Does the United States Compare?" *Quarterly Review* (Federal Reserve Bank of New York) (Winter 1987–1988): 2.

Exhibit 2.6
The Major Differences in Regulatory Segmentation and Functional Supervision in the G–10 Countries

	Regulatory Segmentation for Banking and Securities Activities			Functional Supervision for Banking and Securities Activities
	One Principal Supervisor (One for Both)	Two Principal Supervisors (One for Each)	Multiple Supervisors	Degree of Current or Planned Use
Universal Systems				
France	X*			Low+
Germany	X*			Low+
Italy	X			Low+
Netherlands	X			Low+
Switzerland	X			Limited+
Blended Systems				
Belgium	X			Low
Canada		X		High
Japan		X^		Limited
Sweden	X			Low
United Kingdom		X		High
United States			X	Limited

*The Banking Commission, the principal bank supervisor, shares responsibility for supervising the securities activities of banks with the Stock Exchange Council.

+In universal banking counties, banks are the principal providers of securities activities, so that the need to allocate supervisory responsibility has not spurred the development of functional supervision as it has in some blended system countries.

^ The Banking bureau and the Securities Bureau are both part of the Ministry of Finance, but they operate somewhat independently.

Source: Christine M. Cumming and Lawrence M. Sweet, "Financial Structure of the G–10 Countries: How Does the United States Compare?" *Quarterly Review* (Federal Reserve Bank of New York) (Winter 1987–1988): 8.

The supervisory structure in European countries is quite different from that in the United States: essentially, it is less segmented than in the United States. In the majority of G–10 countries, a single supervisory agency is responsible for both banking and securities firms. "The primary regulator is either a banking commission (Belgium, France, Germany, Sweden, and Switzerland), or the Central Bank (Italy and the Netherlands). In these seven countries the role of the central bank ranges from consultation to principal responsibility for carrying out supervision."[19] Exhibit 2.6 summarizes the major differences.

The separation of financial services is more clear in the United States than in most G–10 countries. However, the lines of demarcation between banking and investment banking are crumbling in the United States as banks and investment banks have figured out, and continue to do so, ways to circumvent the Glass–Steagall Act. This act is discussed below. The predominant forms of financial service integration are summarized in Exhibit 2.7. Only Japan and the United States maintain high levels of separation between banks and investment banks. We now look at the economics of deregulation.

The Economics of Deregulation

The deregulation of financial markets should be considered an investment in the financial well-being of a nation. The payoffs from this investment, although neither certain nor always predictable, are expected to take these forms:

- Increased financial flexibility of firms and households
- Reduced transaction costs, improving the operational efficiency of the financial markets
- Improved allocational efficiency of the financial markets
- New capital attracted to financial intermediaries
- Banking institutions that are stronger and more competitive in a global market
- Better diversified bank portfolios
- The more effective conduct of monetary and fiscal policy
- A fairer market.

Chapter 7 will analyze whether these objectives have indeed been achieved. If they have been, then deregulation would have been justified on economic grounds.

Banking institutions operating in a deregulated environment are faced with a choice between safety and profitability. The safety is reflected in a larger capital base and reserves and in "safer" assets. The profitability is achieved primarily through a better and larger investment opportunity set, but occasionally, and unfortunately, by the bank's assuming undue risk. Any judgment on deregulation must therefore consider whether the risk profile of banking and investment banking institutions has increased as a result of deregulation without a commensurate increase in rates of return.

The economic arguments in favor of and against deregulation are best illustrated in the recent and continuing debate over the Glass–Steagall Act. The act is now examined as a revealing case study.

Glass–Steagall—At the Crossroads

The Banking Act of 1933, enacted in response to the 1929 market crash and the ensuing depression, provided for the Federal Deposit Insurance Corporation. Sections 16, 20, 21, and 32 of the act later became known as the Glass–Steagall Act:

- Section 16 prohibits banks from buying stock for their own account. It places a limit on bank dealing in securities but does not prohibit the activity. However, bank underwriting

Exhibit 2.7
Predominant Forms of Financial Service Integration in the G-10 Countries

	Expanded Bank Powers*	Nonbank Subsidiary of Bank†	Common Holding Company‡	Degree of Integration of Banking and Securities Services§
Universal Systems				
France	X			High
Germany	X			High
Italy	X			High
Netherlands	X			High
Switzerland	X			High
Blended Systems				
Belgium		X		High
Canada		X		High
Japan		X		Low
Sweden		X		High‖
United Kingdom		X		High‖
United States			X	Low

*Single "universal" banks directly provide in-house all banking
and securities services.
†The typical form of integration is for banks to have wholly
owned nonbank financial subsidiaries.
‡A single holding company typically has significant ownership
interests in both banks and nonbank financial firms.
§Either through expanded in-house powers or through
institutional affiliations.
‖Financial structure liberalization recently has increased the
integration of banking and securities services.

Source: Christine M. Cumming and Lawrence M. Sweet, "Financial Structure of the G-10 Countries: How Does the United States Compare?" *Quarterly Review* (Federal Reserve Bank of
New York) (Winter 1987-1988): 4.

of securities is prohibited, and few exemptions are allowed: Banks are allowed to
underwrite U.S. Treasury obligations, obligations of federal government agencies, and
general obligations of states and municipalities (but not municipal revenue bonds), and
to invest in other specified debt instruments, subject to certain restrictions.

• Section 20 prohibits banks from having securities affiliates and from engaging in activities prohibited by Sections 16 and 21 through affiliates.

• Section 21 prohibits any person, firm, corporation, association, business trust, or other
similar organization from engaging in the securities business while receiving deposits to
any extent whatever, except to the extent permitted by Section 16 of the act.

• Section 32 prohibits any interlocking of officers, directors, employees, or partners
between securities firms and banks. Any exception to this will be authorized only by the
Federal Reserve Board.

These prohibitions were circumvented, however, by strong-willed bankers determined to see their business grow and to diversify beyond the prescribed limit of banking as set by the Banking Act of 1933. The results amount to the dismantling of a federal law without an official action by Congress.

The commercial banks of the United States currently engage in the following activities:

- Participating in the private placement of corporate securities
- Holding corporate securities for their own accounts
- Acting as agents for customers in purchasing and selling securities
- Underwriting and dealing in general obligation municipal securities as well as certain types of municipal revenue bonds
- Engaging in trust activities
- Underwriting and dealing in corporate securities overseas

Most of these changes were realized through tough court battles or by the regulators looking the other way. The chronology of the legal battles of the 1980s is shown in Exhibit 2.8. The securities industry has grown timid lately, however.

The May 1987 issue of *Institutional Investor* reported on some ingenious methods banks use to circumvent the regulatory process:

Citicorp, for example, appears to have devised an ingenious end run around the law that would allow it to deal in equities in the U.S. by passing positions to its foreign affiliates. When Citicorp bought Vickers da Costa in London last year it arranged the transition so that the bank—not the holding company—would buy Vickers' New York office. It then won approval from the deregulation-minded office of the Comptroller of the Currency, which oversees national banks, for Vickers in New York to continue making an over-the-counter market in foreign stocks. Through Vickers, Citibank would then be able to place bid and offered quotes on the NASDAQ market system, but it would have to pass orders on to an offshore affiliate immediately.

Shortly after the OCC approved the deal, however, the Federal Reserve—which regulates Citibank's holding company—intervened, worried about possible Glass–Steagall violations. The real reason for the Fed's action, goes the rumor among bank lawyers, is that it felt deceived about the way Citibank acquired Vickers in the first place—that is, without revealing its intentions for the New York operation. Citibank's deal is on hold right now, but bank lawyers are watching it closely. They say that the Fed's okay could open the way for banks to deal in U.S. stocks as well.

The pressures to dismantle Glass–Steagall are coming from unusual sources: state regulators and banking authorities. The state of New York, for example, decided to interpret its own state Glass–Steagall to allow state-chartered banks to engage "in a significant amount of securities underwriting through separate subsidiaries.

Unfortunately, this was not of much direct help to the New York bank holding companies that are federally chartered. The signals were quite helpful, however.

Further pressure is coming from foreign banks. Union Bank of Switzerland was the lead manager of bond issues by Allied-Signal, TransAmerican Financial

Exhibit 2.8
Chronology of New Cracks in the Glass–Steagall Wall

1981: FED IS KEY The Supreme Court upheld a Federal Reserve rule allowing bank holding companies to be investment advisers to closed-end investment companies. The court added that the Fed "Is entitled to the greatest deference" in determining proper banking activities. Later in the year, the Fed reluctantly allowed a Gulf & Western Industries, Inc. subsidiary to acquire a Concord, Calif., bank- the first recognized use of the "nonbank bank" loophole that has set in motion a reevaluation of the limits separating banks from other industries.

1982: A YEAR OF ACTION The Security Pacific National Bank, Los Angeles, began offering discount brokerage services via a joint venture with Fidelity Brokerage Services. The Comptroller of the Currency that year agreed to permit several national banks to acquire or establish brokerage subsidiaries. In August, the Federal Deposit Insurance Corp. issued a controversial policy statement saying that insured banks that are not members of the Federal Reserve System can form securities subsidiaries that can conduct securities activities prohibited to the bank itself under Glass-Steagall. in early 1987, the FDIC's conclusions were upheld by a federal appeals court in Washington.

1983: NEW ADVICE The Fed allowed the BankAmerica Corp. to acquire the charles Schwab discount brokerage firm. And the Comptroller gave the American National Bank of Austin (Tex.) authority to operate an investment-advisory subsidiary.

1984: MORE CHIPS FALL The Supreme Court upheld BankAmerica's acquisition of Schwab. In September, the Senate overwhelmingly approved a banking bill that included expanded securities power, but it dies on the House side.

1985: BRANCHING QUESTION A federal appeals court upheld the ability of a national bank to operate a discount brokerage subsidiary, subject to bank branching restrictions.

January 1986: THE HIGH COURT The Supreme Court upheld the rights of national banks to offer discount brokerage services. Later that month, in the Dimension and U.S. Trust cases, the court gave victories to the nonbank bank movement and heightened debate about banking industry structure.

June 1986: A BUSY FED Bank America's Charles Schwab & Co. unit gets Fed permission to assist in an initial public offering of shares in Schafer Value Trust - perhaps the closest to the underwriting process for a bank affiliate since the 1930s. Later that month, the Fed authorized the National Westminster Bank, London, to offer investment advice and securities brokerage services to U.S. institutional customers. And a Fed letter to the Sovran Financial Corp., Norfolk, Va., cleared the way for bank holding companies to sell shares of mutual funds and unit investment trusts through subsidiaries.

August 1986: JAPANESE PARTNER Japan's Sumitomo Bank announced a plan for a passive investment in Goldman. Sachs & Co., a major Wall Street investment banking partnership. The Fed gave conditional approval in November.

(continued)

Exhibit 2.8 (*Continued*)

November 1986: **MORE COURT VICTORIES** The Supreme Court upheld the
authority of banks to offer a trust service from individual retirement
accounts. The next day, a Washington appeals court ruled against the
Securities and Exchange Commission's Rule 3b9, aimed at forcing banks to
register their securities subsidiaries with the agencies as broker-
dealers.

December 1986: **BANKERS TRUST** After many years in litigation, a federal
appeals court finds Bankers Trust Co.'s commercial paper placement
services to be legal. The next day, the Fed said banks can engage in
modest levels of underwriting activities within a holding company
subsidiary, but it postponed a decision on applications by Bankers
Trust, Citicorp, and J.P. Morgan & Co. to underwrite a broad range of
securities through affiliates. Also, the New York State Banking
Department issued an interpretation of its "little Glass-Steagall Act,"
opening the way for state-chartered banks to participate in currently
impermissible underwriting activities.

January 1987: **NATIONWIDE ACTIVITIES** The Supreme Court upheld the right
of national banks to establish interstate brokerage branches, a decision
that could encourage the development of nationwide securities businesses
by banks.   -Jay Rosenstein

Source: American Banker (2 February 1987). Reprinted with permission from American Bank-
er/Bond Buyer.

Corp., and Borg-Warner Acceptance Corp. Other foreign banks were equally
bold, leading the way, many argue, for U.S. banks.

Congress has not remained passive in the face of all these developments, and
has passed two major deregulation bills: the Depository Institutions Deregulation
and Monetary Control Act (DIDMCA) of 1980, and the Garn–St. Germain
Depository Institutions Act (DIA) of 1982. Both acts were intended to break
down regulatory barriers between different types of depository institutions. Both
gave thrifts broad diversification powers similar to those of banks. Neither act,
however, dealt with nationwide banking, the fusion of commerce and banking, or
the merging of investment and commercial banking. Many bills dealing with
these issues have been debated in Congress, but none has been enacted—yet.

The Fed also became more accommodating in April 1987 when it gave "banks
limited authority to trade in commercial paper, mortgage-backed securities and
certain types of municipal bonds."[20] This ruling was made over the objections of
the Securities Industry Association (SIA).

We now consider the economic arguments in favor of and against the dismantling of Glass-Steagall.

Economic Arguments

The origins of Glass–Steagall, as discussed above, lie in the depression and
the serious abuses by bank/investment bank officers of the trust of depositors and
investors.

Three principal types of abuses common to the investment banking business during the 1920–1930s were:

• Underwriting and distributing unsound and speculative securities
• Conveying untruthful or misleading information in the prospectuses accompanying new issues
• Manipulating the market for certain stocks and bonds while they were being issued.

Examples of the first two types of abuses can be found by examining National City Co.'s involvement in the financial operations of the Republic of Peru. Throughout the 1920s, National City Co. received reports that Peru was politically unstable, had a bad debt record, suffered from a depleted Treasury and was, in short, an extremely poor credit risk.

Nevertheless, in 1927 and 1928, National City Co. participated in the underwriting of three bond issues by the government of Peru. The prospectuses distributed in connection with these issues made no mention of Peru's political and economic difficulties.

As a result, the public purchased all $90 million of the bonds, which went into default in 1931 and sold for less than 5% of their face value in 1933.

While this may be one of the more flagrant examples of these types of abuses, it was generally acknowledged that the extremely competitive banking environment of the 1920s led bankers to encourage overborrowing, particularly by governments and political subdivisions in Europe and South America.[21]

The overaggressiveness of banks is not too dissimilar from what was witnessed 50 years later with the sovereign debt crisis in the United States. This crisis, however, took place with Glass–Steagall still on the books and is being resolved, albeit partially, without a new, tougher version of Glass–Steagall. The abuses of the investment banking industry were attended to by the SEC, which was created precisely for those purposes.

The rationale for keeping the Glass–Steagall Act on the books and for enforcing it is based primarily on the conflict of interest concerns. These can be placed into six categories:

• Bank safety and soundness (i.e., transactions may occur that are detrimental to the bank, but beneficial to an affiliate); or conversely,

• Transactions that are beneficial to the bank at the expense of an affiliate;

• Illegal tie-ins;

• Violation of a bank's fiduciary responsibilities;

• Improper use of insider information;

• The potential for abuse due to the bank's dual role as marketer of services and impartial financial adviser.[22]

The bank safety and soundness concern was dramatically illustrated in the early 1970s when banking institutions came to the rescue of their failing real estate investment trust (REIT) affiliates. A case in point was Chase Manhattan Bank, which suffered huge losses. The answer to this, however, lies not in banning the affiliation, but in better supervising and regulating its nature and extent.

Two safeguards have been introduced in sections 23A (added to the act in 1933 and amended in 1982) and 23B (added to the act in 1987). Both of these sections apply to member and nonmember banks and their dealings with affiliates. Transactions between a member bank and its affiliate are limited to 10 percent of the capital stock and surplus of the bank. Unlike the safeguard that applied to the savings and loans, this one, coupled with vigilant supervision, should render Glass–Steagall unnecessary.

The fear that banks would find a way to unduly enrich themselves at the expense of their affiliates goes back to the 1930s, when, for example, banks dumped bad loans onto their securities affiliates which turned them into bonds sold to investors. The presence of the SEC and the bank regulatory agencies and the resulting close supervision will make this less likely. Furthermore, the securitization of loans goes on in the 1980s without investment banking affiliates. The markets today are much more mature about matters of this sort. This is discussed further in Chapter 8.

The tie-in concerns are exaggerated. There is presently ample room for this to occur in the banking sector and in every other sector. The whole concept of one-stop banking is to provide services "tied" together, and not necessarily for the purpose of self-dealing by bankers. Tie-ins are prevalent in Europe and Japan, and there is no evidence that their banking systems are any less stable as a result or that their customers are any worse off. Unscrupulous banks can also create tie-ins with or without affiliates.

The violation of a bank's fiduciary responsibility as a result of its underwriting activities is possible under the exemptions allowed under the 1933 act. While banks are capable of dumping municipal bonds they underwrite onto their trust departments, there is no evidence of this whatsoever. There is also no reason to believe that American banks will be any less scrupulous than their European counterparts in the management of the relationship between the bank and its securities affiliate(s).

The potential for abuse of insider information is already present in the banking sector. A bank with, for example, GM as a client may choose to inform its trust department about buying GM stock based on inside information acquired as a result of the relationship with GM. There is no evidence that this is taking place, and there is nothing to suggest that an investment banking division will be treated any differently.

The concern over potential abuse due to the bank's dual role as marketer of services and impartial financial advisor is no less exaggerated than those discussed above.

We can conclude therefore that none of these conflicts of interest can support the argument for keeping banks out of the investment banking system. Arm's length dealings between banks and their affiliates can be legislated and carefully supervised so that nonbanking enterprises affiliated with banks would not have an undue advantage over those that are not.

Banks should not be foreclosed from entering the lucrative investment banking

Exhibit 2.9
After-Tax Return on Equity, Comparing Investment Banks and Bank Holding Companies, 1979–1983

	1979	1980	1981	1982	1983	average
Large investment banks	19%	30%	30%	30%	24%	27%
10 largest bank holding companies	16%	16%	14%	13%	13%	14%

Source: J. P. Morgan, *Rethinking Glass–Steagall* (New York: J. P. Morgan, 1984), 20.

industry. Exhibit 2.9 shows that the average after-tax profits in the investment banking sector are about twice those in the banking sector.

Furthermore, there is no evidence to suggest that equity underwriting is more risky than commercial lending, despite evidence that initial public offerings are riskier than existing equity issues.[23] The risk diversification potential of a full-fledged underwriting activity cannot be understated. Because bank profits are the second line of defense after regulatory oversight, the banking system can only become more stable if it is more profitable under an appropriate supervisory umbrella.

The underwriting activity would certainly not be new to U.S. banks. In fact, the division has never been complete since the depression. Exhibit 2.10 shows clearly that banks are already very active in investment banking activities. Those still clinging to the Glass–Steagall Act as effective legislation are dreamers without alarm clocks.

The Achilles heel of this is the quality of supervision and the firmness of supervisors, especially with bankers who have stepped out of line or proved their ineptness. The savings and loan industry case is far from reassuring. Losing S&Ls were kept operating despite the fact they were losing $12 billion a year. The "rescue packages" did nothing but give swaps to a few very shrewd financial engineers.

Furthermore,

Even with the most sophisticated of projection techniques, bank regulators currently are able to project only two-thirds of bank failures a year in advance . . . significantly, our bank regulatory system failed to catch Penn Square (of Oklahoma), Continental Illinois and Seafirst (of Washington) before they failed. The current state of affairs leaves much to be desired. FDIC Chairman, William Seidman, recently acknowledged that his agency is 'significantly behind in its examination schedule.'[24]

What is needed is a whole new concept of supervision, a larger number of well-trained supervisors, and a large supply of political courage. Partially hiding

Exhibit 2.10
Commercial Bank Market Shares, 1986

Activity	1986 market share
U.S. Securities Trading	20%
Municipal Bond Underwriting	27
Private Placements	19
Private Debt Placements	26
Swaps	70
Eurobond Underwriting	10

Source: Jed Horowitz, *American Banker* (2 December 1987): 3.

behind what remains of the Glass–Steagall Act provides for none of these reforms.

In addition, the organizational form within which the investment banking activity will be housed is of importance. The holding company appears to have a few advantages over the bank itself, yet it has been used rather intensively.

Forecasted Consequences

The opinions on the consequences of Glass–Steagall are as varied as the forecasters are. The summary view includes the following probabilities:

- Regional investment banking firms will become attractive takeover targets.
- Regional banks will become better integrated and be in a better position to serve middle market companies.
- Banks will sponsor mutual funds instead of acting merely as agents.
- The new products to emerge are likely to bring about new regulation.
- A major economic downturn could erase most of the things, if not everything, achieved under the banner of deregulation.

The beneficial effects of repealing Glass–Steagall are summarized in an extensive study prepared by the General Accounting Office (GAO) at the request of Edward J. Markey, chairman of the House Subcommittee on Telecommunications and Finance of the Committee on Energy and Commerce.[25] While some of these benefits have been mentioned earlier, a full list is presented, as seen through the eyes of the GAO.

- There would be greater competition, which is, in itself, desirable. Prices charged to businesses and households would be reduced by bidding away any excess profits that might exist, and new and better services would be provided.

- Consumers would benefit from the increased availability of existing and perhaps new financial services. Other existing services might be provided at reduced prices. Consumers might also experience greater convenience in being able to "one-stop shop." For example, a survey cited by proponents indicated that consumers would value the opportunity to purchase mutual funds from their bank instead of from, or in addition to, the current, more remote mutual fund distribution system.[26] A Federal Reserve study has also shown that a substantial number of consumers would like to be able to obtain all their financial services from one location—their bank.[27]

- Business would benefit from improved access to the capital markets. Large firms might pay lower prices for underwriting services as a result of enhanced competition at the national level from the largest commercial banks. Smaller firms would, for the first time, have direct access to the capital markets if regional and community banks offered services previously not available from the highly concentrated set of national underwriters. Results obtained from a 1987 survey of about 700 of 1,700 large U.S. corporations with sales over $250 million found that firms relying on both banks and the commercial paper markets and those with lower credit ratings particularly oppose the retention of Glass–Steagall.[28]

- Smaller firms located away from the New York City home of most investment banks would have better access to the capital markets if their needs could be serviced by the larger regional bank holding companies. This development would improve the regional allocation/distribution of investment funds.

- State and local governments would probably pay lower interest rates on issues of municipal revenue bonds. According to a 1979 review by William Silber of 12 academic studies, underwriting spreads are lower for general obligation bonds, which can currently be underwritten by banks, than for revenue bonds, which most insured banks cannot issue.[29] Some of the reduced issuing costs might be passed on to users of local government services as lower prices, some savings might be used to reduce state and local tax rates, and some savings might be used to provide more services.

- The ability to engage in a more diversified set of activities would allow banks to be more efficient. That is, they might earn higher returns for their current level of risk exposure or reduce their risk exposure at their current rate of return (or a little of both). Even activities that are individually risky could benefit a bank when included to an appropriate degree as part of a portfolio of activities the returns of which are cyclically offsetting.[30] These outcomes may help counter the losses in the domestic commercial banking industry that have been attributed to securitization and globalization in the capital markets.

- If the bank holding company is strengthened by diversification, it may have less need to plunder, in a variety of ways, its banks' capital and profits.

- A stronger banking industry would emerge, reducing both failures and the exposure of the FIDC, as well as the likelihood that the taxpayer would ultimately have to provide funds to meet any underfunded federal insurance guarantees.

- Increased access to the financial markets and lower costs of capital would encourage investment in the national economy, employment, economic growth, and prosperity.

In this writer's opinion, these potential benefits are both very likely and conceptually correct. They should not be overanticipated, however. In particular, the potential benefits of expanded powers to commercial banks should not be exaggerated because of the following considerations:

- While rates of return on equity have historically been higher on average in the investment banking industry than they have in the commercial banking industry, they are also more volatile.

- Although recent investment banking profit rates have been high, the historical gross volume of profits in investment banking is small relative to total profits in commercial banking.[31]

- Therefore, dividing the profits that banks may be able to capture by entry into the securities industry among the participating commercial banks might not increase bank profitability substantially.

- Moreover, returns to investment banking have been declining recently and, according to some analysts, may continue declining through 1992.[32]

The conclusions of the GAO study leave little doubt that the repeal of the Glass–Steagall Act would improve the efficiency of the financial markets, the welfare of consumers, and the stability of a better-supervised banking system.

CONCLUSIONS

This chapter has examined the economics of regulation and deregulation. The arguments are overwhelmingly in favor of continued deregulation, including the repeal of Glass–Steagall. This, however, in no way argues that all regulations are bad and hinder the efficiency of the economic system. What is desirable is rational and balanced regulation. The logic and the fears on which much of the regulatory structure of the United States is based are no longer valid in the 1980s and can unduly harm the stability of the banking industry in the United States and the ability of U.S. banks to compete in an increasingly merciless international environment. Any attempt to hold on to antiquated regulation serves only to mask the glaring weaknesses of the supervisory process. Economic theory has yet to offer a standardized formula for the determination of optimal regulation. Until that happens, we must eliminate bad regulation and supervise very carefully.

NOTES

1. E. J. Kane, *The Gathering Crisis in Federal Deposit Insurance* (Cambridge, Mass.: MIT Press, 1985).

2. Robert Guttmann, "Changing of the Guard at the Fed," *Challenge* 30, no. 5 (November–December 1987): 5.

3. See Franklin R. Edwards, "Can Regulatory Reform Prevent the Impending Disaster in Financial Markets?" *Economic Review* 73, no. 1 (January 1988).

4. Guttmann, "Changing of the Guard," 5.

5. Edwards, "Can Regulatory Reform Prevent the Impending Disaster," 37.

6. George J. Stigler, "The Theory of Economic Regulation," *Bell Journal of Economics and Management Science* (Spring 1971): 3–21.

7. See Douglas Diamond and Philip Dybvig, "Bank Runs, Deposit Insurance, and Liquidity," *Journal of Political Economy* 91, no. 3 (1983): 401–19.

8. James Tobin, "A Case for Preserving Regulatory Distinction," *Challenge* 30, no. 5 (November–December 1987): 11.

9. Anthony Saunders, "Contagion Effects in the Interbank Market" (1988), 226.

10. Sarkis Khoury, "Sovereign Debt Forgiveness: Political Expediency or Economic Rationality?" *Banker International* (forthcoming).

11. Ron Giammarino, (University of British Columbia, 1989, Typescript), 6.

12. R. C. Merton, "The Valuation of FDIC Deposit Insurance Using Option Pricing Estimates," *Journal of Money, Credit and Banking* 9, no. 3 (1977): 446–60.

13. *Wall Street Journal,* 23 April 1987.

14. Khoury, "Sovereign Debt Forgiveness."

15. John Bovenzi, J. Marino, and F. McFadden, "Economical Bank Failure Prediction Models," *Economic Review* (Federal Reserve Bank of Atlanta) (1983).

16. See Robert A. O'Sullivan, "Federal Reserve Bank Examination Procedures," paper presented at Central Bankers Conference, 1987; and Barron H. Putnam, "Financial Warning Systems and Financial Analysis in Bank Monitoring," *Economic Review* (Federal Reserve Bank of Atlanta) (1983).

17. See Edward Altman, "Discriminant Analysis and the Prediction of Corporate Bankruptcy," *Journal of Finance* 23, no. 4 (1968): 589–609.

18. *Wall Street Journal,* 17 January 1989.

19. Christine M. Cumming and Lawrence M. Sweet, "Financial Structure of the G-10 Countries: How Does the United States Compare?" *Quarterly Review* (Federal Reserve Bank of New York) (Winter 1987–1988): 8.

20. "A Plan for America's Thrifts," *Economist* (19 November 1988): 85.

21. *American Banker* (26 August 1987).

22. Ibid.

23. See Ian Giddy, *Deregulating Wall Street,* ed. Ingo Walter (New York: John Wiley & Sons, 1985).

24. Robert Litan, "Which Way for Congress," *Challenge* 30, no. 5 (November–December 1987): 39.

25. Government Accounting Office. *Bank Powers, Issues Related to Repeal of the Glass–Steagall Act* (Washington, D.C.: U.S. Government Printing Office, 1988).

26. Charles Piston (American Bankers Association), statement before the House Committee on Banking, Finance, and Urban Affairs, December 3, 1987, 7.

27. Veronica Bennett, "Consumer Demand for Product Deregulation," *Economic Review* (Federal Reserve Bank of Atlanta) (May 1984): 28–37.

28. Greenwich Associates, *Greenwich Associates Large Corporation Banking 1987 Report to Executives.*

29. A spread is the difference between the price paid to the issuer and the price charged to retail customers by the underwriter. See C. O. Bierwag, George G. Kaufman, and Paul H. Leonard, "Interest-Rate Effects of Commercial Bank Underwriting of Municipal Revenue Bonds: Additional Evidence," *Journal of Banking and Finance* 8, no. 1 (March 1984): 35–50.

30. Data have been presented in several academic studies to show that investment

banking activities may offset cyclical fluctuations in banking. See, for example, Robert Litan, *What Should Banks Do?* (Washington, D.C.: Brookings Institution, 1987).

31. Total net income before taxes in the banking industry was 2.75 times larger than the comparable figure for securities firms.

32. Sanford C. Bernstein & Co., Inc., *The Investment Banking Industry: Strategic Analysis/Financial Forecast* (Sanford C. Bernstein & Co., Inc., October 1987).

3

The Deregulation of the U.S. Financial Markets

The age of deregulation of the U.S. financial markets dawned in the 1960s. It began with neither a bang, nor a whimper. The world and the financial regulators took note of the attempts by large U.S. multinational banks to better manage their liability structure and to force a change in an archaic regulatory system born during the Great Depression—an era of fear, uncertainty, distrust of the market system, and political indecisiveness, creating doubts about the basic economic tenets of the United States.

The deregulatory process has continued unabated until today, and few setbacks have been recorded. Some of the changes realized were predictable, while others were not. Some of the effects were desirable, while others were not. In the 1960s, no one would have predicted that banks would be operating discount brokerage houses or that Japan would be financing the enormous budget and balance of payments deficits of the United States. Wherever there is uncertainty, there is opportunity as well. The U.S. international banks of the 1980s have molded the financial environment, but have also been molded by it. The interaction makes for fascinating study. Also, the internationalization of U.S. banks sheds light on the causality between internationalism and the deregulatory process.

This chapter will look at the origin and nature of U.S. financial regulatory structures (primarily at the federal level), the impetus for regulatory reform, the nature of the financial deregulatory process in the United States, the impact of deregulation, and some cases of reregulation, and then offer general comments and conclusions.

THE ORIGIN OF THE REGULATORY STRUCTURE
IN THE UNITED STATES

Regulation of Banking

The attitude of the U.S. public toward the regulation of banks in the 1800s and 1900s was schizophrenic. Upon the recommendation of Alexander Hamilton, the Bank of the United States was created in 1791. The Bank was a commercial bank with some central banking activity. Its charter was not renewed in 1811; however, another bank charter was issued in 1816 for the Second Bank of the United States. Both banks were established following periods of uncertainty about the banking industry and were intended to increase the safety of deposits. The charter of the Second Bank of the United States was not renewed in 1838, leaving the banking industry totally self-regulated in an era when unconstrained competition was the order of life.

The next initiative came from the states. They basically set up minimum standards for the issuance of a banking license. Some experimented with the deposit insurance system, indicating, once again, the need for a safe system of deposits.

The first federal act, after a long hiatus, was the Currency Act of 1863, which later became the National Bank Act of 1864. Under this act, the Office of the Comptroller of the Currency was formed with responsibility for chartering, supervising, and examining all national banks. The issuance of notes by national banks was then regulated, and any note issued had to be backed by U.S. bonds on deposit with the comptroller. This allowed for a uniform currency for the first time in the United States. This, however, did not stabilize the banking system, and after a series of banking crises, the Federal Reserve Act was passed by Congress in 1913. Under this act, national banks had to become members of the Federal Reserve System, whereas state-chartered banks had the option to join. An agreement was reached in 1917, providing for the Comptroller of the Currency to examine national banks and for the appropriate Federal Reserve Bank to examine state member banks.

The next major legislative initiative dealing with banks and the financial markets was brought about by the Great Depression. Once again, this was a reaction to a major economic downturn—a wrenching reaction. The new laws stemmed from fear and a sudden loss of faith in the free market system. Government laws and guarantees were the answer, and the country was ready for this message, articulated by a strong-willed president: FDR.

The regulatory changes that ensued can be broadly summarized as follows:

- Product regulation
  - No bank sales of insurance
  - No bank underwriting or sales of stocks
  - Limited and insured depository products and services
  - Regulated prices of services
  - No interest on demand deposits

- Interest rate ceilings
- State usury laws
- "Geographical" regulation
  - No interstate expansion
  - Restrictions on interstate branching
  - Regulation of international activities
- Other regulations
  - Asset quality requirements
  - Capital adequacy requirements restricting leverage
  - Separation of banking and commerce and of investment banking and banking
  - Regulation of mergers and acquisitions involving banks
  - Lending limits

The most important legislative acts were the Banking Acts of 1933 and 1935. The following provisions of these two acts effectively ended "free banking" in the United States:

- The creation of the FDIC-member banks that must buy into the insurance

- No interest on demand deposits

- A ceiling on interest paid on time deposits

- Stringent requirements for granting a banking license

- Adjustable reserve requirements at the Fed's discretion

- Branching for national banks limited to the same extent as for state banks

- Separation of banking and investment banking—the Glass–Steagell provisions (That separation was not complete, however, because banks were allowed, for example, to underwrite general obligation municipal bonds. However, the separation was deep and serious enough to create a whole new industry: investment banking.)

Another important piece of legislation, the Bank Holding Company Act of 1956, was drafted to deal with the limitations of the Banking Act of 1933. The 1933 act granted the Federal Reserve Board supervisory and regulatory powers over bank holding companies that owed member banks. The 1933 act did not deal with the formation and expansion of bank holding companies, but the 1956 act remedied this. It defined bank holding companies (BHCs), limited interstate branching through BHCs, separated nonbank activities from BHCs unless the activities are "so closely related to the business of banking or managing or controlling banks as to be a proper incident thereto," and prohibited the acquisition of banks in other states unless specifically authorized by state law. The Bank Holding Company Act of 1956 did not deal, however, with one-bank holding companies. This loophole allowed one-bank holding companies into financial services from which banks were otherwise prohibited.

Regulation of Securities

The securities laws enacted were no less stringent or important than those of banking. The issuance and trading of financial instruments, the underlying contractual agreements between issuer and holder, and the operations of the markets in which these securities are traded are governed by federal and state laws and regulations. Indeed, every phase of the securities industry is regulated in one form or another.

The intent of the various laws and regulations is to prevent fraud and manipulation of security prices and to maximize the flow of accurate and relevant information to the marketplace. Equal access to information, it is theorized, should give every participant in the securities market the same probability of realizing a fair rate of return on his or her investment. The underlying assumptions (weak, if not erroneous ones) are that all recipients of information possess an equal ability to process and act on that information and that the transaction costs for entering and leaving the securities markets are equal for all participants.

The acts and regulations we shall concentrate on are

- The Securities Act of 1933
- The Securities Exchange Act of 1934
- The Maloney Act of 1938
- The Trust Indenture Act of 1939
- The Investment Company Act of 1939
- The Employee Retirement Income Security Act of 1974

The Securities Act of 1933

The Securities Act of 1933 is sometimes referred to as the Truth in Securities Act. Its basic purpose is to ensure full disclosure of information in the registration statement and prospectus for *new* securities. In the language of the act, its intent is "to provide full and fair disclosure of the character of securities sold in interstate and foreign commerce and through the mails, and to prevent frauds in the sale thereof, and for other purposes."

The SEC is the government agency in charge of ensuring full disclosure of all significant material facts concerning a security offered to the public. In so doing, the SEC does not pass any judgment on the investment value (merits) of the security.

Not all *new* issues are subject to the 1933 act. Exempted are

- Intrastate issues sold only to persons residing in one state when the issuer is a resident doing business within that state.
- Securities of any political subdivision of the United States, including those of the federal and state governments and of religious and not-for-profit organizations.
- Issues offered to the public when the total amount is less than *1.5 million*. For these issues, the SEC has adopted Regulation A, which requires notification of the intention to offer such stock to the public. The company must provide certain information to prospective purchasers, however, and the usual registration requirements do not apply. The SEC adopted rules that further eased the guidelines for smaller companies raising money, particularly from accredited investors. An accredited investor is generally defined as one who buys $100,000 worth of stock or as one with a gross income of

$100,000 or a net worth of $750,000. It is theorized that accredited investors do not need the watchful eyes of the SEC as much as the small investors do.

- Securities issued by common carriers subject to the Interstate Commerce Act. These issues are supervised by the Interstate Commerce Commission.
- Annuity contracts issued by insurance companies.

The Securities Exchange Act of 1934

The Securities Exchange Act of 1934 extended the reach of the 1933 act to all phases of trading in existing securities. To enforce its provisions, the act set up the SEC, which consists of five members appointed by the president with the advice and consent of the Senate. No more than three of the five members can be from one political party. The 1934 act also authorized the Federal Reserve System to regulate the use of credit for the purchase or carrying of securities. The Fed has exercised this authority through Regulations T and U.

The Securities Exchange Act of 1934 requires many different groups and organizations to register with the SEC. Among them are

- Corporations with listed securities
- Brokers and dealers involved in interstate commerce and in transactions not consummated on the exchanges
- Securities exchanges—for example, NYSE, ASE. (Strict requirements must be met before approval of registration.)
- Securities traded on the exchanges
- National securities associations

Directors and officers of the issuing corporation and owners of more than *5 percent* of the shares outstanding must file a statement with the SEC. Any changes in ownership position must also be reported within 10 days of their occurrence. Such individuals are barred from establishing short positions in the securities and are required to return to the stockholders any short-term profits realized on inside information. Section 16(b) of the Securities Exchange Act of 1934 requires insiders to return all profits from a purchase and subsequent sale (or a sale and subsequent purchase) that occur within six months of each other.

The 1934 act *outlaws* the use of any "manipulative, deceptive, or other fraudulent *devices or contrivances*" such as churning (making unauthorized or imprudent transactions in an investor's account with the primary intent of generating commissions), matching orders (issuing simultaneous buy and sell orders on the same security by the same person to give the impression of active trading), wash sales (buying and selling the same day in order to establish a tax loss or selling to one's spouse at a lower price in order to purchase the same security later at that lower price), and pooling (setting up a group for the purpose of trading securities within the group with the intent of manipulating the price upward or downward). Manipulative and deceptive devices and contrivances are dealt with in Section 10(b)(1)–(17) of the act.

The act also outlaws, according to SEC statements, the practice of predicting specific results from positions in securities or of recommending securities without adequate inquiry. In addition, the act sets limits on borrowing by member brokers and dealers. The prescribed rule is referred to as the *20-to-1 rule;* that is, a broker/dealer's aggregate indebtedness to all other persons cannot exceed 2,000 percent of net capital. The act also sets the requirements for proxies (transference by the stockholder of his or her rights and privileges to another party) and their solicitation and for the conditions for short sales.

When and if the SEC suspects wrongdoing, it holds an investigation. Everyone who is subpoenaed must testify. If the Fifth Amendment is invoked, testimony is still required. However, the testimony and documents presented cannot be used for prosecution.

The SEC, through its *SEC Statement of Policy,* provides guidelines intended to eliminate misleading statements in literature distributed in the sale of securities.

Regulation T

Regulation T is concerned with the extension and maintenance of credit in the purchase or sale of securities. Cash transactions are expected to be settled within seven days. The margin requirements set by Regulation T specify the maximum percentage of the value of the investment that the investor may borrow from the broker/dealer. Regulation T also identifies those securities that are marginable— purchasable on credit—and those that are exempt. U.S. government securities, municipal bonds, and bonds of the International Bank for Reconstruction and Development are exempt from Regulation T.

The Maloney Act of 1938

The Maloney Act amends the Securities Exchange Act of 1934 by adding Section 15A. This section provides for "the establishment of regulation among *over-the-counter* brokers and dealers operating in interstate and foreign commerce or through the mails to prevent acts and practices inconsistent with just and equitable principles of trade and for other purposes."

National securities associations or affiliated securities associations are required to register with the SEC. Copies of their constitutions, charters, articles of incorporation, and bylaws must be filed with the SEC. Disciplinary action taken against a member of the association can be appealed to the SEC; the commission's decision is then final. The commission can, under this act, suspend (for up to 12 months) or revoke the registration, suspend or expel an individual member, or remove an officer or director of an association who has not enforced the rules.

The Trust Indenture Act of 1939

The Trust Indenture Act of 1939 was intended to protect the holders of debt securities by requiring issuing corporations to live up to the provisions of the indenture agreement (the contract between the bondholder and the bond issuer). The bond issuer, under this act, is required to file periodic financial statements with the trustee. In the words of the act, the intent is "to provide for the regulation of the sale of certain securities in interstate and foreign commerce and through the mails, and the regulation of the trust indentures under which the same are issued and for other purposes."

Some securities are exempted from the act. These include all securities exempted under the Securities Act of 1933 and any securities other than notes, bonds, debentures, and certain other certificates of interest.

The act requires a bond issuer to have one or more trustees clear of conflict-of-interest considerations. The duties of the trustee are specified in the act. A trustee is required to submit a report at least once a year to the indenture security holders, stating among other things the issuer's eligibility and qualifications, any unpaid advances in excess of 0.5 percent of indentured securities, and the inventory of the property and funds in the issuer's possession at the time of such report. The trustee must within 90 days of default give notice to bondholders unless the board of directors or another authorized body instructs him or her, based on the best interest of the bondholders, not to. The trustee is expected to follow the "prudent man" rule—that is, to do only what a reasonable, prudent man would do in the discharge of his duties.

The Investment Company Act of 1940

Part A of the Investment Company Act of 1940 provides for the registration of investment companies with the SEC; Part B, also called the Investment Advisors Act, provides for the regulation of investment companies and investment advisors. The intent of the act is to ensure maximum disclosure of information and fair treatment of those who hold securities handled by investment companies (generally referred to as mutual funds).

The Employee Retirement Income Security Act

The Employee Retirement Income Security Act (ERISA), also referred to as the Pension Reform Act, was signed into law by President Ford on Labor Day, 1974. ERISA replaced all the provisions of the Welfare and Pension Plans Disclosure Act of 1958 and amended sections of the Internal Revenue Code; it supersedes all state laws related to employee benefit plans. ERISA also created the Individual Retirement Account (IRA), under which wage earners not covered by a retirement plan may set aside up to 15 percent of their income or $1,500, whichever is less (limits that were subsequently changed). The contributions to an IRA plan and income thereon are not taxable; however, the sum withdrawn upon retirement is fully taxable. The Economic Recovery Tax Act of 1981 changed the requirements of ERISA with regard to IRA plans. The maximum contribution is now $2,000, and an IRA can now be set up even though the wage earner is covered by another retirement plan.

ERISA covers all pension plans except government plans, church plans (unless an election for coverage is made), unfunded excess-benefit plans, plans set up and maintained outside the United States and benefiting primarily nonresident aliens, and plans set up in order to comply with workers' compensation, unemployment compensation, or disability insurance laws.

Discussed below are some of the major provisions of ERISA that have implications for the securities markets.

Eligibility and vesting. ERISA liberalized the vesting and eligibility requirements. Vesting gives the wage earner a nonforfeitable right to the contributions made to the pension fund. All contributions made by the employee are fully and immediately vested. Contributions made by the employer are vested in accordance with all of the following requirements:

- *Graded vesting.* There is at least 25 percent vesting after five years of service, followed by 5 percent for each of the succeeding five years and by 10 percent each year thereafter. One hundred percent vesting is achieved after 15 years.

- *One hundred percent vesting after ten years.* No vesting is realized at any time before 10 years.

- *Rule of 45.* The rule of 45 deals with the sum of the age of the wage earner and his or her years of service. Under this rule, an employee with five years of service and meeting the 45 requirement must be at least 50 percent vested, with an additional 10 percent vesting each succeeding year. A plan participant with 10 years of service must be 50 percent vested, with an additional 10 percent vesting each succeeding year.

The Internal Revenue Service has the authority to further liberalize the vesting requirements if it deems this appropriate.

The eligibility rule requires that any employee with one year of service who is at least 25 years of age must be included in a pension plan.

The liberalization of eligibility and vesting requirements increased corporate pension contributions and thus decreased net profits. It has been estimated that corporate pension contributions account for about 15 percent of before-tax profits. ERISA also requires that certain plans be subject to minimum funding standards and that these plans maintain an account called the funding standard account (FSA). This account is used to determine compliance with minimum funding standards.

Also, disclosure and reporting requirements were set, as was employer liability. The employer liability clause was at the origin of the legislation. The seeds for ERISA were planted in 1964 when the Studebaker Company declared bankruptcy and left its employees without jobs and without pensions. An employer has a contingent liability limited to the unfunded liability for insured benefits but no more than 30 percent of the firm's net worth. The balance is made up by the Pension Benefit Guaranty Corporation (PBGC), which was created by the act. The PBGC insurance premium is paid by the employer. The maximum guarantee by PBGC is equal to the lesser of (1) 100 percent of the average monthly wages paid to the plan participant during the five highest earning years in the plan, or (2) $750 per month initially with upward adjustments tied to Social Security wage-base increases.

Employers are required under ERISA to reassess their actuarial assumptions in light of actual experience every three years. Employers must also adjust their contributions in accordance with the "experience" of gains and losses.

U.S. Financial Markets 75

Exhibit 3.1
Securities Laws

Scope	Industry Regulations	Antifraud, Deceptive Practices and Manipulation
Stocks, bonds, debentures, investment certificates, variable annuities, and profit sharing interest. Exemptions for deposits, accounts, and CD's in financial institutions; ordinary life insurance and annuity policies; and many pension funds, along with most IRA's and Keogh's in exempt categories. **Registration and Disclosure Disciplines** Securities Act of 1933, Securities Exchange Act of 1934, Public Utility Holding Company Act of 1935, Trust Indenture Act of 1939, Investment Company Act of 1940). Underwriting and Distribution Fed'l registration requirements State Blue Sky laws Administrative enforcement Private remedies Publicly Held Companies Periodic disclosure and reports Proxy solicitations Takeover bids and tender offers Insider trading and "short swing" profits Trading Securities exchanges Self-regulated under SEC supervision Members and specialists	Investment Bankers and Underwriters Disclosure discipline Separation from commercial banking Domestic underwriting Int'l underwriting Broker-Dealer Network (NASD) Responsibilities Net capital rules Segregation of customer funds and securities SEC supervision Securities Investor Protection Corporation (SIPC) Account insurance Assessments and borrowing authority Protective supervision and remedies Investment Companies (including Mutual Funds) Regulated operations Registration and reporting Assets and capital Management restrictions Selling and price restrictions Money market mutual funds Investment Advisors Registration requirements Advisory contracts and compensation restrictions	**Remedies** Administrative enforcement Private remedies (including class actions) Margin regulation Commissions OTC Market NASD trading outside changes National Market System (computer linkage) Other Trading Institutional Trading Other private transactions

Reprinted from Lovett's Banking and Financial Institutions Law in a Nutshell, 2nd Edition, 1988, with permission of the West Publishing Company.

Fiduciary responsibility. ERISA goes a long way in defining the responsibility of those charged with the management of the assets of a pension plan (fiduciaries).

Fiduciaries are expected (among other things) to follow the "prudent man rule" and diversify the portfolio in order to minimize risk. To quote the act, a fiduciary is expected to discharge his or her duties "with the care, skill, prudence, and diligence under the circumstances then prevailing that a prudent man acting in like capacity and familiar with such matters would use in the conduct of an enterprise of like character and with like aims.

In addition, he or she may not make a loan to or acquire securities in a party of interest (the sponsoring corporation for example).

The securities laws discussed above and other securities laws are summarized in Exhibit 3.1. Like their banking law counterparts, these securities laws were intended to calm, to reassure, and hopefully to provide an incentive for individuals to participate in the marketplace. They worked for that time. The question is, however, whether they are still necessary in the 1990s. Before dealing with this issue, let us look more closely at the impetus for the legislative initiatives and their promulgation.

THE IMPETUS FOR BANKING AND SECURITIES LAWS

The near collapse of the banking system in the 1930s was ample incentive for action. The belief in the very foundation of the U.S. economic system was shaken. It was no wonder, as a consequence, that a massive legislative agenda was adopted and simultaneously strong labor unions were started under the leadership of those espousing new economic philosophies that were decidedly socialistic in character.

The swiftness with which many American banking institutions, especially state-chartered ones, were disappearing was most alarming. In the early 1920s, 30,000 American banks were operating. By 1929, 25,000 were still in operation, and by 1933, only 15,000 remained. The Roosevelt administration, inaugurated in 1933, had no choice but to take decisive action. The regulation of banks, securities firms, and markets was a natural reaction and represented only one segment in the process of regulating the entire U.S. economy, either directly or indirectly, with the government appropriating to itself a greater portion of economic activity—referred to by economists as "priming the pump." The problem was aggravated by massive debt default and exchange rate disturbances, reflecting the shaken confidence in the U.S. economic system.

The thrust of all banking legislation was primarily anticompetitive. The free market cannot protect depositors, nor can it ultimately protect the banking system. Safety nets had to be installed. Thus, the Federal Reserve System acted as lender of last resort and overseer of banking operations, and the FDIC served as a guarantor to depositors.

Many other laws were adopted and institutions set up or modified in response to the evolution of the United States after the depression, and particularly after World War II. Savings and loan associations were set up to answer the housing need of Americans, especially after the war; ERISA was enacted to affirm the rights of workers to dignified and secure retirement; the Voluntary Credit Restraint Act was enacted to limit capital outflows from the United States; and so on. In practically all these cases, the legislation and regulations were reactive rather than proactive. They reflected the fears and concerns of regulators rather than their imagination and foresight.

The strong links (albeit out of control) among banks, financial markets, and the macroeconomy became dramatically obvious and may explain many of the causes of the depression:

It is widely agreed that these monetary factors were central to its singular depth and long duration. The inability of the Federal Reserve to prevent widespread bank failures, along with its inability to interrupt the linkages running back from bank failures to financial markets and to the macroeconomy, is a central explanation for the severity of the crisis in the United States. Thus, one reason for the exceptional depth of the Great Depression in the U.S. was that policy was used less effectively than in other countries to prevent the transformation of financial market disturbances into a generalized financial crisis.[1]

The control of the financial system through laws and regulations was the only viable short-term option. This control was so pronounced and so widespread that it left little choice for bankers and investment bankers but to try to nibble at it gradually and forcefully to eliminate the excesses and make the system more consistent with the new realities in the United States and in the rest of the world economy.

The regulations discussed thus far have dealt with economic conduct. The other set of regulations (including truth in lending laws, regulations on loans to insiders, etc.) deals with ethical conduct. Both these regulatory initiatives stem from considerable pressures from various fronts:

One suggested pressure is that high profitability and easy capital mobility would attract a large number of dishonest firms that must be carefully excluded from the business. A second related pressure is that personal customer greed would lead individuals to make "irrational" decisions, so markets must be designed to prevent excessive speculation, gambling, or other types of chance-rewarded behavior. A different type of pressure arises from the historical production function forms in this industry. The complex transaction process for securities requires codification and standardization of procedures if the system is to operate smoothly. Another type of pressure comes from preconceived notions about what is the best industry structure for our economy. Thus some argue that for efficient capital raising in this country we need a securities industry with many firms, and competition would substantially reduce the number of firms in the industry. A final illustration of felt pressures is the attempt to create regulations so that certain types of risk will appear to be absorbed by industry firms rather than transferred directly to customers. Thus customers are protected by market makers from abrupt stock fluctuations and by regulations on firms' capital structures from bankruptcy risks for funds and securities left on deposit.[2]

All these pressures, while real and valid, are not necessarily arguments for regulation because there is no evidence to suggest that regulation is always the optimum response to every form of pressure—although it occasionally offers the illusion of action, and that may be a sufficient reason for its existence. Supervision and market competition may indeed be the superior alternative. Yet, even after deregulation, the urgency to go back to regulation is ever present. The fact of reregulation is quite evident.

Today, despite all the regulatory changes documented below, U.S. banking is

the most heavily regulated industry in the country and one of the most decentralized. All banks are chartered by the federal or a state government, most are inspected by several sets of government examiners, all can be shut down or given orders about important operating procedures. There are three federal agencies primarily concerned with regulating banks: the Office of the Comptroller of the Currency (which regulates bank holding companies and state banks that are members of the Federal Reserve System), the Federal Reserve System, and the Federal Deposit Insurance Corporation (which regulates state

Exhibit 3.2
Insurance Regulation System

Scope	Industry Regulations
Insurance Companies--	Chartering and Authorization
Life, Annuity, Disability Pensions and Health	Chartering requirements
Property, Marine, Liability	Out-of-state insurers
Surety and Fidelity	Agent activities
	Capital, Reserves and Solvency--
State Regulation	Minimum capital
Key States and Industry Associations	Reserves requirements
National Association of Insurance Comm'rs (NAIC)	Liquidation procedures
Trade Groups	Examination and valuation
Main Themes-	Rate Making and Filing-
Standard Form Contracts	Property-Liability
Capital and Reserves	Prior Approval
Investment Regulation	Open Competition
Authorization and Marketing	Direct Writers
Rate Filing System	Life and Group
Socialized Risks	Health and Disability
	Standard Contracts--
	Standardization
Entry, Underwriting and Marketing	Limits on Harshness or Cancellation
Life and Health	Socialized Risks--
Life and Annuity	Extreme Costs
Health CAre	Limited Incomes
Disability	Unaffordability
	Taxation--
	Premium taxes
Property, Marine Liability	Assessments
Surety, and Fidelity	Contributions
Multiples Lines and merger activity	
	Federal Regulation
	McCarran Act
Competition With Other Financial Intermediaries	Antitrust exemption
	Socialization of Risk
Banks and Trust Departments	Social Security
Investment companies and Mutual Funds	Health CAre
Securities Broker-Dealers	Flood Insurance
Pension Funds	Crime Insurance
Government	Export Financing
	Potential Regulatory Expansion
	State Regulation Problems
	Industry Influence on Regulatory Process
	Reduced Antitrust Exemption

Reprinted from Lovett's Banking and Financial Institutions Law in a Nutshell, 2nd Edition, 1988, with permission of the West Publishing Company.

banks it insures that are not members of the Fed). And that's not to mention the fifty state banking agencies, or the federal agencies that regulate the savings-and-loans, which make mostly home-mortgage loans (as opposed to commercial loans—loans to business— which is what banks mostly make).[3]

The insurance industry in the United States did not escape the regulatory rope either. We shall look at this only briefly because it is not the focus of this research. The primary motivations for insurance regulation are to protect policyholders and to encourage ethical and due diligence behavior by the insurance industry. In this regard, the regulation is very similar to that of banks and securities firms. Insurers must have a charter, adhere to certain restrictions on their portfolios, meet capital and solvency requirements, adhere to certain standards of rate making, and regularly report their financial results. All these requirements are enforced exclusively by the state in which the insurance company resides. The supervision is exercised by a commission or department of insurance. Insurance regulation is summarized in Exhibit 3.2.

The involvement of the banking industry in insurance has been a great temptation for banks, a marriage unacceptable to regulators, and a concern to the insurance industry, if only for competitive reasons. Security Pacific Bank of California managed to crash all the barriers on February 3, 1989, when it announced that, as a result of the approval of Proposition 103 by the voters of California, it had decided to enter the insurance business (auto, life, health, and other types of coverage) through a state-chartered subsidiary. The timing of the entry was interesting because the constitutionality of Proposition 103, which mandated a 20 percent rollback of insurance rates, has yet to be resolved. Security Pacific's entry was immediately challenged in the courts by insurance agents and brokers, arguing that the entry creates unfair competition and gives "banks coercive powers over their customers because they have access to loan files." It appears, though, that Security Pacific may have succeeded in becoming the first bank to enter the insurance industry in the lucrative California market.

We now look at the deregulation of the U.S. banking and securities industries. We shall consider each deregulation and the impetus for its evolution and adoption.

THE DEREGULATORY PROCESS

The regulation of financial institutions and markets appears, on the surface, to be totally inconsistent with the concept of free markets. Economists argue that in a truly free and efficient market, the banking industry represents a market failure and banking regulation an accentuation of this failure. Individuals could enter directly into transactions to transform assets, to assess risk and lend money, and to accept deposits from other individuals. Whether banks do allow for a more efficient execution of these transactions is the issue. If they do—and no one has figured out how to rid society of banks—then the issue becomes the optimal size of banks. Having determined the optimal size, the issue shifts toward determining whether society's welfare is enhanced or hindered by regulation. Should regulation be endorsed, as this writer has done to a limited degree in Chapter 2? Then the question is one of the optimal regulatory burden. The market, the Congress, and the regulatory agencies appear to have concluded, not independently it seems, and not without the pressures of common sense and basic economics, that the regulatory burden on banking institutions in the United States was excessive. The reduction of that burden began in earnest in the early 1970s and proceeded vigorously through the 1980s.

The context within which the deregulatory process was born and matured deserves careful consideration because it allows the observer to develop a perspective on the impetus and the impact of any given change in regulation.

The deregulations of the early 1980s represented a convergence of various interest groups, the Congress, the efforts of the Reagan administration (which preached the fundamentals and values of a freer market economy), and public and consumer pressures. All these factors combined to redefine even the concept of regulation. One must keep in mind the hospitable environment created by the Reagan administration in terms of the philosophical tone and agenda it set for the nation. The deregulation of the financial markets thusly becomes a key component of what is referred to as the "Reagan Revolution." The earlier, successful (at least in part) experiments with deregulation during the Carter administration (airlines, the 1980 Depository Institutions Act, etc.) helped the deregulatory process along. The mood was positive indeed.

The other factors that contributed significantly were these:

• Very high, and highly volatile, interest rates prevailed from 1979 to 1981. In the United States, the banking industry, and especially the savings and loan industry, suffered immeasurably. Unable to pay market rates, S&Ls began to lose deposits (about $200 billion) to money market funds. This process, referred to as disintermediation, threatened the very survival of the S&L industry. Something had to be done, especially as the remaining portfolio of S&Ls became riskier than ever before as a result of interest volatility combined with a management too inexperienced to deal with it. The regulators of these institutions were all too clear on the developments within their industry and the implications, and they pressed Congress for regulatory relief.

• Technological developments allowed information to be accessed instantaneously and huge pools of funds to be shifted from one country, one location, and/or one currency to another, making deregulation much easier to implement and even helping bring it about.

• The banking/investment banking community was run in the early 1980s by a more sophisticated and internationally minded management cadre eager to deploy its skills and compete in a tough international market. The human resource element was a powerful stimulus to deregulation and responsible to a large degree for many of its sad consequences.

• Risk diversification also played a part as financial institutions sought to reduce their dependence on traditional banking business.

These are the general factors. The specific ones attributed to a given deregulatory effort will be discussed below.

DEREGULATIONS/INNOVATIONS AND THEIR IMPETUS

The major developments on the deregulatory front and some of the major product innovations introduced by the banking industry are listed in Exhibits 3.3 and 3.4. This section identifies the main motivations for these developments.

Several innovations and deregulations were the byproducts of restrictions on capital flows, on interest payments on deposits, and on the types of products banks could offer their clients, especially when compared with investment banks.

Exhibit 3.3
Regulatory Developments, 1978–1982

1972   NOW accounts were authorized for thrift institutions in Massachusetts. In the next few years, all New England thrifts were allowed to issue NOWs.

1973   The wild card experiment: The first use of ceiling-free, small denomination certificates of deposit. The certificate had a minimum maturity of four years; the experiment lasted four months. All depository institutions were allowed to participate.

1975   California state-chartered savings and loans were authorized to issue variable-rate mortgages. At the same time, a few national banks in California began to issue variable-rate mortgages.

1978   California federally-chartered savings and loans were authorized to issue variable-rate mortgages.

May 1978 Federal regulatory agencies authorized commercial banks and thrift institutions to issue Money Market Certificates, effective June 1.

These certificates have a 26-week maturity, a minimum denomination of $10,000 and interest ceilings indexed to the 26 week Treasury bill rate, with a differential between commercial banks and thrift institutions.

September 1978 The International Banking Act of 1978 was enacted.

The legislation aimed at leveling the playing field between U.S. banks and branches and agencies of foreign banks.

December 1979 Federal regulatory agencies authorized commercial banks and thrift institutions to issue Small Saver Certificates, effective January 1, 1980.

These certificates have 30 to 48 month maturity, no minimum denomination and interest ceilings indexed to the average 2 1/2-year yield for U.S. Treasury securities. Thrift institutions enjoy a ceiling differential.

March 1980 The Depository Institutions Deregulation and Monetary Control Act was enacted.

This legislation authorized NOW accounts nationwide, extended reserve requirements to nonmember banks and other depository institutions, expanded the tiers of thrift institutions, and created the Depository Institutions Deregulation Committee (DIDC). The DIDC was charged with gradual elimination of Regulation Q.

October 1980 The DIDC authorized a new category of 14 to 90 day time deposit.

It established the ceiling on that account and NOW accounts at 5 1/4 percent, with no differential between commercial banks and thrift institutions. At the same meeting, the DIDC issued final rules governing premiums, finders fees and prepayment of interest on regulated deposits.

(continued)

Exhibit 3.3 (*Continued*)

June 1981 **The DIDC adopted a schedule for gradual phase-out of interest ceilings, beginning with longer term accounts.**

July 1981 **The U.S. District Court of the District of Columbia invalidated the phase-out schedule which the DIDC had adopted.**

August 1981 **The Economic Recovery Tax Act of 1981 was passed.**

This act authorized depository institutions to issue All Savers Certificates, effective October 1, with interest paid exempt from Federal Income Taxes and broadened eligibility for IRA and Keogh Accounts, effective January 1, 1982.

September 1981 **The DIDC increased interest ceilings on passbook statement savings accounts by 50 basis points, effective November 1.**

At the same meeting, it authorized a ceilingless instrument for IRA and Keogh Accounts.

October 1981 **The DIDC postponed indefinitely the scheduled increase in passbook and statement savings account interest ceilings.**

March 1982 **The DIDC adopted a new schedule for gradual phase-out of interest ceilings, beginning with accounts with maturity of 3 1/2 years or longer.**

At the same meeting, it authorized a new 91-day savings certificate with a $7,500 minimum denomination and interest ceilings tried to the 13-week Treasury bill rate. The ceilings give thrift institutions a one-quarter point differential.

1983 **Introduction of the Super NOW accounts**

Lowering of minimum deposit on short-term certificates of deposit to $2,500. Elimination of ceiling rates on remaining time deposits.

Sources: Daniel J. Vrabac, "Recent Developments at Banks and Nonbank Depository Institutions," *Economic Review* (Federal Reserve Bank of Kansas City) (July–August 1983):35; Federal Reserve Bank of Minneapolis, *Annual Report* (1981).

These problems became very acute when inflation reached unprecedented levels toward the end of the Carter administration, producing negative rates of return on bank and thrift deposits. The increasingly aware and better-informed depositors had to act to prevent the erosion of their wealth. Money market funds were quickly created to attract these depositors, and the net results during the relevant period were dramatic, as Exhibit 3.5 shows. In 10 years, money market funds became a $200 billion industry, thanks largely to the regulation of the thrift industry, and specifically to Regulation Q.

The conditions for banks and especially thrift institutions were untenable. The Massachusetts thrifts were the first to take action in the early 1970s. They introduced the NOW (negotiable order of withdrawal) account, which was effec-

Exhibit 3.4
Selected Recent Financial and Technological Innovations of Commercial Banks

Innovations	When Introduced
Consumer time certificates	1950s
Eurodollars	1960s
Credit cards	1960s
Leasing	1960s
Federal funds	1960s
Repurchase agreements	1960s
Certificates of deposit	1961
Variable rate term loans	1970s
Remote service units	1974
Money market certificates	1978
Swaps	1980
Notes issuance facilities	1981
Currency options	1982
Forward rate agreements	1983

Source: Kerry Cooper and Donald R. Fraser, *Banking Deregulation and the New Competition in Financial Services* (Cambridge, Mass.: Bellinger, 1984), 57.

tively the equivalent of an interest-bearing checking account. This bold action was subsequently sanctioned by a federal regulation authorizing all New England thrifts to issue NOW accounts by 1976. These accounts became available nationwide in October 1980 with the passage of the Depository Institutions Deregulation and Monetary Control Act of 1980 (DIDMCA). This act authorized all depository institutions to issue, in effect, checking accounts that can pay interest. Three years later, the Super NOW accounts were introduced, lowering the minimum deposit on short-term certificates of deposit to $2,500.

Exhibit 3.5
Assets of Money Market Funds, 1973–1983 (Billions of dollars)

Year	Total Assets	Percent of Household Deposits
1973	-	0.0
1974	2.4	0.3
1975	3.7	0.4
1976	3.7	0.3
1977	3.9	0.3
1978	10.8	0.8
1979	45.2	3.1
1980	74.4	5.1
1981	181.9	N.A.
1982	206.9	N.A.
1983[a]	176.2	N.A.

[a]1983 data are as of the end of the second quarter.
Source: Board of Governors of the Federal Reserve System, 1983.

The pressure to further the playing field (the competitive arena) for financial institutions and those competing for their deposits persisted, however, as the hemorrhaging was, manifestly, continuing. Some of the pressure was applied by small depositors who successfully argued that Regulation Q amounted to discrimination against small savers (depositors). In May 1978, the federal regulatory agencies authorized financial institutions to issue money market certificates, effective June 1, 1978. This allowed the "flow of funds to be reintermediated."

None of these actions, however, helped significantly to solve the problem of thrifts' inflexible portfolios and their mismatched balance sheets. This was resolved, at least in part, by permitting thrifts to issue variable rate mortgages. This was further extended under the 1980 act and the Garn–St. Germain Depository Institutions Act of 1982. The latter increased the ability of regulators to come to the rescue of distressed financial institutions, provided for competitive deposit accounts at financial institutions, and broadened the lending powers of S&Ls, allowing them to diversify their loan portfolio, but not to the same extent as that of commercial banks. The deregulation of the asset side of the balance sheet was a logical and necessary consequence of the deregulation of liabilities.

All these legislative and regulatory changes served to protect the financial institutions and simultaneously the depositors. Title IV of the Depository Institutions Deregulation and Monetary Control Act (DIDMCA) of 1986 simplified and reformed earlier truth in lending legislation. Consequently, depositors were better informed and received competitive rates, despite attempts by some industry groups to keep the lid on interest rates—that is, to keep Regulation Q away from the $500 billion that the industry still had on deposit, despite the disintermediation. The monopoly rent derived from deposits at below-market rates was slowly vanishing. The burial date for Regulation Q was set for March 1986.

The above also makes clear that deregulation was "a result rather than a cause of the more intense banking climate." It was the bankers who brought about the change, and the regulators simply transformed, in most cases, de facto deregulation into de jour deregulation. Every type and size of financial institution looked for, and often found, a way around regulatory constraints. This is the nature of the regulatory process. The usefulness and effectiveness of regulations ebb and flow. There is no legislation that is permanently and consistently desirable and effective.

The pressure for change was imported into the United States via foreign banks. The growth of foreign banking in the United States, documented in Chapter 1, brought about radical changes in the opportunity set for banks in investing their resources and in sourcing funds within and outside the regulatory boundaries. We have already documented the reasons behind the development of the Euromarkets (primarily to circumvent Regulations Q and D and capital controls—actual and prospective); offshore banking facilities (to allow for international activities without having to set up an entity in a foreign country); tax havens (to escape tax regulations); and various off-balance-sheet innovations such as swaps, options, NIFs, etc. (to escape the regulatory taxes imposed in the form of capital requirements).

Foreign financial institutions in the United States were intent on competing at every level with U.S. banks. They were skilled, aggressive, and very price competitive. They also had traditions of excellence and quality customer service, in many cases, and huge resources from their parent company and home market. In brief, they presented a tremendous challenge to U.S. banks.[4] The wheels of change were suddenly turning faster as these institutions were demonstrating their ability to compete effectively and simultaneously, and the unregulated Euromarkets were growing at a fast pace without any major problem to whet the appetite of regulators.

Foreign banks operating in the United States had, some argued, more freedom than U.S. banks. They were able, prior to 1978, to operate banking facilities in two or more states, own securities affiliates, and make equity investments in U.S. commercial companies. These advantages, considerably exaggerated by U.S. bankers at the time, put more pressure on the U.S. Congress to act—which it did in 1978. The International Banking Act of 1978, signed by President Carter on September 17, 1978, was aggressively lobbied for by U.S. banks. The act brought foreign banks fully under the U.S. regulatory umbrella and afforded them whatever privileges and rights were available to U.S. banks, such as eligibility for Fed membership and FDIC insurance. Nonbanking activities were also restricted as foreign banks were subjected to the Bank Holding Company Act of 1956 and to Sections 105 and 106 of the Bank Holding Company Act Amendment of 1970. A grandfather clause applies to banks engaged in nonbanking activities not permitted to U.S. banks prior to July 26, 1978. This fact, incidentally, turned out to be a significant concession to foreign banks. Today, 15 foreign banks are underwriting securities in America—an activity from which U.S. banks are partially, but significantly, barred. This is not the case throughout Europe, especially after the Big Bang, as the marriage between banking and investment banking appears to be a happy and profitable one. The authorities empowered under the 1978 act to supervise, audit, and carry out the provisions and purposes of this act are the Comptroller of the Currency, the FDIC, and state banking authorities. However, the Federal Reserve has residual authority to examine foreign banking operations. Foreign banks, now full members of the system, began to work to change it from within through the Institute of Foreign Bankers. Indeed, foreign banks in the United States were responsible for many changes that occurred later in the banking sector (see Chapter 1). Some argue that foreign bankers have helped redefine the concept of banking.

The only other U.S. legislation dealing with international banking (because all banks operating in the United States after 1978 were "domestic" banks, regardless of their national origin) was the International Lending Supervision Act of 1983. This act was a response to the sovereign debt crisis, indicating, once again, that regulation is likely to follow financial crises. The act requires banks to hold special reserves against the risks present in certain international credit and directs federal regulators to assess foreign country exposure when assessing capital adequacy and to establish minimum capital requirements for banking institutions.

U.S. banks also managed to circumvent two major regulations: interstate branching and the separation between banks and investment banks. The latter has already been discussed in Chapter 2. We need only add the dramatic entry of Bankers Trust in the sale of a new issue of junk bonds in September 1989 using a carefully structured and a creative legal set up.[5] Interstate branching was achieved utilizing three avenues. The first was the 1966 amendment to the Bank Holding Company Act of 1950. This amendment made the acquisition of a banking institution in another state contingent on whether that state's law permitted acquisitions by out-of-state bank holding companies. While restrictive in appearance, the amendment did not stop interstate acquisitions as one state after another gradually began to eliminate restrictions on entry by out-of-state banks.

The second avenue was through the acquisition or de novo establishment of "nonbank banks" which can perform all basic functions except accepting deposits and making commercial loans. An example of this is the Edge Act corporation or limited service bank set up by Merrill Lynch, Sears, Gulf & Western, etc. Edge Act corporations may be set up across state lines for the sole purpose of entering into international and foreign business. They may own stock in certain corporations, undertake investment banking activities, and participate in banking consortia without violating the antitrust laws. The Edge Act has been in effect since 1919.

The third avenue for interstate expansion was the acquisition of distressed banks and thrift institutions—e.g., the acquisition of Ohio's failing thrifts by New York thrifts. According to Donald Savage, the impetus for interstate branching lay in

- The desire to attract new capital to the state
- The belief that strong regional banks enhanced economic development
- The desire to allow for greater competition, and hence stronger institutions and more fairness to depositors and borrowers
- The need to inject vitality and quality management into troubled local financial institutions
- The desire to keep a state competitive with the other states that have already taken the step to permit interstate banking[6]

The one-bank holding companies (OBHCs) were the institutions most involved in interstate banking because of a major loophole in the 1956 Holding Company Act. This act did not cover companies controlling only one bank. As a consequence, OBHCs were establishing loan offices and selling debt instruments bearing market rates of interest across state lines. This loophole was closed in 1970 through an amendment to the Bank Holding Company Act of 1956. However, this in no way hindered the growth of bank holding companies and their resistance to regulatory constraints.

The other major deregulatory step—and a giant one at that—was the gradual dismemberment of the Glass–Steagall Act, which separates banking from investment banking. This process was extensively discussed in Chapter 2.

The evolution of the banking regulatory framework in the United States is traced in Exhibit 3.6, which shows the purpose(s) of the regulation (law), how it was circumvented or eliminated, and whether, as a result, a new regulation or law was implemented (passed). Deregulatory changes were not restricted to the banking sector. As banks gradually acquired investment bank characteristics, investment banks were acquiring banking characteristics and competing effectively with banks in various areas of banking. The regulatory changes dealing specifically with the investment banking activity also had a significant impact on the conduct of investment banking firms.

Exhibit 3.6
The Evolution of the Banking Regulatory Framework in the United States

OLD REGULATION	CIRCUMVENTION OR ELIMINATION	NEW REGULATION
Ban on interstate banking (McFadden Act 1927)	Circumvented through:	
	(a) bank holding companies which owned subsidiaries in several states;	(a) a 1966 Douglas Amendment to BHCA (1956) applies nearly the same restrictions to BHC's as to banks;
	(b) one bank holding co. loophole which allowed BHC's controlling only to use "non-banks" across state lines.	(b) A 1970 amendment of BHCA closed this loophole. The one bank amendments also set standards for the approval of closely related nonbanking activities.
	(c) Automatic teller machines networks are used for interstate expansion.	
	Many states either eliminated or relaxed restrictions on expansion of out-of-state banks.	
Companies operating in non-banking industries are prohibited from owning banks.	Circumvented through use of non-bank banks (which accepted demand deposits or made commercial loans but not both).	A 1970 amendment to BHCA closed this loophole.
Capital adequacy requirements.	Off-balance sheet financing.	Risk-adjusted capital ban (proposed).

(Continued)

Exhibit 3.6 *(Continued)*

OLD REGULATION	CIRCUMVENTION OR ELIMINATION	NEW REGULATION
Ban on insurance activities of banks	BHC's own insurance companies	Title VI of the Garn-St. Germain Act explicitly BHC's from insurance activities.
Interest rate ceilings (Regulation Q)	Circumvented through: (a) certificates of deposit (first offered by Citibank in 1961) (b) money market mutual funds DIDMCA provided for gradual elimination of in rate ceilings between June 1981 - March 1986	
Prohibition of interest on demand deposits (GSA 1933)	Negotiable order of withdrawal (NOW) accounts are initiated by mutual savings banks in the early 1970's in Massachusetts and spread throughout New England. The prohibition is eliminated by DIDMCA (1980)	
Separation between investment and commercial banking (Glass Steagall Act 1933)	Partially eliminated by a court ruling 1975 (banks can offer brokerage and automatic investment services) and by a host of other court rulings, deregulatory changes and maneuvers by banks.	
State usury laws limits on interest rates charged on certain types of loans	Banks established credit card subsidiaries in South Dakota and Delaware (these two states passed special legislation to attract capital)	

Exhibit 3.6 (*Continued*)

OLD REGULATION	CIRCUMVENTION OR ELIMINATION	NEW REGULATION
Fixed securities commission rates	Circumvented to some extent through non-price competition. Completely eliminated on May 1, 1975.	
Margin requirements on securities loan (1934 Act).	------------	No Change
Real Estate Loan restrictions (on size and interest rates)	Most eliminated by 1983 (Comptroller of the Currency).	
Selective credit controls	Were used only during brief periods during the 1960's and 1970's	
Controls on credit quality		No Change
Limits on loans to single borrower		No Change
Loans to insiders		No Change
Restrictions on types and maturity distribution of securities held as investments		No Change
Restrictions on credit transactions with non-banking affiliates		No change
Reserve requirements (applies to member of FRB)		DIDMCA (1980) extends requirements to all depository institutions on an equal basis
CAMEL rating system (p. 79)		No change
Reporting requirements (on quarterly basis)		No change

(*continued*)

Exhibit 3.6 (*Continued*)

OLD REGULATION	CIRCUMVENTION OR ELIMINATION	NEW REGULATION
Entry regulations (charters) administered by Comptroller of the Currency on state authorities		No change
Restrictions on bank ownership		New restrictions imposed on bank owner-ship by individuals by the Changes in Bank Control Act (1978)
Regulation of management interlocks (only for FRB members)		The Depository Inst. Management Interlocks Act (1978) extends restrictions to all depository institu-tions.
Restrictions on bank mergers (Bank Merger Act of 1966) - The opinion of the Department of Justice on any competitive factors regarding bank mergers is required.		No change
Regulation of international expansion of U.S. banks		Supervisory procedures have been strengthened by the International lending Supervision Act (1983)
Foreign bank entry into U.S.		The Glass-Steagall restrictions on separation between investment and commercial banking apply to foreign banks (Int'l Banking Act-1978)
Truth in Lending Act (1968)(Regulation Z) requires accurate disclosure of lending terms	10 years after enactment, 80% of banks were not in compliance	The regulations are simplified in the Truth in lending Simplification and Reform Act (1980)

Exhibit 3.6 (*Continued*)

OLD REGULATION	CIRCUMVENTION OR ELIMINATION	NEW REGULATION
Consumer Leasing Act (1976)(Regulation M) requires accurate disclosure of the terms of personal property lease		No change
Real Estate Settlement Procedures Act (1974) requires lenders to inform potential homebuyers in writing of settlement charges (Regulation X of HUD)		No change
Electronic Funds Transfer Act (1978) (Regulation E) applies to personal accounts		In 1984, the regulattions were extended to debit card transactions.

Three major changes in the regulatory environment for investment banks have taken place. The first is the move toward negotiated commissions, which began in 1971 and culminated with legislation mandating the deregulation of all brokerage commission charges by May 1, 1985. This cut commissions drastically (over 50 percent in some cases), brought about a whole new industry (discount brokers), and put a large number of small, undercapitalized firms out of business.

The second major change was authorized by the Securities and Exchange Commission on March 5, 1982. This marked the birth of Rule 415, or shelf registration. Prior to that, every time primary securities were to be issued, disclosure documents had to be prepared, no matter how short the time period separating them. Under Rule 415, one disclosure document is sufficient for securities issued against it for up to two years. This permitted underwriters to better time the issuance of securities, depending on market conditions.

The third major change is the gradual but sure incursion of investment banks into banking territory. Merrill Lynch now operates "nonbank banks" and allows clients to write checks against their credit balances in the margin account. This appears to be the trend in an industry which is rather tightly knit and well led by its top 10 firms. The Capital Markets Association has only 100 members, compared with 14,000 banks in the United States. The top 4 investment banking firms underwrite 60 percent of corporate securities in the United States, and the top 10 underwrite almost 95 percent of corporate securities. Their expansion into traditional banking business is, therefore, understandable as they seek new business opportunities that are "available" and profitable. Expansion within the industry is possible but riskier.

All the developments in the regulation of banks and investment banks and the attempts by banks and investment banks to circumvent existing regulations were enhanced by the technological changes that ushered in the "information age."

Technological improvements have facilitated the ability of bank holding companies to locate certain bank operations in other states. The availability of electronic data transmission and funds transfers and other communication facilities no longer requires that all banking operations be located in the vicinity of the majority of a bank's customer.[7]

The age of high-speed computers, personal computers accessible to practically every bank employee, automated teller machines, credit cards acceptable (and verifiable) all over the world, telephone, telefax, and telex machines coupled with computers, teleconferencing, networking, data sets and services that put every conceivable piece of information at one's fingertips, and sophisticated, well-trained computer operators who make it all work have resolved the communication and transportation problems that historically justified the location of banking offices near the client or not too far from headquarters. Suddenly, geographic distance shrank toward zero as the speed of information flow approached instaneousness.

Nowhere was the effect of technology more dramatic than in the financial markets, the securities markets in particular. The selling and buying of securities became possible using a PC, and no broker needed to be involved. Worldwide arbitrage and arbitrage between one market and another (e.g., cash and futures) became the order of the day because they require the simultaneous purchase and sale of securities. Computers make this possible. "Program trading," which allows investors to arbitrage between the stock index futures market and the underlying cash, is possible only with computers. It was born in 1982 with the advent of stock index futures. The "program" allows a trader to profit without bearing any risk the minute prices of futures diverge from their normal relationship to the value of the underlying.

While this technology contributes to the efficiency of the stock market, some argue, others point to the October 19, 1987, crash and the alleged evidence that program trading may have caused it, at least in part. *The Wall Street Journal* reported that during 1987 "index arbitrage trading accounted for 1% to 19% of Big Board daily volume, according to a Big Board study."[8] That means that on a typical day, when 175 million shares change hands, index arbitrage can represent as much as $1 billion of trading.

Technology is critical in the implementation of computerized trading, in which very complex models were developed to trigger buy and sell orders for stocks. Thus, the computer is put in the place of a portfolio manager in terms of making decisions on portfolio composition. This form of portfolio management has its critics who claim that it contributed to the October 19, 1987, crash. One variation of computerized trading has become known as portfolio insurance. This strategy is designed to protect stock portfolios against market downturns by selling stock index futures as stocks fall. The profits from the short futures position are expected to offset, given a carefully calculated hedge ratio, the losses in the cash position.

Technology is also partially responsible for the internationalization of portfolios as it links the world financial markets. One single screen has all the information a trader needs to trade anywhere in the world. The execution is practically instantaneous. One needs to visit a trading room to feel the awe of technological advances. Their value is considerable, but their perils are also present. An electrical blackout, equipment failure, sabotage, computer hackers, and other perils could disrupt the financial system in ways not entirely predictable.

We now look at the impact of deregulation.

THE IMPACT OF DEREGULATION

The impact analysis, requiring statistical methods and dealing with macroeconomic issues, is presented in Chapter 7. In this section the remaining issues are examined, beginning with the securities industry.

The Securities Industry

The increased acceptance (and evidence) of the net benefits of international diversification, the quantum leap and spread of technology worldwide, and the deregulation of financial markets in practically every country increased interdependence (correlation in performance) among national markets. The net effects were largely positive as spreads narrowed throughout, commission costs dropped throughout, reaction time to market events narrowed to a fraction of a minute, and costs of funds adjusted for exchange risk became equal or were brought close to equity by sharp-eyed arbitragers and their computers.

The increased price competition observed in the market did not come about instantaneously. It represents an evolutionary process which started in the early 1950s and culminated in a very competitive market, providing investors with a wider range of products at more competitive prices and a higher quality of service. Exhibit 3.7 traces that evolution.

Price competition replaced nonprice competition (e.g., toasters and TVs), and pricing schedules were increasingly based on costs. This may have adversely affected the small client with small and infrequent orders and benefited those institutions with large and frequent orders (with a very low cost per unit).

The negative side of interdependence is that increased correlation reduced the value of international diversification and increased the speed with which bad and even distorted news was transmitted on a worldwide scale. The crash of October 19, 1987, was a perfect example. Regardless of what one thinks its causes were, or whether it originated in Japan or in the United States, the fact that it was a worldwide overreaction to economic developments is unquestionable. Exhibit

Exhibit 3.7
Evolution of Price Competition

1. Give-ups, special services for institutional business (1950s)
2. Load and no-load fund competition (1960s)
3. Institutional off-board trading (1960s)
4. Direct discounting of very large orders (1971)
5. Dividend reinvestment plan extensions (1970s)
6. Reduced odd-lot fees (1970s)
7. Competitive commission rates (1975)
8. Discount brokers and other noncommissioned-salesmen-type firms (late 1970s)

Source: Michael Keenan, "The Scope of Deregulation in the Securities Industry," in *The Deregula-tion of the Banking and Securities Industries,* ed. Lawrence G. Goldberg and Lawrence J. White (Lexington, Mass.: Lexington Books, 1979), 123.

3.8 shows how widespread and deep the damage was and how similar, in many cases, the magnitudes were.

The Wall Street Journal, in its November 13, 1987, issue, accented the behavior of market participants as they reacted to the dramatic and unexpected October 19 event:

In the wake of the October 19 stock crash, Continental European markets were rocked by U.S. speculators scrambling to meet margin calls in their home markets and by mutual funds managers dumping shares to meet redemption orders. Portfolio managers were scouring the world to sell shares wherever they found good liquidity at the best prices.[9]

Exhibit 3.8
World Markets' Collapse

Percentage change in Morgan Stanley's index for each market between August 25, 1987—the record high for the U.S. market—and Wednesday, October 21, 1987

	% Change (in local currency)
USA	-27.8%
Japan	-19.8
UK	-27.2
Germany	-38.4
Canada	-28.4
France	-34.7
Switzerland	-30.5
Australia	-43.4
Italy	-18.7
Netherlands	-33.6

Source: Morgan Stanley Capital International Perspective, December 1987.

The post-crash analyses provided many answers as to causes and effects. Some blamed index arbitrage, others absolved it. In fact, Richard Roll argued "Thus, taken as a characteristic in isolation, computer directed trading such as portfolio insurance and index arbitrage, if it had any impact at all, actually helped mitigate the market decline."[10]

However, the February 18, 1988, issue of *The Wall Street Journal* reported that

the New York Stock Exchange has voted to restrict index arbitrage any time the Dow Jones Industrial Average moves 50 points in a day. The rule, which has been put into effect on a voluntary basis pending Securities and Exchange Commission approval, is a step toward "reinforcing investor confidence in the integrity, fairness and efficiency" of the market, says John T. Phelan, Jr., the Big Board's chairman.[11]

This action by the NYSE could not have been based on the belief that index arbitrage and portfolio insurance had salutary effects on the market. No matter its causes, the increased volatility of the market is not healthy, especially for the smaller investor whose mistrust of the market has never been greater.

The deregulation of banking institutions improved their position vis-à-vis investment banks but did not completely close the gap. The securities industry has steadily increased its share of the value-added volume of financial institutions. This improvement came not at the expense of commercial banks, but at the expense of savings and loans and other thrift institutions.[12]

The investment banking firms were not satisfied with invading the turf of banks. They moved into direct acquisition of major corporations in deals referred to as leveraged buyouts (LBOs). Exhibit 3.9 shows that 9 of the top 10 leveraged buyouts during the 1980s involved investment banking houses.

This trend continues despite the howls of protest from several corners about the huge profits being realized in the process, the decapitalization of America (limited capital resources going to acquisition instead of de novo investment), and the effect of LBOs on the stock market, most especially on the bond market.

Exhibit 3.9
Top 10 Leveraged Buyouts

Date announced	Target	Acquirer	$bn
October 1988	RJR Nabisco	Kolhberg Kravis Roberts	20.3
October 1985	Beatrice Co	Kolhberg Kravis Robert	6.2
July 1986	Safeway Stores	Kolhberg Kravis Roberts	5.7
April 1987	Borg-Warner Corp	Merrill Lynch	4.2
July 1987	Southland Corp	Saloman Brothers & Goldman Sachs	4.0
February 1987	Viacom Int.	National Amusements	3.9
March 1988	Montgomery Ward	GE Capital and Kidder, Peabody	3.8
October 1985	R.H. Macy & Co.	Goldman Sachs	3.7
December 1986	Owens-Illinois	Kolhberg Kravis Roberts	3.6
June 1988	Fort Howard Paper	Morgan Stanley	3.6

Source: The Economist (29 October 1988): 69.

The Economist argued that "leveraged buy-outs have become so huge that investors now realize that almost every company's bonds are under the threat of instant conversion into junk."[13] An excellent example of this is the RJR Nabisco case in which existing bondholders holding $5.4 billion incurred an $800 million loss as a result of the LBO by Kolhberg Kravis Roberts. This is typical because from 1985 through 1987 "30 billion worth of bonds were downgraded from investment grade to junk."

The adoption of Rule 415 also had a significant impact. The study by Robert J. Rogowski and Eric Sorensen[14] showed that the investment banking industry has become more competitive despite increased concentration (due largely to an acquisition drive by the industry) and that the risk-adjusted returns in the investment banking industry may have declined as a result of lower underwriter spreads.

The Banking Industry

The deregulation of the banking industry has had extensive impact. Because this book is too small to cover every effect in a comprehensive fashion, only the major points will be highlighted.

The bank advertisements one watches throughout the United States and the cynicism and sarcasm they engender about banking services illustrate the plight of the small depositor. Today, a depositor at some banks is charged a fee for speaking to a live teller. He/she is regularly penalized through lower (or zero) interest payments on deposits or through fees charged for checks written in the event the deposit size falls below a certain level. The smaller the CD, the lower the rate of interest earned. Detailed statements of account activities are no longer issued on demand. There is a flat fee for cashier's checks to the maximum allowed, making it a very regressive cost to the smaller investor. Even cashing a check at some banks costs a substantial sum (up to $10 in some places). Spreads on small transactions are much higher than those on larger transactions. One needs only to examine the spreads on sums under $1,000 versus those on sums that are much larger. So important has account size become that banks set up separate divisions for substantial clients. This cost-driven fee structure has left the individual with small savings practically outside the banking system. This attitude toward smaller depositors is quite universal across banks and thrifts.

The passage of DIDMCA has produced another phenomenon, the blurring of the difference between banks and thrifts. Also, the dismantling of Glass–Steagall blurred the difference between banks and investment banks. We are therefore moving toward a financial industry in which the demarcation lines between types of institutions are so indistinct as to make them irrelevant. The day of true financial supermarkets, where any financial service can be had in one location, is dawning. This diversified service center could be owned by a bank, an investment bank, or an insurance company, and, until a recent reversal, by Sears. This will increase competition and lower the prices consumers must pay for services rendered. The problem, however, as was pointed out earlier, is the tiering of clients. Clients do not pay the average or the marginal cost to the institution; they pay the marginal cost within a given tier, which is much higher for small depositors.

The benefits to everyone lie in the higher interest rates that depositors have been receiving from their banks. Savings accounts compete with money market accounts after adjustment for FDIC insurance, the convenience factor, and explicit transaction costs. Also, savings accounts have become more liquid, and one can earn positive, real rates of return while still being able to withdraw money on demand.

Viewed from the bank's perspective, deregulation has had mixed effects. Among the many reasons are the following:

- The liabilities of the banks have become more costly, but variable rate loans were introduced to transfer interest rate risk to the borrower. The innovations that produced deregulation allowed risk to become tradeable. The increased liquidity of bank portfolios allowed banks to adjust their assets and liabilities (adjust the gap) in such a way as to keep a natural hedge. This was enhanced by new hedging tools such as swaps, options, and futures contracts.

- Interstate branching has put pressure on banks to become more competitive. Today's bankers, as a result, are much more sophisticated and much more responsive to changes in the marketplace. Donald Savage found that the hypothesis that interstate branching can lead to increased concentration in the banking industry is supported (but not strongly) in the banking industry. The top 100 banking institutions controlled 57.7 percent of domestic banking assets in 1985, compared with 50.4 percent in 1970.[15] The consolidation was necessary in some cases to save certain institutions from liquidation and to effect an immediate presence in a given market. However, there is no evidence to suggest that increased concentration has translated into "greater control over the allocation of credit." The increased concentration did not hurt the ability of well-run, smaller banks to compete because the banking industry does not appear to be particularly affected by economies of scale.

- The new products introduced by aggressive and progressive banks discussed throughout this book put enormous pressures on smaller, less sophisticated banks and thrifts. Some learned to cope quickly, some learned slowly, and the rest never learned, explaining (but only partially) bank and thrift failures. The strategies, the nature of the decisions, and the scope of the problem with which bank and thrift managers suddenly had to deal were truly revolutionary. A new age has dawned.

New financial products challenge the thrifts to make decisions they never before had to make. In the traditional thrift business, mortgage prices were dictated by the market and deposit offers were dictated by the regulatory structure. Location of branches was basically the only real decision facing the thrift manager. Now, deregulation has brought a whole range of financial products that the thrift and its competitors can offer, and a variety of chartering options that force the savings institutions to decide the best form in which to operate.[16]

The five years following enactment of DIDMCA, a major legislative initiative, showed that the banking industry was not getting better in terms of quality of assets and return thereon. Exhibit 3.10 shows that the position of commercial banks worsened considerably in many cases. To attribute this solely to deregulation is neither wise nor accurate, and even if it were, it does not

Exhibit 3.10

Key Performance Indicators: All Insured Commercial Banks, 1980–1985

	1980	1981	1982	1983	1984	1985
Return on average assets	.82%	.81%	.74%	.67%	.65%	.64%
Percent of banks with good return on assets (over 1.0%)	60.47%	56.56%	53.07%	48.14%	43.03%	43.14%
Percent of banks with negative return on assets (under 0%)	3.71%	5.14%	8.33%	10.99%	13.82%	16.16%
Net charge offs as percentage of average total loans	.38%	.37%	.57%	.69%	.78%	.86%
Loss reserves as a percentage of average total loans	1.06%	1.10%	1.15%	1.26%	1.35%	1.51%

Source: William L. Seidman, "Issues in Bank Regulation," (Spring 1987): 2.

necessarily spell disaster because this may be the adjustment period during which U.S. banks will become truly competitive internationally in an environment that allows only the fittest to survive. The U.S. banking industry did not do much better through 1987. During the first six months of 1987, U.S. banks led by Citicorp set aside $21.2 billion in reserves and recorded a $106 billion loss—the worst loss in any six-month period in the industry's history. Thankfully, the results for 1988 were quite good and reassuring.

• The thrift industry, especially the S&Ls, has experienced a wrenching change, mostly voluntary, in the composition of its asset portfolio. The result is a more stable portfolio with less emphasis on mortgages (Exhibit 3.11). This took place without any credit rationing in the mortgage market; there is no evidence that credit availability has been a problem for mortgage seekers. The high mortgage rates were indeed a disincentive in the mortgage market. Interestingly, mortgage rates fell markedly during the Reagan years—a period of major regulatory changes.

• The further internationalization of the U.S. banking industry is another source of deregulatory changes. U.S. banks compete worldwide, and foreign banks from every country are trying to find a niche in the U.S. market. A deregulated environment allows for quick reactions by international banks to changes in market conditions and for an enlarged set of tools for capitalizing on opportunities, whether actual or perceived. All these affect the risk/returns tradeoff on the bank portfolio. The distinction between domestic and international banking has disappeared for all practical purposes as all markets, investment opportunities, and sources of funds become multinational in character:

Their home state (in the case of U.S. banks) or their home country (elsewhere) was essentially a franchise granted by them, which protected them from others in return for restricting their expansion. But those days are gone. There are few barriers to entry in most banking markets: no one has any patents or copyrights.[17]

Exhibit 3.11
Share of Funds Allocated to Mortgages, 1976–1984 (Quarterly)

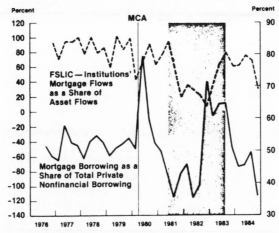

Source: FRBSF Weekly Letter, August 2, 1985.

This reality has had wide-ranging effects. It has affected the soundness of the U.S. banking system, the convenience and welfare of depositors, the ability of the Fed to conduct monetary policy, the profitability and stability of U.S. banks, the organizational structure of banking firms, and the macroeconomy through capital flows, employment, and interest rates.[18] The banking industry has finally reached the global state of commercial and industrial firms as it has unshackled itself from its regulatory chains. The results are not too clear, and this is precisely what concerns the U.S. Congress, the regulators, and even the bankers themselves. This is what has laid the groundwork for reregulation.

RETHINKING DEREGULATION

The October 19, 1987, crash produced a litany of proposals, all intended to place restrictions on the market. There were the calls and the subsequent decision to stop the computerized entry system if the Dow Jones Industrials move by 50 points or more in one day. There were the calls to close the exchange if the Dow falls by a certain number of points (300). There were the calls to place price limits on index futures. However, these and other proposals were never implemented. Those who argued for a hands-off policy are breathing easier because the stock market has adjusted considerably since the crash and since various studies, like the Katzenbach report, have vindicated futures contracts as culprits in the increased market volatility. Nevertheless, the fact remains that the central conclusion in the Brady Commission's report was that the absence of a central regulatory agency could have exacerbated the market decline. The call for a "super agency" like that in Japan still goes unheeded, however.

The Federal Reserve System, concerned about the growth of the junk bond market, decided to curb the use of junk bonds in corporate takeover cases.

On the banking side, several market observers have argued that the deregulation of financial markets is a "mirage." Indeed, they suggest that a careful examination of the laws passed during the 1980s would show that these acts were as much attempts to regulate the market as they were attempts to deregulate the market. The 1982 Garn–St. Germain Act released the S&L industry from certain constraints on its assets and liabilities structure, but "it also tightened up substantially on bank holding companies' powers to get into insurance agencies."[19]

The off-balance-sheet activities of U.S. banks increased the risk to their insurer, the FDIC. The regulatory responses were intended to reduce the banks' incentive to increase asset risk and then shift that risk onto the FDIC. Minimum capital was set at 6 percent of assets for banks and bank holding companies with assets less than $1 billion and at 5 percent for those institutions with assets exceeding $1 billion. The Federal Reserve later proposed and subsequently adopted risk-adjusted capital asset ratios that use a certain conversion factor to effectively turn off-balance-sheet items into balance-sheet items. In addition, bank regulators became more vigilant in their examination of assets and liabilities. Also, DIDMCA expanded the Fed's regulatory powers and its ability to intervene when bank problems were induced by sovereign debt.

The suspicion of deregulation in banking has its roots partially in the results of deregulation of the airline and telephone industries. While rates have declined in both industries, the quality of service and the stability of the industry have not improved, according to most studies. The failures of S&Ls are attributed by some (who are not well informed) to the departure of the industry from its traditional focus on the mortgage business—that is, to deregulation. That is why it appears that the revamping or elimination of the Glass–Steagall Act has yet to go anywhere, even after many bills were introduced and thousands of hours were spent in debate. The spirit of deregulation is dissipating. Several lawmakers are calling to turn the clock back and to give more regulatory powers to the Fed (over banks) and to the SEC and the CFTC (over securities, options, and futures contracts).

Lest we overlook this, the 1970s and 1980s also witnessed a goodly number of legislative acts intended to protect consumers. Among them are the Electronic Fund Transfer Act of 1978, which establishes the rights and responsibilities of participating parties so the interests of consumers are protected; the Consumer Learning Act of 1978, which requires accurate disclosure of the terms of personal property leases; and other laws and provisions requiring more disclosure to the public so their decisions may be more enlightened. The problem, however, is that the increased information relates to very complex issues. As a result, there appears to be no net improvement in the ability of the average investor/depositor to assess the risk profile of a bank or an investment bank. That is why depositors waited until February 13, 1989, to line up in front of two S&Ls in California to receive their deposits from the FDIC. Every one of those standing in long lines could have shifted his/her funds well before that day to another institution. Those interviewed did not realize that the S&L was in trouble until the last minute. Increasing the flow of information is one thing; understanding and acting responsibly on that information are another.

On the international level, the 1978 and 1983 acts dealing with international banking have dealt with only a few of the problems. There still is no international system of supervision that corresponds to the reality of international banking and to that of the interbank market, which is an excellent vehicle for transmitting beneficial policy effects as well as disaster. The impact of the growth of international banks in the United States documented in Chapter 1 has yet to be fully understood. What if the Japanese acquire the top five U.S. banks in the next 10 years. Will the banking industry be as secure? Will the conduct of monetary policy be unaffected? What are the full political implications? It appears, thus far at least, that the United States is operating on the premise that more direct investment is better. This is bound to change. The stock market crash of October 19, 1987, showed, among other things, the fragility of the banking system. The banks in the United States responded well. Would the response have been as rapid and massive if the banks were owned by foreign interests? One cannot be sure.

Also, the new measures such as the International Lending Supervision Act of 1983 did not change the conditions of U.S. banks for the better with respect to sovereign debt. Net exposure by U.S. banks to sovereign debt increased markedly between 1983 and 1988, and no permanent solution to the debt crisis is in sight. When sovereign debt is resolved permanently, the American taxpayers will pay for it, just as they did for the solution to the S&L crisis. Deregulation has not improved the competitive position of U.S. banks and investment banks in the world markets. They are slipping on almost every level, with Japanese and European firms taking the lead (see Chapter 1). The problem is certainly deeper than regulation/deregulation.

CONCLUSION

This chapter has reviewed U.S.-specific regulatory issues. Our focus has been on the various regulations, the corresponding deregulations, and the reregulations, with the statistical and macro issues saved for Chapter 7. The impact of all this has been examined in order that the reader can develop a perspective on the merits of the arguments in favor of or against certain positions. In many cases, the issues could not be sorted out in a crisp fashion. The regulation of banks and its impact has a lot of grey areas.

NOTES

1. Barry Eichengreen and Richard Portes, "The Anatomy of Financial Crisis," in *Threats to International Financial Stability* ed. Richard Portes and Alexander K. Swoboda (Cambridge: Cambridge University Press, 1987), 10–57.

2. Michael Keenan, "The Scope of Deregulation in the Securities Industry," in *The*

Deregulation of the Banking and Securities Industries, ed. Lawrence G. Goldberg and Lawrence J. White (Lexington, Mass.: Lexington Books, 1979), 117.

3. Nicholas Lemann, "Change in the Banks," *Atlantic Monthly* (August 1985): 60.

4. Sarkis J. Khoury, *Dynamics of International Banking* (New York: Praeger Publishers, 1980).

5. *International Herald Tribune,* 23–24 September 1989, 14.

6. Donald T. Savage, "Interstate Banking Developments" *Federal Reserve Bulletin* (February 1987): 79–91.

7. *Chicago Fed. Letter* no. 10 (June 1988): 2.

8. Kevin G. Salwen, "Divided Street," *Wall Street Journal,* 18 February 1988.

9. Michael R. Sesit, "Stock Crash Highlights the Perils of a Linked Market," *Wall Street Journal,* 13 November 1987.

10. Richard Roll, "The International Crash of October, 1987" (UCLA, 1988, Typescript).

11. Salwen, "Divided Street."

12. See Robert O. Edmister, "Securities Industry Market Share Trends after Banking Deregulation," *Financial Analysts Journal* 42 (March–April 1986): 9.

13. "Corporate America Snuggles Up to the Buy-out Wolves," *Economist* (29 October 1988): 69–72.

14. Robert J. Rogowski and Eric Sorensen, "Deregulation in Investment Banking: Shelf Registration, Structure and Performance," *Financial Management* 14, no. 1 (Spring 1985): 5–15.

15. Donald Savage, *Federal Reserve Bulletin* (February 1987).

16. John Tuccillo, "Deregulation and Thrift Strategies," *Business Economics* 20, no. 3 (July 1985): 23.

17. Serge Bellanger, "Going Global," *Bankers Magazine* 170, no. 2 (March–April 1987): 68.

18. For a detailed analysis, see Khoury, *Dynamics of International Banking.*

19. *Euromoney* (June 1986).

4

The Deregulation of the Japanese Financial Markets

The deregulation of the Japanese financial markets started much later than that of U.S. markets and moved at a much slower pace—at times grudgingly. Some of the changes may be considered revolutionary, especially from Japanese historical and cultural perspectives, and others insufficient or inadequate. There was no Big Bang similar to Britain's, and there is not likely to be one in the foreseeable future.

The deregulation of the Japanese market was inevitable, considering Japan's meteoric rise in the world economy, its large balance of payments, the surpluses it has accumulated over the years (Exhibit 4.1), and the increased prominence of the Japanese yen (Exhibit 4.2) as an international currency. The last, it can be argued, is more a consequence rather than a cause of deregulation. This question will be addressed later.

A rich, confident standardbearer of economic development based almost exclusively on human capital, run by a well-educated sophisticated cadre of professionals less burdened by the tragedy of World War II, determined to compete in all countries and at all levels, urged to assume a major share of its defense and that of the region, and intent on exercising political power (with its corresponding prestige) commensurate with its economic power, Japan had no choice but to deregulate its financial markets. The flow could not have been unidirectional. The West was as intent on enjoying the fruits of the East as the East was on enjoying the fruits of the West. Japan could not have achieved the world stature clearly demonstrated during the funeral of Emperor Hirohito by maintaining a fortress, ethnocentric mentality.

Deregulation was also a necessary strategic component as Japan sought to

Exhibit 4.1
Japan's Merchandise Trade, 1980–1987 (US$, billion)

(US$,billion)	Total Japanese Merchandise Trade			with US			with SE Asia		
	X	M	Bal	X	M	Bal	X	M	Bal
1980	130	141	-11	31	24	7	30	31	-1
1981	152	143	9	38	25	13	34	32	2
1982	139	132	7	36	24	12	32	30	2
1983	147	126	21	43	25	18	35	28	7
1984	170	137	34	60	27	33	37	32	5
1985	176	130	46	65	26	39	33	30	3
1986	209	126	83	80	29	51	42	29	12
1987	229	150	80	84	31	52	53	39	14

```
Legend: X - exports
        M - imports
        Bal - balance
```

Source: Japan Tariff Association, *The Summary Report: Trade of Japan* (Tokyo, 1988).

diversify its exports and the sources of its imports: both products and raw materials. The multinationalization of the Japanese corporations led to the multinationalization of Japanese banks. Prior to 1978 Japanese banks entered the U.S. market on terms that gave them a competitive advantage even over indigenous U.S. banks. After the passage of the International Banking Act in 1978, Japanese

Exhibit 4.2
International Use of Yen (%)

		1980	1986	1987
Ratio of nation's currency used in merchandise trade	Japan-Exports	29.4	36.5	33.4
	Imports	2.4	9.8	10.6
	West Germany-			
	Exports	82.3	82	–
	Imports	42.8	52	–
Currency components in international bond issues	US$	66.5	62.7	35.8
	Yen	1.5	10.0	14.1
	DM	17.5	9.0	8.1
Currency components in world's foreign exchange reserves	US$	69.0	66.6	–
	Yen	4.5	6.9	–
	DM	15.6	14.8	–

Sources: International Monetary Fund, Bank for International Settlement, Ministry of Finance, Ministry of International Trade & Industry, Bank of Japan, OECD.

banks were able to operate just like any other banks in the United States in every area of banking. This required reciprocal behavior, and the Japanese opened their doors, but only a crack, as a result. Now, the doors are being pushed to open wider. The Ministry of Finance (MOF) of Japan has always insisted on reciprocity when it has been approached by a foreign entity seeking to do business in Japan. However, as shown below, the reciprocity provided by Japan is more form than substance in many cases.

We now look at the full set of forces that produced dramatic changes in Japan.

THE IMPETUS FOR DEREGULATION

The post–World War II financial system of Japan reflected an inward-looking, yet determined country, a regenerated system, and the need to have every Japanese pay his/her fair share to rebuild a shattered economy. The Japanese had their way of doing things as they proceeded to move their economy from a military foundation to a capital/consumer goods economy.

The philosophy that gripped Japan immediately after the war was one of maintaining order and discipline. This meant that everything had to be regulated—including the financial sector. Control meant stability to the Japanese, and this was a necessary ingredient in the ambitious reconstruction program.

The massive cost of reconstruction necessitated a high savings rate at a very low cost to the Japanese government. Thus, strict controls on capital flows and a tight ceiling on interest paid to depositors were imposed. The investment opportunities were also limited, leaving savers with savings accounts as the only alternative to the "mattress."

The third element in the strategy was the compartmentalization of the Japanese financial institutions. Certain types of banks were allowed certain possibilities on the assets and liabilities sides, and a strict separation was to be maintained between banking and investment banking. The latter could have been a reflection of the American philosophy at the time and the American experience with Glass–Steagall.

The creation and branching of financial institutions were also restricted, interest on loans and types of loans were strictly regulated, exchange rates were fixed and rigid, direct investment in Japan was prohibited, and only certain categories of imports were allowed. The expansionist policy of Japan was replaced by a solemn isolationist policy focused on economic development so Japan could rise from the ashes.

As a result, the transformation of Japan's financial markets could not have come at the same speed as the deregulation of U.S. markets. Japan needed to put the memory of the war behind it (significantly, if not completely), reassure itself that it was on a firm economic footing for the long run, and convince itself that the formula that has served it so well and brought it unprecedented and enviable economic prosperity required modification. The recent wave of deregulatory steps taken by Japan was intended, some argue, simply to lessen the world resentment toward Japan, which keeps its markets relatively protected while achieving monopoly or near monopoly positions in many products and in many markets outside its boundaries.

The first major motivation for deregulation in Japan was the oil crisis of 1973–1974, which brought an abrupt end to Japan's rapidly increasing economic prosperity. As a consequence, Japan's real GNP growth declined from 10 percent per year to 3.6 percent, and its budget deficit, which accounted for only 2 percent of GNP in 1973, was at 7 percent of GNP by the end of 1975. To deal with the economic slowdown, Japan began to borrow large sums of money to finance its rising budget deficit. It did this by issuing 10-year bonds, using the government bond underwriting syndicate (GBU), a syndicate made up of banks, investment banks, and insurance companies.

The evolution of this debt and the conditions for its placement led to the first crack in the Japanese regulatory structure.

Rather than sell the increasing volume of government debt on the open market, the MOF placed the debt directly with a "captive" syndicate of banks and other institutions that were required to purchase the debt at below-market rates and to hold it for as long as one year. Syndicate members did not resist the procedure prior to 1975 largely because the amount of debt was small. Also, the BOJ was willing to repurchase the debt from banks at prices that guaranteed no capital loss, and the MOF allowed securities companies to use the debt to support a repurchase, or "Gensaki", market as it is called in Japan. After 1975, when the size of the debt rose, the MOF met with increasing market resistance and was forced to make a number of concessions to market forces, which officially started the liberalization process.[1]

The massive government borrowing crowded out loans to the private sector. With banks required to buy as much as 80 percent of the government bonds issued, their loans and discounts to the private sector dropped from 82 percent of assets in 1974 to 74 percent in 1979.

The increased attention of banks to the fiscal problems of the central government put pressure on corporations to lessen their dependence on banks as their sole source of funds. This meant tapping the financial markets directly, and, thus, the corporate securities markets were born. Corporations, after 1977, were able to improve the returns on their liquid assets by shifting funds from the banks with their below-market rates on deposits to government bonds with competitive rates. This further diminished the dependence of corporations on their banks for the performance of their liquid assets. Banks, for a long time, needed alternatives, and their first one arrived without any lobbying effort—a natural consequence of the government's attempting to deal with a fiscal crisis.

The economic slowdown also had a marked effect on consumers. The limited investment opportunities and the below-market rates on deposits suddenly became glaringly inadequate. The maintenance of their standard of living and the realization of their economic expectations necessitated a reduced savings program and/or a higher return on existing savings. The latter was the easier alternative. Individual considerations had to be placed at par with national considerations. The long years of sacrifice had to end, in some respect, for Japanese investors. The economic success realized by then was considerable and robust enough to withstand some freedom for the financial markets.

Other pressures to deregulate the financial markets came from Japanese banks that had tasted freedom in the overseas markets and were able to compete successfully through their branches and subsidiaries. Japanese banks in London did not operate in a regulated interest environment, were able to hedge their portfolios using financial futures and other instruments, and could involve themselves in the securities industry. In the United States, Japanese banks could act as primary dealers in the U.S. government bond market. Yet these same banks were denied access to these types of activities in their domestic market. The gap had to be bridged.

The decision by President Nixon in 1973 to float the U.S. dollar put further pressure on the Japanese to liberalize their financial system. Japan could not have hoped, or be allowed, to maintain a strict, fixed exchange rate while the rest of the world's nations were allowing their currencies to float. To allow flexibility for the yen value, capital inflows and outflows had to be permitted and interest rigidities reduced or eliminated. Japan, having integrated its production and commercial sectors internationally, could no longer avoid to do much less for its financial sector.

In 1980, Japan amended its foreign exchange and foreign trade law to lift regulations on capital inflows to and outflows from Japan. Sensitive and well attuned to international trends and concerns, Japan responded to the outside pressures, especially those coming from the United States. Several agreements were concluded with the United States, including a May 1984 agreement under which the United States was expected to put its fiscal house in order and Japan to further the deregulation of its financial markets. U.S. bankers, deprived of equal access in the Japanese market at a time when Japanese banks were enjoying full and equal opportunity in the United States, added to the pressures on the Japanese government.

The Japanese hypothesis that financial deregulation begets instability was proved wrong in the U.S. markets and in several European markets. While this lesson was not lost on the Japanese, their changes were more deliberate than those of their western counterparts. Also, the phenomenal success Japanese firms achieved in the industrial and trade sectors provided added reassurance. Japanese firms that came to hold a major share or even dominate certain product markets set an example of successful international economic expansion for financial firms to emulate. Japanese banking firms could do no less. They had to reflect the character (structure) of their multinational corporate clients for competitive reasons, at least initially. They were concerned about the possibility that a loss of the account of the industrial subsidiary overseas may lead to the loss of the account of the parent at home.

Adding to the drive to deregulate the Japanese financial markets was the desire to capitalize on the locational advantage in a region with explosive growth (the Four Tigers) and to play a leadership role in the political and economic transformation of the region; the will to expand trade in China after the opening of relations between China and the United States; the vast resources available to Japanese banks managed by well-trained managers (many from leading schools in the United States), confident and ready for international competition; and the excellent mastery by the Japanese of highly advanced and complex technology. Japan could not have realized these ambitious international dreams while remaining a protected market. One-sided internationalism was neither possible nor a stable long-run condition.

THE NATURE AND COMPONENTS OF JAPAN'S FINANCIAL DEREGULATION

The original Japanese financial system resembled that of the United States with few, but major differences. The similarities were these:

- Restricted portfolio choices for financial institutions
- Interest rate ceilings on deposits and loans
- Direct or indirect credit allocation schemes
- Stiff opposition to all regulatory changes from affected interest groups
- Significant restrictions on capital flows (abandoned quickly in the United States)

The major difference between the two systems lies in the role the Japanese government plays in the transmission of savings to users of capital. The Postal Savings System (PSS) receives deposits at 2,500 post offices throughout Japan and holds about 30 percent of all Japan's deposits. Holding ¥177 trillion at the end of 1987, the PSS is the largest financial institution in the world by any measure. These savings are paid below-market rates, but until recently they received a special tax treatment (Manuyu). The PSS is exempt from paying corporate taxes and savings insurance, and does not pay dividends to shareholders. Its operations are completely regulated (predictable) on the asset and the liability sides. The major recipient of PSS funds is the Ministry of Finance (MOF) of Japan. The MOF uses these resources to fund government projects and for political purposes. Its lending operations are conducted through its Trust Fund Bureau.

Japan also imposed strict controls on capital flows, Euroyen activities, and access to the Japanese markets by foreign financial institutions. In fact, every aspect of Japan's financial regulations has experienced change in the last 15 years, with most of the changes coming in the last 5 years. Some of these changes were real, while others were superficial, as will be demonstrated below. First, we consider the banking structure in Japan.

The MOF exercises control over the banking sector through its banking bureau, while the Bank of Japan (BOJ) implements monetary policy and regulates loan rates to banks and interest rates for private institutions. The BOJ (actually, an appropriate bureau therein) must consult the MOF (again, the appropriate bureau therein) and the Interest Rates Adjustment Council before implementing certain monetary measures. The PSS is controlled by the Ministry of Post and Telecommunications. Some regulatory control is also exercised by the Ministry of International Trade and Industry.

This compartmentalization of functions is also reflected in the banking and securities sector. Japan has five major categories of banks: long-term credit banks, foreign exchange banks, city banks, trust banks, and thrifts.

- The Bank of Tokyo, for example is a special case, long-term bank. As such, it can obtain long-term funding. Its domestic and international operations are driven primarily by foreign trade.
- Commercial banks were authorized under the banking law of 1927 (amended in 1981). They operate deposit and loan facilities, discount commercial bills, deal in foreign exchange, and sell CDs, repos and bonds.
- City banks, of which there are 13, operate a national branch network. Their funding sources are deposits, borrowing from the BOJ, interbank borrowing, CDs and Gensaki bonds, and foreign funding. Their transactions must have a maturity of three years or less. The BOJ is a major buyer of CDs issued by city banks.
- The trust banks can obtain long-term financing. Their loan portfolio is heavily committed to plant and equipment. Their unique feature, and one that is very attractive to foreign banks, is the management of pension funds.
- The thrifts are mainly mutual banks and credit associations. Their assets come primarily from small business loans, and their liabilities are primarily in the form of time deposits.

Unique to the Japanese financial system is the PSS. Insurance companies also play a major role, with a clear separation between life and nonlife insurance companies.

The securities industry is dominated by the Big Four: Nomura, Nikko, Daiwa, and Yamaichi. They are the major underwriters of bonds and stocks in Japan.

The securities finance corporations comprise another important financial group. Three major firms—Japan Securities Finance Company, Ltd. (JSF), Osaka Securities Finance, and Chebu Securities Finance—dominate this market. JSF, the largest, is privately owned and acts like a central bank. Its largest shareholders are Mikko Securities, the Tokyo Stock Exchange Regular Members Association, and the Industrial Bank of Japan. JSF controls 72 percent of the securities financing market.

All the various segments of the Japanese financial markets have specific functions to perform, and each is run by an oligopoly with a dominant firm: Daichi Kangyo for banks, Nomura Securities for investment banks, and JSF for securities finance corporations.

DEREGULATORY SCOPE

The deregulation of Japan's financial markets was aimed at relaxing, and in some cases abolishing, interest rate constraints. It gave Japanese institutions greater freedom in structuring their portfolios, allowed new securities to emerge

Exhibit 4.3
The Process of Decontrol in Japan

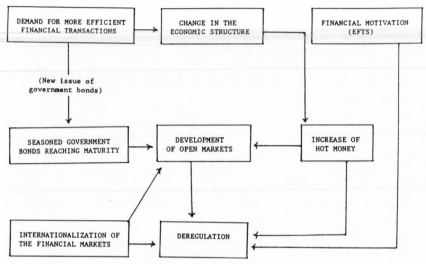

Source: Banker (January 1985). Reprinted with permission.

in the private and public debt markets, and widened and deepened the participation of foreign banks. It introduced derivative products, such as futures and options contracts, to allow for hedging and price discovery; allowed the Japanese yen to play a role in the foreign exchange markets (as both a reserve and a vehicle currency) commensurate with Japan's position in the world economy; and broke down the barriers between banks and investment banks and different types of banks.

The process of deregulation is illustrated in Exhibit 4.3.

The Bond Markets

The most important Japanese bond market is the Japan government bond (JGB) market. The other markets detailed in Exhibit 4.4 are maturing faster under the careful eyes of the MOF.

We will now examine the specific deregulatory steps taken in the money and capital debt markets, the Euroyen market, the equities markets, the futures markets, and the banking sector, both domestic and foreign.

Interest Rate, Money Market, and Capital Debt Market Deregulation

The deregulation of interest rates in Japan coincided with the introduction of money market instruments and continued to evolve as more consumers and corporations demanded market rates on their investment funds. The regulators

Exhibit 4.4
Japanese Bond Classification (Public and Private Placements)

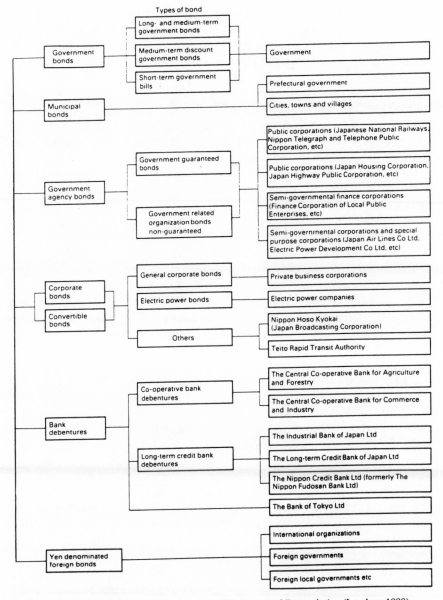

Source: Helen Thourghton, *Japanese Finance: The Impact of Deregulation* (London, 1988).

allowed the introduction of various money market instruments, although the initial conditions, as is typical in Japan, were very restrictive. As these markets matured, the constraints began to weaken.

The Japanese money markets may be classified into two categories: the interbank markets and the open markets. The first consists of call monies and bills discounts. The bills discounts, which date back to 1971, are paper sold at a discount by commercial and industrial firms. Their maturity is typically one month or more, and they are an excellent source of short-term financing. The call monies, dating back to World War II, are uncollateralized loans for financial institutions.

The open markets consist of the Gensaki market (the repo market for government bonds), negotiable CDs, bankers acceptances, and money market certificates (MMCs). All rates on these instruments are exempt from the temporary interest rates adjustment law.[2] And all these instruments have widened and deepened the Japanese financial markets.

The pattern of these changes is typical for Japan and thus is predictable. First comes the approval of the instrument with the appropriate set of constraints (issuer, size, maturity, etc.). Then, should the market succeed, the constraints begin to disappear gradually (faster for certain instruments than others).

The changes in the money markets are chronicled in Exhibit 4.5. The gradual nature of the changes is quite visible, but nonetheless, these changes are dramatic. Until June 1989, however, small depositors in Japan did not have access to these markets. They were able to earn only 3.64 percent on two-year time deposits. The minimum size of CDs and MMCs continues to come down substantially. In early 1989, the minimum CD size was ¥20 million, and that of MMCs was ¥10 million. It will not be long before all constraints are removed, following the U.S. and the European experimentation, and this will have significant effects on the PSS of Japan.

In late 1987, the commercial paper (CP) market was born in Japan. Originally, only 180 companies were allowed to issue CP. Foreign firms were given permission to issue yen-denominated CP in Japan in January 1988, the first foreign issuer being Dow Chemical. All issues were subject to national taxes and stamp duties, and as a result, the competitiveness of the market was very much in doubt at the outset. The forecasts proved wrong, however. By the end of 1988, the MOF had increased the number of firms allowed to issue CPs to 400, though of these, 300 were required to secure back-up lines from banks. The market exploded in one year to $73.6 billion. Some of the issues were indirect methods for financing the assets of Japanese banks. The proceeds for certain CP issues were used immediately to purchase MMCs issued by the same banks that brought the CP issues to market. CPs were therefore used as a tool for arbitrating the interest market. One can observe from this instrument the step-by-step, methodical approach the Japanese employ in the transformation of their markets.

The JGB market, born in 1966, experienced its fastest expansion in 1973. In 1975, deficit financing bonds were introduced, and in 1978, the first discount and zero coupon bonds were issued. The market was supplemented by the bond

Exhibit 4.5
Deregulation of Money Markets, 1984–1987

Jan.1984 -	Reduction of the minimum denomination of CDs (Y=500 million ⌐ Y=300 million)
Apr.1984 -	Enlargement of the ceiling on CD issues (gradual enlargement from 75% of each bank's net worth to 100% by Apr.1985)
Mar.1985 -	Introduction of Money Market Certificates (MMC) for mutual banks and credit associations (Y=50 million or more, with maturity 1-6 months)
Apr.1985 -	Introduction of MMC for other banks (Y=50 million or more, with maturity 1-6 months)
·	Reduction of the minimum denomination of CDs (Y=300 million ⌐ Y=100 million)
·	Relaxation of restriction on CD maturities (minimum maturity shortened from 3 months to 1 month)
Oct.1985 -	Decontrol of interest rates on deposits of Y=1 billion or more with maturity 3-24 months
·	Enlargement of the ceiling on CD issues (100% ⌐ 150% of each bank's net worth)
·	Enlargement of the ceiling on MMC issues (75% ⌐ 150% of each bank's net worth)
·	Interest rate on time deposits of Y=1 billion or more liberalized. (The minimum will be reduced to Y=50 million early this year.)
Apr.1986 -	Decontrol of interest rates on deposits of Y=500 million or more
·	Relaxation of restrictions on CD maturities (maximum maturity extended from 6 months to 12 months)
·	Enlargement of the ceiling on CD issues (150% ⌐ 200% of each bank's net worth)
·	Enlargement of the ceiling on MMC issues (150% ⌐ 200% of each bank's net worth)
Sep.1986 -	Decontrol of interest rates on deposits of Y=300 million or more
·	Reduction of the minimum amount of MMC (Y=50 million ⌐ Y=30 million)
·	Enlargement of the CD issues (200% ⌐ 250% of each bank's net worth)
1987 ·	Decontrol of interest rates on deposits of Y=100 million or more
·	Reduction of the minimum denomination of CDs (Y=100 million ⌐ Y=50 million)
·	Relaxation of restriction on the CD maturities (minimum maturity to be less than one month)
·	Relaxation of restriction on the MMC maturities (maximum maturity to be extended 12 ⌐ 24 months)
·	Enlargement of MMC issues to 200% ⌐ 300% of each bank's net worth
·	Introduction of small denomination MMC (Y=3 million ⌐ Y=10 million)

Source: Bank of Tokyo, Ltd., Economic Research Division, 1988.

futures market on the Tokyo Stock Exchange in October 1985, and the Japanese government began issuing six-month discounted paper with an initial minimum purchase size of ¥100 million in February 1986.

The daily turnover in the JGB market is ¥7–8 trillion on a bull day. The issuance process is through auction by the MOF and implementation by the BOJ. The buyers are members of a syndicate made up of 788 financial firms, which until October 1984 did not include foreign institutions. Foreign investors accounted for about 2.4 percent of all purchases and sales of JGB in the secondary market during 1987.

The wealth of Japan brought in many foreign firms seeking financing in Japan denominated in yen. The market that evolved was dubbed the Samurai bond market (yen-denominated bonds issued in Japan by foreigners). The first issue was a 7.4 percent Asian Department Bank issue in 1970. The market grew fast enough to "threaten" the attempt by the Japanese government to adequately finance its budget deficit in 1973. As a result, the market, which is not subject to withholding tax, had to be shut down by the MOF in 1974. It resumed in the late 1970s but lost its luster quickly because of the pervasive call provisions in the issues and the emergence of the Euroyen market. By 1987, the market had fallen to below ¥2 trillion.

All the Samurai securities met with very tough competition from the Euroyen market. The MOF authorized this market in April 1984—an approval that was long overdue. This coincided with the liberalization of the yen forward market and was immediately followed by the elimination of the limits on swaps involving the yen. Once again, the gradual process was very much in evidence. The number of issues was initially limited to six per year, the minimum was ¥15 billion, the issuer had to be qualified in accordance with strict guidelines, and a lockup period of 90 days was imposed during which Japanese investors could not buy new issues.

The growth of this market has been strongly motivated by the swap market. In fact, 80 percent of Euroyen issues are swapped upon issuance. Also, the market is characterized by nonconventional issues. Twenty-one percent of the issues are dual currency bonds, for example.

The chronology of the developments in the yen money and bond markets and in the related (in some cases) foreign exchange markets appears in Exhibit 4.6.

We now consider the developments in the Japanese stock market.

Exhibit 4.6
Chronology of Money and Credit Markets Deregulation in Japan, 1984–1989

May 1979 - Issuance of CDs of Y=500 million or more. (The minimum will be reduced to Y=50 million early this year)

Dec 1980 - Foreign Exchange Control Act amended

Apr 1982 - Banking law revised to promote expansion and liberalization of financial markets

Apr 1983 - Direct sales of public (including Government) bonds by banks started

Apr 1984 - European bond issues by residents allowed

- Start of domestic sales of foreign CPs and CDs

- Approval of automatic transfer between Chukoku Funds with securities firms and deposit accounts with credit associations

- Relaxation of guidelines on unsecured bonds

- Eligible foreign banks allowed to participate in syndication of Japanese government bonds

- Lifting of real demand rule in forward exchange transaction

- Liberalization of yen-dominated loans with maturities over one year to non-residents

- Approval of Euroyen bond issues by Japanese residents

- Relaxation of guidelines and qualification standards of Samurai bonds (followed by further relaxations in Jul 84, Dec 84 and Apr 85)

- Currency swap transactions allowed. "Real demand rule" in forward exchange transactions eliminated

May 1984 - Two reports released by the Japan-U.S.Yen-Dollar Ad Hoc Committee and the Finance Ministry concerning the internationalization of the yen and financial liberalization.

Jun 1984 - Restrictions on conversion of foreign currencies into yen abolished. Dealing in public bonds by banks started

- Japanese banks allowed to deal in Japanese government bonds

- Lifting of the swap limit

- Liberalization of Euroyen loans with maturity one year or less to Japanese residents

Jul 1984 - Elimination of the designated company system limiting the total percentage of stock which foreign investors are permitted to purchase in any of 11 companies in defense-related and other fields

Oct 1984 - Foreign banks in Japan allowed to deal in Japanese government bonds

Dec 1984 - Foreign securities firms permitted to lead-manage Euroyen bond issues

- Approval of Euroyen CDs with maturities of six months or less, not to be purchased by Japanese residents

- Relaxation of guidelines and qualification standards for Euroyen bonds issued by non-residents (followed by further relaxation in Apr 1985)

- Guidelines on issues of Eurobonds by non-residents eased.

Mar 1985 - The end of the ban on a bank being both borrower and lender at the same time in

Exhibit 4.6 (Continued)

		bill discount market
	-	Approval of access to investment consulting business by banks
	-	Approval of issues of convertible bonds by banks
	-	Money-market certificates (MMCs) of Y=50 million or more introduced. (The minimum is now Y=20 million)
Apr 1985	-	Eligibility standards for Euroyen issues eased. Withholding tax repealed on Euroyen bonds by Japanese issuers for non-residents
	-	Lifting of withholding tax on non-residents' interest earnings on investment in Euroyen bonds issued by Japanese residents
	-	Relaxation of restriction on seasoning period of Euroyen bonds (shortened from 180 days to 90 days)
	-	Introduction of new features to Euroyen bonds issued by Japanese residents
	-	Credit rating system by recognized agencies fully introduced for the qualification standards of Samurai bonds
	-	The liberalization of Euroyen loans with maturities over one year to Japanese residents is now being studied by the MOF
	-	Setting up bond rating companies
	-	Reduction of stockbroking commission for large orders
	-	Liberalization of Euroyen loans with maturities over one year to non-residents
Jun 1985	-	Introduction of new features to Euroyen bonds issued by non-residents
	-	Full dealing allowed for banks in Government and Government-organization bonds
	-	Variations of Euroyen bonds allowed for non-residents:

1. Euroyen floating-rate notes
2. Euroyen dual currency
3. Euroyen zero coupon
4. Deep discount bonds

	-	Dealing in Government securities by foreign banks allowed
	-	Approval of dealing in CDs by securities firms
	-	Approval for securities firms to advance stand-by loans using government bonds as collateral
	-	Dealing in Japanese government bond permitted to more banks
	-	Approval of full-scale dealing in Japanese government bonds by eligible banks
	-	Approval of direct entry into trust business by nine foreign banks
	-	Start of yen-dominated BA market
	-	Start of five and six-month contracts in bill discount market
Jul 1985	-	The first foreign-currency-denominated convertible bonds issued by city banks in overseas market
	-	Removal of collateral requirement in call market
Aug 1985	-	First issue of domestic corporate bond with 15-year maturity
	-	Start of two and three-week loans in call market
Oct 1985	-	Start of bond futures market
	-	Foreign banks allowed to open trust banking subsidiaries
Nov 1985	-	Further relaxation of guidelines on unsecured bonds
Dec 1985	-	Start of new type of trust funds by trust banks
Feb 1986	-	Start of auction for short-term government bonds
Apr 1986	-	Dealing in Japanese government bonds permitted to more banks
	-	Credit rating system by recognized agencies fully introduced for the qualification standards of Euroyen bonds
	-	Approval for securities firms to participate in yen-denominated BA market
	-	Trust funds allowed to invest in short-term government bonds
	-	Relaxation of restriction on maturities of Euroyen CDs (up to 6 months - up to 12 months)
	-	Japanese companies allowed to issue floating issue bearer bonds and currency conversion bonds. 180 day lock-up period cut by half to 90 days with the exception of dual-currency bonds
Jun 1986	-	Approval of Eurobonds issued by Foreign banks
	-	Euroyen bond issues for foreign banks allowed
Dec 1986	-	Start of Japan Offshore Market (JOM) (Initial size of the market US $51.5 billion, with 181 participants)
Mar 1987	-	Foreign Securities Companies received a 380% boost in the amount of Japanese government bonds they could underwrite--still less than 0.2% of total bonds issued.
Sep 1988	-	Foreign underwriters fixed share of the syndicated portion of each bond offering was increased to 8% from 2.5%
Apr 1989	-	The Japanese government sells 40% of a 10 year issue through competitive bid system

Source: Bank of Tokyo, various releases.

Stock Market Deregulation

The Tokyo Stock Exchange (TSE) is now the premier stock exchange in the world in terms of the market value of the shares listed thereon. It now trades stocks, futures on Japanese government bonds, and the Tokyo Stock Price Index (TOPIX) futures contracts. Membership on the TSE is very small. Only 93 firms were members in 1987, compared with 600 in New York. In this tightly controlled club, change does not come easily in terms of new products, new trading rules, and new members (foreign members especially).

The fixed commission rates of the TSE remain in full force. Lower commissions were observed after 1985, and since then, the reduction has continued, especially for large transactions ($100,000 or more). After the October crash, the TSE cut commission rates by 10 percent to make the rates competitive with the negotiated rates of London and New York.

In 1985, six seats on the TSE were issued to foreign firms. Merrill Lynch was among the U.S. firms able to purchase a seat. In June 1987, the Osaka Stock Exchange opened futures trading using a quasi-stock index known as the Osaka 50. TSE followed in September 1988 with its own stock index futures contract.

In December 1987, 16 foreign houses gained membership on the TSE. The American houses were Salomon Brothers, Inc.; Prudential-Bache Securities, Inc.; Shearson-Lehman Brothers, Inc.; Kidder Peabody and Company; Smith Barney Harris Upham and Company; and First Boston Corporation. This opening followed intense political pressures.

The Futures Markets

The futures markets in Japan are still in their infancy in terms of diversity of products when compared with those in the United States. The TSE began trading bond futures in 1985. The underlying is a 10-year JGB. In September 1986, almost six years after their introduction in the United States, stock index futures began trading on the TSE. On June 9, 1987, futures trading in the Kabusaki 50 index, designed to correlate with the Nikkei stock average, began trading on the Osaka Stock Exchange. Program trading is allowed, but, interestingly, only to foreign firms. Index arbitrage is also allowed.

The cash settlement index contract found instant success. The first day of trading saw 200,000 contracts traded at a value of $36.7 billion.[3] The highest trading volume for the Kabusaki 50 futures contract between June 1987 and September 1989 was 700 contracts per day.

Late in 1988, the Tokyo Commodity Exchange began admitting foreign trading companies, but not as full members. An associate membership status was introduced for this purpose. This status does not allow its holder to trade directly on the floor of the exchange.

The Financial Futures Exchange of Tokyo was inaugurated in the summer of 1989. It should prove quite a match for its American equivalent.

One additional liberalization with respect to the derivative market is the permission granted by the MOF on March 22, 1989, to 332 Japanese financial institutions to trade options on physical in markets outside Japan. The over-the-counter option market in currency has been growing at a reasonable rate. During 1989 three index options contracts began trading. One is based on the TOPIX, the second on the Nikkei Dow 225, and the third on a new 25-stock index designed to track the TOPIX and the Nikkei Dow 225 index. The latter trades on the Nagoya Stock Exchange.

The precedent for this was set in November 1988 when the MOF permitted banks to trade currency options but not stock, bond, and stock index options. This proved to be a bonanza for the Philadelphia Stock Exchange and the Chicago Board Options Exchange.

FOREIGN AND DOMESTIC BANKING INSTITUTIONS IN JAPAN

The deregulation of the banking sector in Japan has been slow, but significant. Foreign banking institutions have made major inroads, but nowhere near those realized by Japanese banks overseas. Japan is not ready yet to fully assimilate foreign banking institutions into its financial system.

Foreign banking institutions in Japan can deal in the JGB market (October 1984), participate in the trust banking business (December 1985), own a membership on the TSE, deal in the Euroyen market, and even own up to 50 percent of securities firms (compared with 5 percent for domestic firms). However, ownership is one thing; full access is another.

Entry by foreign banks, however, is still subject to severe restrictions. Approval takes a very long time. During the application period even the floor plans are checked. Foreign banks are still limited to wholesale banking and are barred from a few markets such as the call market where borrowing and lending between banks of unsecured short-term foreign currency take place. Foreign banks are also obliged to bring funds from overseas and to rely on the domestic wholesale market which is expensive.

Domestic banks were allowed greater freedom. Antimonopoly laws were applied less strictly to permit mergers and takeovers of institutions in financial difficulties. Restrictions on CDs were largely eliminated, and money market certificates were allowed. Yen-denominated bankers acceptances were also permitted as of April 1986. Offshore banking units were allowed, but they were required to pay stamp duties and local and national taxes, and were forbidden to engage in any underwriting activities.

Domestic banks were also allowed to deal in government bonds as of June 1984. This marked the beginning of their entry into the investment banking field despite strict separation between banking and investment banking in Japan.

The major developments within the Japanese banking industry were to a large degree booked as off-balance-sheet items. This led to a new set of guidelines for banks:

- A new two-tier system of capital asset ratios
- Liquidity ratios for assets and liabilities with three and six months' life remaining

- Tighter rules on large-lot loans
- Regular reporting of off-balance-sheet transactions
- Regular reporting on overseas subsidiaries
- Systematic data on funding through market instruments and assets deployed in floating-rate instruments

These plus the new risk-adjusted capital ratios parallel developments in the United States and Canada. Some new regulations were being introduced from the back door as new regulations were being forced out the front door.

We now look at the separation between banking and investment banking in Japan.

Article 65

Article 65 is the Japanese equivalent of the Glass–Steagall Act in the United States. Japan has maintained strict separation between banks and investment banks. The irony of this is that Japanese banks are heavily involved in underwriting activities in foreign countries while being denied the same in their home market. Despite the tenacity of Japanese regulators, however, the walls of separation are being systematically dismantled. Today, banks in Japan compete with investment banks in underwriting and selling government bonds and in trading bond futures, certificates of deposits, bankers acceptances, and yen-denominated commercial paper. Banks can still participate in the securities industry through direct ownership or through joint ventures. The limit is 5 percent, yet banks have managed to acquire larger stakes in the securities industry. Maruman, a long-term credit bank, owns 26 percent of Daichi Securities, for example. The aggressive moves, however, are in the opposite direction as investment banks attempt to invade the lucrative field of Japanese banking, especially the area of pension asset management.

Banks—and trust banks in particular—are permitted to manage huge equity and bond portfolios, which is a lucrative portion of the investment banking business. Trust banks along with insurance companies have an exclusive hold thus far on the pension fund market, estimated to reach $450 billion in 1996.

The banking industry will continue to evolve. Whether the cracks in the regulatory structure become gaping holes or whether they disappear will depend on the experiences of other countries that deal with Japan and on the world's economic and political conditions.

THE IMPACT OF DEREGULATION

The character of the Japanese financial system has changed so dramatically as to upset every prediction ever made about it. The transformation has been wide and deep.

The Banking Investment Sector

Foreign bank operations in Tokyo (79 in 1987) have not been very profitable. Lack of experience, traditional Japanese thinking about dealing with those whom you know, incredibly expensive office space, huge salaries and benefits for nationals working in Japan, and keen competition in every sector account for this performance. Fully one-third of the foreign banks operating in Japan in 1985 registered losses. Those that realized profits did so largely as a result of foreign exchange trading and dealings in Japanese government bonds. Profits fell again to 38.5 percent in 1986, and the picture in 1988 was not that much more reassuring.

The fact that nine foreign banks were granted permission to open trust banking subsidiaries in October 1985 did not improve matters markedly. Foreign banks had much to learn about the special nature of the bank/client relationship in Japan.

The limited engagement that foreign banks have in the trust business, their lack of access to low-cost consumer deposits, and the Japanese custom of emphasizing long-term banking relationships will continue to affect the profitability of foreign banks adversely. Foreign banks, despite years of trying, control only about 2 percent of the Japanese banking market.

The domestic Japanese banks found (or put) themselves in a much more competitive environment. They were competing more intensely in every business and at every level, a phenomenon accounted for by the decreased compartmentalization of the banking sector. While competition reduced margins in certain areas, the new opportunities to banks, such as JGB dealing, improved the profitability of Japanese banks.

City banks were treading on the turf of small and medium-size regional banks or were acquiring them whenever possible. Two examples are the mergers between Heiwa Sogo Bank and Sumitomo Bank and between the 11 credit cooperatives in Kumamoto in 1985. City banks were particularly keen to attract business from small and medium-size companies. The shares of funds going to these size companies grew from 30 to 50 percent of their assets between 1977 and 1986.[4]

Maturity mismatching in bank balance sheets became more serious as interest rates were deregulated. Under the old regime, the government insured that the short rates were always lower than the long rates. The new regime of freely determined yield curves and short-term money market instruments funding very long term loans (as much as 20 years) made for riskier bank portfolios.

On the investment banking side, competition also became more intense. Investment banks successfully invaded banking domains. The Big Six continued to exercise heavy influence on the securities markets, accounting for 80 percent of all trades on the TSE.

The deregulation of the world financial markets and the aggressiveness and wealth of the Japanese firms operating from a freer domestic market have allowed Japanese investment banks to dominate the underwriting of debt, especially that denominated in dollars and yen. This has been documented in Chapter 1. It is safe to say that Japanese securities firms are in control and will continue to control the underwriting of Eurobonds for a long time to come.

The competition from foreign securities firms also affected the character and the results in the market. Foreign underwriters successfully broke into new issues of domestic Japanese companies. Six issues were comanaged by foreign firms in 1988.[5] The experience of these firms and their ability to place shares "strategically" with foreign as well as domestic investors made for a critical difference. In the past, foreign firms were excluded from underwriting new issues

because Japanese companies often establish close relations with the securities firms that manage their initial offerings, and stick with them through the years. Unlike new issues in many Western markets, however, the number of managing firms in a Japanese initial offering is usually very small, sometimes only a handful.[6]

Lest we get overenthusiastic about the implication of this "crack" in equity underwriting in Japan, it will be a long time before foreign companies get a firm foothold in the Japanese market. If and when they do, some restrictions will be imposed by the Japanese government—as it has done in many cases before. In any case, the operating results of securities firms operating in Japan have been quite dismal. The February 1989 issue of *Euromoney* reported that most foreign firms lost money in 1987 and 1988. Of the American firms, five were reasonably successful as Exhibit 4.7 shows.

The above limited successes on the trading floor of the TSE were not without blemishes. In December 1988, the MOF launched an investigation into the role of Morgan Stanley in a futures driven stock rally based on index arbitrage transactions. As of mid-1989, no pronouncements have been made.

Money and Capital Markets

The impact of deregulation on the bond markets has been extensive and not altogether predictable. Some markets (CDs, MMCs, Euroyen bonds) prospered, and others [yen-denominated bankers acceptances and short-term government bonds (six months discounted paper)] fizzled.

The trading in JGBs (the largest market behind the U.S. government bonds market) grew at astronomical rates. In 1987, 93 percent of total trading on the Tokyo Stock Exchange involved government bonds.[7] The Gensaki market exploded from ¥22 trillion in 1977 to over ¥8,000 trillion in 1987. To curtail this astronomical volume, the Japanese government imposed a tax on all transfers of government bonds.

The explosion in bond volume took place despite the fact that Japan lacks a clearing system like Euroclear and Cedel which clear Euroyen bonds, despite the fact that most securities require physical delivery, and despite the transaction tax on short selling and Gensaki trading. This tax adds as much as 150 basis points to a typical trade.

Exhibit 4.7
A Few U.S. Firms That Have Succeeded in Tokyo

Revenue of Japanese operations (in millions of dollars)*

	1986	1987	1988	1989
Salomon Bros.	$100.9	$167.9	$157.3	$158.0
Morgan Stanley	54.3	99.5	125.6	93.1
Merrill Lynch	76.9	98.8	92.4	54.3
Goldman Sachs	36.0	67.0	84.7	67.8
First Boston	20.5	39.5	55.7	48.7

Pretax income (in millions of dollars)*

	1986	1987	1988	1989
Salomon Bros.	$34.8	$47.5	$31.3	$53.6
Morgan Stanley	8.6	10.8	.4	5.8
Merrill Lynch	11.8	25.5	8.0	1.0
Goldman Sachs	1.1	9.3	?.7	12.8
First Boston	5.2	4.7	5.6	7.3

*Converted from yen at recent rates
NOTE: Fiscal years ended Sept. 30, except 1989 figure, which measures six months to March 31

Source: Wall Street Journal, 16 August 1989, A1.

The huge volumes and associated profits account for the clamoring by foreign investment banking houses for a greater share of the bond market. Japan's MOF, however, hands out the carrots one at a time.

Volume on the equity side has been no less breathtaking than in the bond market. Once again, foreign firms were not participating to the desired extent. The equity volume transacted by foreign members on the TSE is shown in Exhibit 4.8.

The volume of 1.9 billion shares for October and November 1988 transacted by the 22 foreign member firms, while appearing significant, is a small percentage of a market that trades one billion shares in a slow day. The volume held by foreign firms accounts for less than 5 percent of total volume and is less than uniformly distributed across foreign firms. Morgan Stanley is by far the most active in this market with 16 percent of foreign members' total volume. The need for a large share of the market is a matter of survival for foreign firms burdened by huge entry costs (setup costs plus $10 million for the seat) and operating costs. So competitive and difficult has the equity market become that several foreign firms are losing substantial sums.

Prosperity abounds in Japan, with no clear indication that it is due to any specific deregulation. The Nikkei Index reflects this prosperity. It closed at 31,938 on March 7, 1989, up from 30,159 at the end of 1988 and 21,564 at the

Exhibit 4.8
The TSE Steeplechase, 1988–1989

Equity volume (millions of shares) of Tokyo Stock Exchange foreign members in the first two months of 1988-89 financial year.
(Financial year begins October 1)

Company	October	November
Baring Securities	149.68	137.15
WI Carr	126.42	109.35
Country NatWest	45.96	61.61
DB Capital	N/A	N/A
Dresdner ABD	13.77	24.26
First Boston	134.25	138.06
Goldman Sachs	166.02	176.23
Jardine Fleming	95.04	128.72
Kidder Peabody	49.53	37.58
Kleinwort Benson	30.69	47.50
Merrill Lynch	62.15	92.68
Morgan Stanley	342.37	330.94
Prudential-Bache	90.84	71.36
Salomon Brothers	152.32	177.68
Schroder	42.19	52.57
Shearson Lehman	79.82	75.69
Smith Barney	44.75	49.75
Sogen	14.64	17.59
Swiss Bank	26.97	38.33
UBS	56.54	55.78
Vickers	75.09	88.46
SG Warburg	92.61	87.65
Total	1,882.65	1,998.94

Source: TSE member firms.

end of 1987. Foreign interest in Japanese equity certainly helped in this growth, and there is no evidence to suggest that deregulation in general has been anything but helpful to the Japanese economy and specifically to Japanese institutions. The yardstick for the latter is the number of policy reversals taken by the MOF, which is always ready to act when things do not go as desired. This number is small because the MOF proceeded very cautiously, and whenever it was not sure, it introduced nominal liberalization measures instead of real ones.

On the futures side, the picture is also bright. JGB futures, which were introduced in October 1985, proved their merit as excellent hedging tools for bond price risk. In July 1988, futures contracts on the super-long-term JGB (20-year maturity) were introduced to help hedge the risk resulting from the massive redemption of 10-year bonds issued in the late 1970s. The latter market had limited volume because of the thinness of the underlying cash. The former experienced healthy growth initially, yet by March 1989, open interest amounted to only 66 contracts.

The stock index futures contracts traded on the TSE were also popular. Total open interest on TOPIX was 14,616 contracts at the end of 1988. This volume compares favorably with that on the CBT covering the S&P 100 contract. Japanese and foreign portfolio managers with Japanese securities have discovered and confirmed the value of index futures as a hedging tool for portfolio risk.

Other Effects

The continuing liberalization of the Japanese and other markets and the pressure on Japan to import more and export less to certain countries produced a wave of mergers and acquisitions (M&A) overseas. M&A is the fastest and occasionally the cheapest and most effective way for penetrating a market. Also, it is, in some cases, an excellent alternative to portfolio investment, which normally yields no capital gains and allows for no control. Foreign M&A deals involving Japanese firms, buoyed by their new wealth and by a strong yen against practically all currencies, increased by 330 percent in 1986 and by 100 percent in 1987 and 1988 in money terms. Contributing to this phenomenal growth is 1992, when Europe comes together as an economic unit.

The international activities by Japanese banks increased dramatically, and these banks now dominate international banking, with American banks running a distant second in many areas. The share of Japanese banks as a percentage of international banking activity rose from 31 percent to 35 percent in the third quarter of 1988, as reported by the Bank of International Settlement (BIS). The statistics from the BIS were quite dramatic.

Japanese banks continue to dominate international banking, as they have since eclipsing U.S. banks' leadership role two years ago. The Basel, Switzerland-based BIS acts as a central bank and research unit for the world's major central banks.

In its latest quarterly report of international banking developments, the BIS said Japanese banks increased their lending abroad 70% to $231 billion in the year ended Sept. 30. The banks lent yen valued at $42.5 billion during last year's third quarter alone.

International clients more than doubled deposits in Japanese banks to $173 billion for the year. These clients deposited yen valued at $39.5 billion during the third quarter.

The BIS also said cross-border lending of Euroyen by banks in major industrial countries increased 40% to the equivalent of $122 billion in the year ended last September.[8]

The more international Japanese banks became, the more they had to adhere to international standards, including those on capital adequacy. The new agreement between the central banks of 12 industrial nations on uniform capital requirements meant an increase in the capital/asset ratio to 8 percent by 1992 for all banks involved in international activities. This translated into an increased capital requirement for the top 32 Japanese banks equal to $50 billion. The question is what to include in the definition of capital. Japanese banks would like to include hidden reserves, of which they hold considerable sums, in the definition of capital.

Japanese firms in the United States have been expanding as well, regardless of capital rules. Their particular focus is California where they appear to be in every community and in every banking activity. At the end of 1987, Japanese banks owned 4 of the top 10 banks in California, with 21.7 percent of the total assets of all banks, agencies, and branches. And the expansion continues in California and other parts of the United States, as was documented in Chapter 1.

Japanese banks have also used foreign markets as incubators for testing the effects on eliminating Article 65. They have been doing so in the United States for a long time. In September 1988, three Japanese banks—Fuji, Sumitomo, and Mitsubishi—received approval from the MOF to apply for universal banking licenses in West Germany, their intent being to break into the deutsche mark securities market. Similar observations can be made about the Japanese bank presence in London.

In sum, Japanese banks will pursue business anywhere, anytime, at any level, and in whatever language or currency. Their deregulation has unleashed a competitive force that has taken the world by storm and the consequences of which have yet to be accepted or dealt with.

As to the yen's role in the world, it has expanded considerably. In 1987, yen-denominated bonds accounted for 14.1 percent of all issues, up from 1.5 percent in 1980. The Japanese yen reserves accounted for 7.5 percent of world monetary reserves in 1987. The Japanese exports were increasingly denominated in yen: 33.4 percent in 1987, up from 29.4 percent in 1980. The use of the yen as an international currency is beginning to correspond to the role Japan plays in the international economy.

CONCLUSIONS

The deregulation of the Japanese financial market has been deliberate in some cases and a response to foreign pressure in others. In either case, it has been measured and applied with considerable safety valves. The MOF has played a constructive role generally, but a manipulative one occasionally. What it gave in one hand in terms of liberalization, it took, sometimes, with the other in terms of restrictions, taxes, and duties. Foreigners were allowed in, but strictly on Japanese terms. Their conduct is carefully circumscribed so it can always be controlled whenever the interests of the Japanese are involved. The only certainty in all of this is that deregulation in Japan will continue and Japanese institutions will be even more prominent in a more integrated world economy.

NOTES

1. Thomas Cargill, *Weekly Letter* (Federal Reserve Bank of San Francisco), 17 May 1985.

2. See "Japanese Finance: The Impact of Deregulation," Special *Euromoney* Report (1986).

3. *Wall Street Journal,* 6 September 1988.

4. *Banker* (January 1987).

5. *Wall Street Journal,* 2 September 1988.

6. Ibid.

7. *Euromoney* (January 1988): 61.

8. *Asian Wall Street Journal,* 5 September 1988.

5

The Deregulation of the U.K. Financial Markets: The "Big Bang"

The British financial markets were turned on their heads by the new disciples of Adam Smith. Stodgy and traditional approaches were to be dismantled in favor of new ideas and programs which could secure a firm foothold for Britain in the new age of global competition and information. The new face Britain was to assume was vastly different from its traditional one. The change was dramatic and not altogether predictable.

Today, London ranks as the world's third largest capital market behind New York and Tokyo. Since the 1950s, it has been the home of the Euromarkets where by June 1988 the Eurocurrency deposit market totaled $3 trillion. London is also the world's leader in insurance and reinsurance, in shipping contracts, and in trading in many commodities. A new financial futures exchange—the London International Financial Futures Exchange (LIFFE)—opened in 1982 and was trading in January 1989 an average of 16,389 contracts a day on the Financial Times Stock Exchange 100 index, one of the many contracts traded thereon. All in all, London represents a $600 billion-a-year market in exchange-traded stocks and bonds.

In addition, $600 billion in assets are managed through the city. European governments raise more money in London than in any capital on the continent. London had 458 foreign banks operating within its limits in 1987. Of these, 429 owned branches and subsidiaries, and 29 had stakes in bank consortia.

London's reputation as a financial center was on the decline until recently. The importance of London as a capital market was due primarily to its huge Euromarkets, which are dominated by foreign institutions. London's role as an equity market, though still the largest in Europe, had been steadily declining.

The strict restriction of foreign membership and the adoption of fixed commission rates had caused the London Stock Exchange to be both uncompetitive and expensive. In addition, compared with New York and Tokyo, the London Stock Exchange was very small, with most stockbroking and jobbing firms highly undercapitalized. For example, Japan's Nomura Securities has a stock market capitalization of around $30 billion, and America's Salomon Brothers has around $6 billion, compared with way under $1 billion each for Warburg, Kleinwort, Bensons, Hill Samuel, and Hambro.[1]

The decline of London as a financial center may be observed in the following facts:

- Between 1979 and 1984, $29 billion worth of portfolio investment left Britain, more than half of it through non-British brokers.[2]

- Trading of U.K. shares by big institutions was executed more outside the exchange than on the exchange. For example, more than 60 percent of the trading in ICI shares in 1984 took place in New York, mostly through American brokers.[3]

- Between 1979 and 1983, British investors bought some £12 billion worth of foreign securities—90 percent of which were purchased through foreign brokers.[4]

London realized the inefficiencies of its capital markets and, on October 27, 1986, launched a dramatic deregulation effort. This became known as the "Big Bang" because it transformed the nature of the British financial markets and the range of products traded therein.

THE IMPETUS FOR DEREGULATION

The London Stock Exchange (LSE) is a central market for equities, domestic corporate bonds, gilt-edged (government) bonds, and other public sector securities. In addition, LSE also trades Eurobonds and equities and bonds of foreign companies and governments. Exhibit 5.1 shows the distribution of trading activities prior to the Big Bang. The market value of the shares of non-U.K. companies traded on the LSE was almost three times that of the shares of U.K. companies. Active trading in the securities of non-U.K. entities was concentrated in particular types of stocks (e.g., Australian Shares) that account for a relatively modest proportion of the total.[5]

In 1986, there were 5,009 LSE members, 207 stockbroker firms, and 18 jobbing firms. In addition to arranging deals for a minimum commission, brokers also managed investment portfolios and provided investment management services. Although the 20 largest brokerage firms accounted for 70 percent of the market in terms of commission income, the brokerage market was not particularly concentrated in that no one firm had more than about 10 percent of the whole market. On the other hand, the jobbing system was highly concentrated. Only 5 of the 18 firms handled deals of institutional size, and 2 of these firms dominated the gilts market and also had a large share of the equity market.[6]

Exhibit 5.1
Distribution of Trading Activities in London

	No. of Securities	Market Value (billions of £)	% of Market Value
UK public sector	385	127.1	11.8
Non-UK public sector	260	9.9	0.9
Eurobonds	1,184	75.6	7.0
UK-registered stocks	4,402	233.8	21.7
Non-UK-regist. stocks	696	626.7	58.2
Sub-total main market	6,927	1,073.1	99.6
USM company securities	324	3.6	0.4
Total	7,251	1,076.7	100.0

Source: *Bank of England Quarterly*, Bulletin (December 1985): 545.

Before the Big Bang, the LSE's trading rules were as follows:

- Fixed commission rate on equity and gilts (Exhibit 5.2).
- Strict separation between brokers (those who buy and sell shares for investors) and jobbers (those who make markets on the floor of the exchange). This system was called the *single capacity system*.
- Strict restriction of foreign ownership of member firms. Foreign ownership was limited to 10 percent of equity. In 1982, this limit was increased to 29.9 percent.[7]
- Restricted access to the gilt market. Only two major dealers (Wedd Durlacher and Akroyd & Smithers) controlled 75 percent of the gilt market.[8]

All these restrictions conspired to bring about a change—and a dramatic one at that. The seeds of London's financial revolution were planted in 1979 with the inauguration of the Conservative Thatcher government.

Shortly after arriving in power, Sir John Nott, the Secretary of State for Trade

Exhibit 5.2
LSE Fixed Brokerage Commission Rates before the Big Bang

1.65 %	first	7,000
0.55	next	8,000
0.5	next	115,000
0.4	next	170,000
0.3	next	600,000
0.2	next	1,000,000
0.125	remainder	

Source: "Flinging Open the Doors of Change," Supplement to *Euromoney* (Aug. 1986): 2.

and Industry, began litigations against the LSE and presented the LSE's Rule Book to the Restrictive Practices Court. At the heart of the dispute were the following charges:

- Commissions on stock transactions were fixed rather than negotiated.
- Membership in the stock exchange (and hence ownership of stock exchange firms) was prohibited to external firms such as commercial banks, merchant banks, insurance companies, and the like.
- The LSE's single capacity system restricted competition to the detriment of the consumer.

In response to this attack, the LSE capitulated by agreeing to permit negotiated commissions, allow outside members to take over member firms, and end the single capacity system—all by December 1986. The abolition of fixed commissions and the elimination of barriers to entry by noninvestment banking firms required a stronger capital base for investment firms because they had to take much larger risks and compete with bigger, well-capitalized institutions. The need for larger capital prompted many of the LSE's member firms to seek and admit "outsiders" as full participants in their capital structure.

The motivation for deregulation also came from a deeply felt British desire to regain the leadership London once enjoyed as a major world financial center. The increasingly global character of all major financial markets had left traditional London well behind. For example, when Britain's eighth largest industrial conglomerate, BTR Industries PLC, wanted to issue new equity abroad in 1985, the LSE pronounced the act "inappropriate" because, according to the old rules of the exchange, British companies listed on the exchange must give the existing shareholders the first option on any new shares. But BTR turned to Swiss Bank Corporation International and issued convertible Eurobonds so structured as to readily force conversion of debt into equity. The issue was worth about $300 million.[9] As this case makes clear, business will gravitate toward centers with the lowest transaction costs, the highest liquidity, and the most efficient mechanism to consummate transactions. In this case, business was moving out of the "City." This type of flow was central to the eventual changing of the rules, if London hoped to remain a major player in the global financial markets.

The grounds were thereby laid for one of the most comprehensive changes in the City's financial markets in recent history. Interestingly, the mandate was not market driven, but forced by the government on a very reluctant, traditional market. This development is a far cry from the mechanism through which the deregulation of the U.S. market was effected.

THE NATURE OF DEREGULATION

Deregulation fever touched every segment of the British financial markets. We begin with a look into the equity markets.

Equity Markets

The Big Bang began on October 27, 1986. It brought about the following changes in the London equity markets:

- Fixed commission rates were abolished.
- Barriers between order-taking brokers and risk-taking market makers were broken down. This dual-capacity system allows a single investment firm to perform either the broker function or the jobber function. The new dual-capacity system applies to equities and to gilt-edged and other fixed-interest securities.[10] This means that brokers are now forced to risk their own capital to buy securities in the hope of selling them at higher prices.[11]
- The existing informal system of regulation was replaced by a private version of the United States' SEC, called the Securities and Investments Board (SIB). This self-regulating body was backed by the Financial Services Act.

As a result of these changes, the investment community expected to see a steep reduction in trading commissions and a move to offer clients a full range of underwriting, research, and trading services.

Starting March 1, 1986, even before the Big Bang went into effect, new rules were introduced permitting foreign/outside members to own 100 percent of a member firm, thus removing the earlier 29.9 percent ceiling.[12] Also beginning on March 1, 1986, the LSE lifted a moratorium imposed in July 1984 on the creation of new member firms without outside financing. This enabled non-exchange entities to set up new firms de novo, without having to buy into an existing firm.

As a result, an influx of outsiders, including U.K. and foreign banks, began acquiring stock exchange member firms. Of the 20 largest brokers, only Cazenove & Co. retained independence, and all 5 of the City's jobbers merged with well-capitalized partners. Out of just over 200 original member firms, more than half became part of larger groupings. Exhibit 5.3 shows the effects of mergers and takeovers on the original membership of the LSE.

Of the 65 outside entities with stakes in these stock exchange firms, more than half are commercial or investment banks, mainly from the United States, the U.K., and the rest of Europe. Among the nonbanks acquiring controlling interests, firms from the financial services sector are prominent.

Parallel with the ownership patterns described above, the exchange attracted a number of direct new entrants, among them U.K. subsidiaries of some of the largest U.S. and Japanese securities houses. By January 1987, the membership of the exchange had increased to about 360.

In addition, the new equity market structure abolished the traditional floor-based market in favor of a quote-driven, competing-market-maker system (similar to NASDAQ), where transactions are made by telephone. Market makers will be obliged to maintain two-way quotes for deals of normal market size (1000 shares) at all times on the Stock Exchange Automated Quotations (SEAQ) system.

Exhibit 5.3
Participation in the Original Stock Exchange Member Firms

	Outsiders	Jobbers	Brokers	Total
UK banks	14	9	17	26
Other UK				
Fin. institutions	16	1	30	31
Other UK entities	6	-	9	9
US commercial banks	4	1	9	10
US investment banks	3	1	2	3
European banks	12	3	13	16
Other foreign banks	4	-	5	5
Other	6	-	6	6

Source: Bank of England Quarterly Bulletin, February 1987.

SEAQ screens, carrying the quotes of individual market makers, are to become available to both member firms and major investors. However, they will be
limited to information dissemination and will not be used to consummate transactions. Deals between market participants will be consequently arranged by telephone or on the floor of the exchange. The floor may remain important for the
transaction of small deals, but it will probably decline in importance for the
handling of large blocks of stock.[13]

The exchange also created four categories of stocks for SEAQ purposes:

• *Alpha* stocks, which are the most actively traded U.K. equities

• *Beta* stocks, which are less actively traded than alphas

• *Gamma* stocks, which are less actively traded than betas

• *Delta* stocks, which are in the least liquid category[14]

Exhibit 5.4 lists the different categories of equities and the number of equities per
category.

Gilt Market

The gilt market had considerable depth. It amounted to £15 billion and accounted for about 80 percent of the overall volume on the LSE in 1986. The
futures market on gilts was no less deep. The amount of open interest in gilt
futures on January 25, 1989, reached 30,321. Several changes have also taken
place since the Big Bang. Among them are the following:

• New contracts, including medium gilt futures, German government bond futures, and
  options on three-month sterling interest rate futures, were introduced on the LIFFE in
  1988.

Exhibit 5.4
SEAQ Classification of U.K. Equities: Number of Equities per Category, 1986

	October 27, 1986	December 31, 1986
Alpha	62	76
Beta	427	534
Gamma	1,240	1,296
Delta	244	244
TOTAL	1,973	2,150

Source: Bank of England Quarterly Bulletin, February 1987.

- The market is now made up of 27 primary dealers (14 are British, and the remaining 13 are international, with no less than 10 U.S.-controlled) in place of the previous 2 major dealers. (Wedd Durlacher is now part of Barclays de Zoete, Wedd, and Akroyd & Smithers has been integrated into Mercury International).[15]

- Commissions totally disappeared; there is now a net trading instead, as in the case of the U.S. government bond market.[16]

- The traditional trading floor gave way to a fast-moving telephone system.

- Brokers/dealers in gilts came under rules similar to those for equities dealers; such firms were then able to deal in both gilts and equities. Market makers in the gilts market were permitted, however, to deal only in sterling fixed-interest, floating-rate, or indexed securities and related instruments (e.g., gilt futures and options) and in approved sterling money market instruments.[17]

Other Developments

Commercial Papers

In May 1986, the sterling commercial paper (CP) market was born. The signs were hopeful because commercial paper rates were lower than London Interbank Offer Rate (LIBOR) rates. According to the Bank of England, sterling CP amounted to £50 million as of June 18, 1986. During July 1986, £175–200 million worth of CP were issued.

Issuers of CP may be U.K. or overseas companies listed on the LSE with a net worth of £50 million or more. Alternatively, they may be wholly owned by an approved company, provided their obligations are guaranteed by the listed parent company. However, if a company is already able to issue CDs, it may not issue commercial paper. CP must have a minimum denomination of £500,000 and may have a maturity of between seven days and one year.

Until the passing of the Financial Services Act, it was stipulated that issuers in the U.K. would have to comply with the normal prospectus disclosure requirements for debt securities. It has been noted that to avoid these requirements, some CP has been issued "orally" without offer documentation.

New Regulations for the Euromarkets

One of the more interesting developments in recent years is the host of "new regulations" aimed at the Eurocredit markets. Although the aim of the Financial Services Act is to "protect private investors," it laid down rules for all securities business in Britain.

The Department of Trade and Industry proposed new rules for the new issues market in Eurobonds and shares. In 1987, the Bank of England published three discussion papers dealing with the following issues:

- Capital backing for swap exposures.
- A proposal that a bank that decides to underwrite an issue worth more than 60 percent of its capital must notify the Bank of England upon doing so, and that a bank involved in a deal worth over 150 percent of its capital must notify the Bank of England in advance.
- The regulation of the wholesale financial market, the proposed capital requirements being so stringent that it put the Bank of England at odds with the Securities Association, a self-regulatory watchdog.

The proposal in the second paper also dealt with the bank's capital adequacy requirements for gilts and Eurobonds: "an inventory of gilts of one to five years' maturity must be backed by capital worth six percent of their value. And an inventory of gilts of more than five years' maturity must be backed by capital equivalent of nine percent of their value."[18]

The capital requirements for Eurobond issues were

- 11 percent backing for Eurobonds with one to five years' maturity.
- 12 percent for those with maturity of more than five years.

The intent of these new measures was to deal with two types of risks:

- Credit risk—the borrower may default.
- Market risk—prices may collapse.

In 1987, *The Economist* reported that the squabble between the Bank of England and the Securities Association about the amount of capital that firms must have was finally won by the Securities Association.[19] Therefore, in lieu of the rules of the Bank of England, new capital adequacy rules were adopted by the association for its members. Under these rules, members must have three types of capital:

- *Position-risk capital* to ensure against sudden market downturns. This requirement is based on an analysis of the volatility of each security over the past seven years.
- *Base capital* equivalent to 25 percent of the firm's annual costs to ensure against a sudden drop in profitability.
- *Counterparty capital* to ensure against credit risk in the settlement system.

The Securities Association also ruled that merchant banks must set aside separate capital for securities and banking businesses. These new capital requirements added to the issuance costs of securities and, in the process, may have reduced the profitability of Eurobond underwriting.

British Investors' "Bill of Rights"

Until recently, Britain's financial business was conducted under a set of old laws that stipulated what the market participants should not do. For example, insider trading and other forms of fraud were prohibited. Now, however, the regulatory system clearly establishes who is allowed to sell and trade investment products, in what manner these products are to be sold and traded, and how much information is to be disclosed to investors.

The Financial Services Act (FSA) set up the Securities and Investments Board (SIB) to oversee securities trading. Costs resulting from the FSA are paid by the industry. The Bank of England still maintains its authority over banking, the gilts market, and the foreign exchange market—markets that do not have many private investors.

The primary job of the SIB is to oversee the honesty, competency, and solvency of the investment community. Exhibit 5.5 illustrates the new structure.

Also in May 1986, the LSE proposed to establish a "third market" to complement its existing markets for listed and unlisted equities. The new market opened for business on January 26, 1987, and in particular provided small, untested companies with access to the financial markets.[20]

THE IMPACT OF DEREGULATION

The effects of deregulation are many. This section will deal with the more important ones.

Insider Trading

Coincident with the Financial Services Act and the Big Bang has been the addition of new computer systems to the London Stock Exchange that help monitor suspicious stock tradings. Since the Big Bang, the new market makers must submit computerized records of all deals, including the time—often a vital piece of information in proving insider trading. Before October 1986, deal records were not time-stamped. "Before Big Bang it took six weeks to find out who bought what, when and for whom in any share transaction. It now takes less than two hours."[21] Although weaknesses still show and some wrongdoing is often uncovered, the new requirement is a step in the right direction because it can only enhance the efficiency of the market.

Private-Client Stockbrokering

Before the Big Bang, almost all of the City's big stockbrokerage partnerships had private-client divisions. When the new foreign firms arrived, this business

Exhibit 5.5
New Market Structure

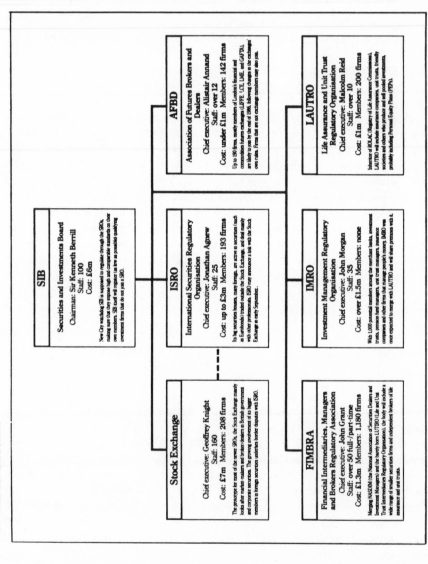

SIB

Securities and Investments Board

Chairman: Sir Kenneth Berrill
Staff: 100
Cost: £6m

New City watchdog SIB is supposed to regulate through the SROs, making sure that they impose high and comparable standards on their own members. SIB itself will register (as few as possible) qualifying investment firms that do not join a SRO.

Stock Exchange

Chief executive: Geoffrey Knight
Staff: 160
Cost: £7m   Members: 208 firms

The prototype for most of the newer SROs, the Stock Exchange mainly looks after market-makers and broker/dealers in British government and corporate securities. The growing involvement of its bigger members in foreign securities underlies border disputes with ISRO.

ISRO

International Securities Regulatory Organisation

Chief executive: Jonathan Agnew
Staff: 25
Cost: up to £3m   Members: 193 firms

Its big securities houses, many foreign, are active in securities (such as Eurobonds) traded outside the Stock Exchange, and deal mainly with other professionals. ISRO may announce a link with the Stock Exchange in early September.

AFBD

Association of Futures Brokers and Dealers

Chief executive: Alistair Annand
Staff: over 12
Cost: under £1m   Members: 142 firms

Up to 190 firms, mostly members of London's financial and commodities futures exchanges (LIFFE, LCE, LME, and GAFTA), are likely to join by the end of 1986, following changes in the exchanges' own rules. Firms that are not exchange members may also join.

FIMBRA

Financial Intermediaries, Managers and Brokers Regulatory Association

Chief executive: John Grant
Staff: over 50 full-/part-time
Cost: £1.3m   Members: 1,180 firms

Merged NASDIM (the National Association of Securities Dealers and Investment Managers) and the barely born LUTIRO (Life and Unit Trust Intermediaries Regulatory Organisation), the body will include a wide range of smaller securities firms and independent brokers of life assurance and unit trusts.

IMRO

Investment Management Regulatory Organisation

Chief executive: John Morgan
Staff: 35
Cost: over £1.5m   Members: none

With 1,000 potential members among the merchant banks, investment trusts, pension fund managers, unit trust managers, insurance companies and other firms that run other people's money, IMRO was once expected to merge with LAUTRO and will share premises with it.

LAUTRO

Life Assurance and Unit Trust Regulatory Organisation

Chief executive: Malcolm Reid
Staff: over 10
Cost: £1m   Members: 200 firms

Inheritor of ROAC (Registry of Life Assurance Commitment), LAUTRO will include insurance companies, unit trusts, friendly societies and others who produce and sell pooled investments, probably including Personal Equity Plans (PEPs).

Source: Economist (30 April 1988). © 1988 The Economist Newspaper Ltd. Reprinted with permission.

appeared lucrative, and some existing firms sold these operations at large premiums. The new conglomerates thought that the private-client business would offer easy money. The government's privatization and a bull market under way were the basis for optimism and the high premiums. However, many newcomers found making money a lot more difficult than they initially thought it would be. This was so because many private-client brokers found that their management and settlement systems were inadequate to cope with a surge in demand. Back offices were clogged up, and some stock deliveries were taking up to three months. As a result, brokers frequently had to borrow money to pay for the shares. The interest payment on that debt wiped out most firms' profits. Eventually, many firms gave up, including Kleinwort, Security Pacific's Hoare Govett, and Sheppards.[22]

The Big Bang led institutions to begin the practice of negotiated commissions. Many firms discovered that they could no longer afford to cross-subsidize other operations, including private-client stockbrokering. Managers woke up to the fact that the retail part of their business was costing them dearly, and they started raising prices. This increase in some cases has been as much as "1.65% for bargains of up to 7000 pounds."[23] Thus, the small client is feeling the brunt of this adjustment.

Life Insurance Firms

Britain's life insurance industry is confronted with an upheaval that is mainly a byproduct of the 1986 FSA. Two provisions of the FSA—polarization and best advice—have harmed many small independent firms. In the past two years, 4,000 smaller firms have either closed their doors or tied themselves to selling the products of just one firm.[24]

Polarization means that agents must either be tied to one company, selling its products exclusively, or be qualified as fully independent. To be an independent, an intermediary must prove that it regularly researches a large number of rival policies and that it only recommends *best advice*. Many small firms lack the resources to carry out enough research to convince regulators that they are indeed delivering the best advice.

FSA is also increasing the costs of many independent financial intermediaries. The provisions of FSA regarding new capital requirements and the need for record keeping, quarterly returns, and computer systems generated new costs for many small, old, independent firms. Agents tied to an insurance company simply do not have to worry about this escalation of new costs because all regulatory costs are referred to the company they represent.

Another byproduct of the new regulatory environment has been an industrywide agreement on maximum commission rates for the life and pension business. Again, this hurts the independents that have to rely on higher-than-average commissions from insurance companies. It specifically affects independents because insurance companies can pay their tied agents as much as they want. All this gives a big incentive to be tied.

Another factor helping to thin the ranks of the independents is increased competition from financial conglomerates. Increasingly, banks, building societies, and insurance companies are competing on each other's turf, and this new competition has hurt the independents. Only time will tell if independent intermediaries are a species worth preserving.

The Equity Market

The impact of the Big Bang on the equity market has been considerable. This is reflected in the following factors.

Lower Transaction Costs

As of October 27, 1986, the stamp duty was lowered from 1 percent to 0.5 percent. This plus the more competitive environment overall decreased commissions substantially. In many cases, big institutions were able to deal on a net-of-commission basis. An informal survey by the Bank of England suggests that since the Big Bang, commission rates have fallen from about 0.4 percent to 0.2 percent for equity deals in the range of £100,000–1 million. On very large deals (more than £2 million), rates are even lower—0.125 percent.[25] Exhibit 5.6 compares transaction costs before and after the Big Bang for an alpha stock.

It should be noted, however, that the commission paid on small transactions by individual investors was not expected to fall significantly under the new trading agreements because the cost associated with brokerage institutions tends to be fixed. For example, for investors buying £1,000 worth of shares, the commission rate remained at 1.65 percent in most cases, the same as that before the Big Bang; but a number of firms have cut their rates to 1.5 percent, and a few have even cut them to 1 percent for an execution-only service (service equivalent to that of a discount broker in the United States). The LSE introduced an automatic small-order execution system in 1987, which implied reduced transaction costs for small investors.

The new arrangements generated new pressures leading to a narrowing of the

Exhibit 5.6
Equity Transaction Costs before and after the Big Bang for a Liquid Alpha Stock

	Purchase value at: 1,000 pounds		500,000 pounds	
	Before	After	Before	After
Stamp duty	1.0	0.51	.00	.5
Commission	1.7	1.50	.40	0-0.2
Market touch (halved)	0.4	0.30	.40	.4
Total	3.1	2.31	.80	.9-1.1

Source: Bank of England Quarterly Bulletin (December 1985): 61.

Exhibit 5.7
Market Makers' Touch before and after the Big Bang (Percentage of share price)

Category of stock	Alpha	Beta	Gamma
Pre-Big Bang:			
Average touch at normal size	0.8	1.8	3.4
Post-Big Bang:			
Average touch at 1,000 share	0.6	1.4	2.8
Average touch at largest SEAQ quote	0.8	1.7	3.2

Source: Bank of England Quarterly Report (February 1987): 59.

market touch, the difference between the best bid and the best offer prices. For investors purchasing shares, this implicit cost is represented by half of the market touch—that is, the difference between the best offer price and the midmarket price. A comparison of market touch before and after the Big Bang is presented in Exhibit 5.7.

Exhibit 5.7 shows that alphas had the narrowest market touch, averaging 0.8 percent. In general, the more actively a stock is traded, the narrower the touch will be because the market maker will be reasonably confident of being able to reverse a position quickly. At the same time, however, the touch tends to widen for large-size quotations, reflecting the risks to the market maker of unbalancing his book.

The behavior of the market touch as quote sizes increase can be taken as an indication of the depth of market liquidity; the less the touch widens, the deeper the market is for the shares in question. The market touch survey in Exhibit 5.7 shows that alpha stocks have greater market depth than do beta or gamma stocks, and that the Big Bang boosted the liquidity of the market.

Increasing Turnover Rate

The value of daily turnover in U.K. and Irish equities between October 27, 1986, and the end of that year was about 21 percent higher on average than that of the first 10 months of 1986. Also, the number of bargains was up by 40 percent.[26] Exhibit 5.8 shows the change in this regard.

The Gilt Market

The post–Big Bang gilt market was characterized by the following factors.

Lower Costs and a Higher Turnover Rate

For big institutions, trading is based on net dealing prices. This, combined with a much larger number of market makers, resulted in lower dealing costs.[27] The total daily turnover in the gilts market in 1987 after the Big Bang was running at £3 billion, a rise of 50 percent over 1986.[28]

Exhibit 5.8
Stock Exchange Turnover: U.K. and Irish Equities, 1980–1986

Year	Average daily turnover (Millions pounds)	Average daily bargains (1,000's)	Average Value per bargain (1,000's)
1980	121.3	16.7	7.3
1981	128.5	15.7	8.2
1982	147.9	15.3	9.6
1983	222.7	18.8	11.9
1984	289.0	19.2	15.1
1985	417.2	22.0	19.0
1986 Q1	710.1	31.4	22.6
Q2	653.2	27.2	24.0
Q3	571.7	21.3	26.8
October	578.8	34.6	19.1
November	774.3	36.4	21.3
December	767.8	40.1	19.1

Source: Bank of England Quarterly Bulletin (February 1987): 61.

Much Lower Profits for Gilt Dealers

After the Big Bang, there were 27 gilt dealers instead of the 2 major dealers in the pre–Big Bang era. In the U.S. Treasury market, by contrast, there are 38 primary dealers, but the market is much larger. In the U.S. government debt market, the value of turnover is about $80 billion per day in a $1.5 trillion market. In the United Kingdom, on the other hand, market turnover averaged between £1 and £1.5 billion per day during the period 1984–1986.[29] According to *Banker* magazine, few gilt market makers have made any profits since the Big Bang. Of the 27 gilt traders, Lloyds Merchant Bank gave up after incurring losses of $11 million, and Orion Royal Bank also pulled out in October 1987. Citicorp's Scrimgeor Vickers, Kleinwort Grieveson, and Morgan Grenfell admitted to losses in the market as well.[30]

This heightened competition has benefited institutional investors. Before the Big Bang, they had to pay an average commission of 0.1 percent on all bargains, whereas now at least four-fifths of customer business is done directly with market makers without commissions. The spreads on these deals are now about half of what they were before deregulation: 0.06 percent versus 0.1 percent.[31]

Move to Positioning

Because of the tough competitive conditions, gilt dealers were forced to become speculators. Their financial survival required that they assume a correct view of the market and position themselves accordingly. The increased risks unfortunately did not produce corresponding returns in many cases.

Merger and Acquisition

The impetus for M&A in a deregulated market is relatively easy to identify. In a recent study of the U.S. trucking, airline, and financial industries, the consulting firm of McKinsey and Co. identified three fundamental pressures that typically develop in a deregulated market:

- The first force is development of overcapacity as new entrants flood the market. This gives rise to the second factor.
- Declining profitability in areas that were previously profitable is the byproduct of increased competition.
- The above two factors give rise to a most important result: increased demand for capital.

In London's case, one can find strong support for the above hypotheses in most market areas. To begin with, prior to the Big Bang, there were only six market makers in the gilt market. After the Big Bang, the number of gilt market makers increased to 27. The overcapacity can also be seen in the fact that in 1988, market makers have each committed about £25 million ($42 million) to trading equities, with a total capital committed to equities now well over £800 million, compared with about £100 million before the Big Bang. The average return on capital in 1987 was about 5 percent, compared to the yield on gilts of 10 percent.[32] The commission for equity transactions in London had at the same time tumbled by as much as 50 percent since the Big Bang.[33]

The total revenues that securities firms earn in the four markets of the International Stock Exchange (domestic equities, foreign equities, gilts, and options) have shrunk by almost two-fifths from the pre–Big Bang levels.[34] This was prior to the stock market crash.

As a result of increased competition, many new entrants will have a higher need for new capital to satisfy their various new demands: buying talent, specialist skills, and technology, and at times even acquiring the opposition. In the case of London, due to the smallness of domestic merchant banks, the acquirers of British securities firms came largely from outside, especially from the United States. Big, foreign commercial and investment banks bought participation in the gilt market, as was documented earlier. (The British government permits banks to operate both commercial and investment banks.) In this highly competitive environment, smaller and inefficient firms are forced to merge or to cease business.

The Futures Market

Even during the months leading up to the Big Bang, the transformation of financial markets was already visible. Since its inception in 1982, business on the LIFFE has been steadily growing. The Big Bang exploded the volume. At the end of July 1986, volume on the LIFFE for the first 7 months of 1986 was more than 3.8 million contracts, surpassing the 3.6 million recorded during the whole of 1985. The average daily volume rose from 14,058 contracts to 25,671 in the first 8 months of 1986. After the Big Bang, the long gilt futures contract reached 30,000 contracts a day, and the average turnover in November 1986 exceeded 1 billion daily.[35]

Trading patterns have also shifted since the Big Bang. Prior to that time, most banks were simply customers for other brokers; now they can compete on equal terms and are playing a major role in the market.

Another important change is the newly gained ability to go short on the cash market. This means that a gilt player can now hold a bear position. Arbitrage opportunities between futures and the cash market have narrowed, and potential profits are much smaller. In addition, the market has now provided greater liquidity and lower price volatility for several instruments.

Although the gilt futures contracts have turned into a highly successful contract as a result of the Big Bang, the performance of the Financial Times Stock Exchange 100 index (Footsie) futures and options has been somewhat discouraging. However, the volume has picked up lately, and open interest in this contract reached 16,389 by January 25, 1989. Three factors have contributed to the initially discouraging start:

- The absence of arbitrage program tracking
- Tax considerations
- Competition between two basically similar FTSE-100 option contracts (one belonging to the LIFFE, the other to the LSE)[36]

Merchant Banking

The City's old merchant banks have shown remarkable resiliency in the face of the new market conditions. Long-lasting relationships between corporate finance chiefs and their bankers seem to have outlasted the lure of the new financial supermarkets.

Foreign Equity

According to *Euromoney,* the number of foreign stocks actively traded in London grew to 584 between 1986 and 1987, or about 40 percent. A growing number of institutional investors from different money centers of the world have been eager to include foreign equities in their portfolios. This is due partly to the boom of domestic equity prices in the early eighties and partly to the deregulation of financial flows. One of the interesting features has been the enthusiasm shown by the British regulatory authorities (unlike those of the other centers) in promoting new business—almost as much as shown by the banks themselves.

Security Trading Profitability

The Economist of January 24, 1987, reported that during the previous week Giles & Overbury, one of London's oldest independent brokerage houses, went bankrupt.[37] Many other firms have been under financial stress. Since the Big Bang, which abolished fixed commission rates and the separation between brokers and jobbers, "almost half of all trading in British equities in London is free

Exhibit 5.9
Comparison of LSE Members' Estimated Income before and after the Big Bang

Date	Turn Over (Billion pounds)	Average Commission	Annualized Income (million pounds)	
1985	97.76	0.5%	Broking/Jobbing	643
Jan-Sept. 86	113.87	0.43%	Broking/Jobbing	893
Sept. 86	11.66	0.43%	'' ''	823
Nov. 86	14.09	0.26%	Broking *	242
			Net prices *	76
			Inter-member *	93
			Total	411
Dec. 86	14.25	0.26%	Broking *	245
			Net prices *	77
			Inter-member	94
			Total	416

*Implied commission on trades.

Source: Economist (24 January 1987).

of commission," a fact that is having considerable effect on the profitability of investment houses. Exhibit 5.9 illustrates the differences in jobbing revenues before and after the Big Bang.

The Midland Bank also decided to pull out of making equity markets in London in early 1987. It was losing money at the rate of £2 million a month.

By another account, the amount of capital devoted to the gilt-edged market rose by 600 percent after the Big Bang, yet in the subsequent year, average commission rates fell by 90 percent. This would not have been so bad if firms had been able to make money on increased volume. Total revenues fell by 82 percent, however.[38]

Future Developments

The reforms of the London financial markets will continue well beyond the Big Bang. Financial innovation is likely to continue, the market for futures and options will grow more rapidly.[39] The LSE through more sophisticated technology has already become linked with other international exchanges, especially the exchanges in the United States (Chicago in particular). A wider range of products will be traded on the LSE in the future as financial instruments continue to proliferate.

Corporate and industry restructuring will continue through mergers and acquisitions. Much consolidation will also be observed. The number of market makers in gilts has already shrunk from 38 to 22 (the last to leave was Citicorp's Scrimgeor Vickers Securities Ltd.). New players will take their place. As of August 1, 1988, Nomura International Ltd. joined 22 other market makers in gilts, and another Japanese firm, Daiwa Securities, became a gilt market maker in October 1988.

Looking to parallels in the United States following "May Day" 1975, when commissions became negotiated, commissions fell by 40 percent, stabilized, and then fell again, driving some 35 firms out of business in 7 months. However, the next 10 years were among the most profitable ever on Wall Street, and firms that survived now provide more effective and efficient service to their clients than ever before.[40] Although the Big Bang's explosion and its aftershocks have caused many casualties, London's role as a financial center will be successfully maintained, despite the emergence of Tokyo as a contender for the top spot.

The evidence so far indicates that deregulation has increased competition in both equity and gilt markets, lowered transaction costs, and increased market liquidity. In addition, the U.K. economy has been growing strongly. Some believe this strong growth could lead to overheating, however.

Concerned voices are also raised as a result of deregulation. The potential problem lies in the conflicts of interest between securities firms and their customers, because deregulation has resulted in the creation of large financial services conglomerates that can provide various services, including market making, fund management, and corporate finance and banking. The possibility for potential conflicts of interest between market making and giving investment advice is great indeed.[41] Research provided by brokers might lose its objectivity because brokers can profit by pushing their own inventory.[42]

The securities watchdog, SIB, has promulgated strict rules on front running, including the requirement that a firm giving recommendations state "clearly and comprehensively" that it has taken a position in the stock and state the amount held, the price paid, and the period the stock has been held. The trouble is that this rule applies only to firms that are directly licensed by the SIB.[43]

All these measures are steps in the right direction. However, no one has figured out how to make any system permanently foolproof. The temptations to undermine the system will always be present.

NOTES

1. "Capital of Capital," *Economist* (11 October 1986): 13.

2. "All Change in the City," *Economist* (7 December 1985): 70.

3. Salomon Brothers, *International Equity Flows, 1988* (September 1988).

4. "Big Bang Supports LIFFE Volume," *Banker* (October 1986): 41.

5. "Change in the Stock Exchange and Regulation of the City," *Bank of England Quarterly Bulletin* (December 1985): 545.

6. Ibid.

7. Ibid.

8. Ian Verchere, "Flinging Open the Doors of Change," Supplement to *Euromoney* (August 1986): 2.

9. *Wall Street Journal*, 28 February 1986.

10. "Change in the Stock Exchange and Regulation of the City," *Bank of England Quarterly Bulletin* (February 1987).

11. "Looking for Parallels in America," *Institutional Investor* 20, no. 6 (June 1986): 258.

12. Ibid.

13. "Change in the Stock Exchange and Regulation of the City," December 1985, 547.

14. For further discussion of these stocks, see "Change in the Stock Exchange and Regulation of the City," February 1987, 58.

15. Ian M. Kerr, "Big Bang," *Euromoney* (1986).

16. "Looking for Parallels," 258.

17. "Change in the Stock Exchange and Regulation of the City," December 1985, 547.

18. "Tying Down the Euromarkets," *Economist* (25 April 1987): 73.

19. "Britain's Capital Rules for Securities Easier than Expected," *Economist* (July 18, 1987): 76.

20. "Change in the Stock Exchange and Regulation of the City," February 1987, 56. A. W. Mullineux, *UK Banking after Deregulation* (London: Croom Helm, 1987), 91.

21. "Insider Trading in London," *Economist* (7 February 1987): 74.

22. "Hard Time for Britain's Small-Client Brokers," *Economist* (12 November 1988): 95.

23. Ibid., 96.

24. "Death of Britain's Financial Intermediaries," *Economist* (5 November 1988): 95.

25. "Change in the Stock Exchange and Regulation of the City," February 1987.

26. Ibid.

27. Kerr, "Big Bang," 95.

28. Edi Cohen, "Deregulation, Back to the Futures," *Banker* (January 1987): 101.

29. Kerr, "Big Bang."

30. Michael Blanden, "One Year On," *Banker* (November 1987): 49.

31. "Market Focus: Overcrowding in Gilts," *Economist* (16 January 1988): 71.

32. "London's Beleaguered Securities Firms," *Economist* (20 August 1988): 67.

33. *Euromoney* (April 1987).

34. "London's Beleaguered Securities Firms," *Economist* (20 August 1988): 67.

35. Edi Cohen, "Deregulation, Back to the Futures," *Banker* (January 1987): 101.

36. For a complete discussion of the impact of the Big Bang on the futures market, see "Deregulation, Back to the Futures," January 1987, 101.

37. "Has Big Bang Knocked City Profits Flat?" *Economist* (24 January 1987): 69.

38. *Economist* (25 June 1988).

39. Mullineux, *UK Banking,* 121.

40. "Big Bang," *Barclays Briefing.*

41. "Change in the Stock Exchange and Regulation of the City," 544.

42. "Looking for Parallels in America," 261. Kerr, "Big Bang," 106.

43. "First off the Starting Blocks," *Economist* (21 March 1987): 88.

6

The Deregulation of the Other Financial Markets

Because the deregulation of financial markets is a worldwide phenomenon, the discussion of the evolution of every market is not possible. Therefore, the most interesting cases—Hong Kong, Australia, and Canada—have been selected. Hong Kong is an excellent case for studying the regulation of a market that was one of the freest in the world at a time when other markets were being deregulated. The Australian case is also very interesting because the deregulation of the Australian financial market was actively pursued and implemented by a socialist labor government. The Canadian case will be briefly discussed in order to explore the effects of the changes taking place in the United States on its neighbor to the north.

THE CHANGING HONG KONG FINANCIAL MARKETS

The Hong Kong financial markets have relied on market forces to discipline market participants. In this respect, they resemble the U.S. financial markets prior to 1913. Add to this the plush office towers and the high speed technology, and you get Hong Kong of the late 1970s and very early 1980s. All was not well in the capitalist's paradise, however. Changes had to take place, driven by several banking crises, securities crises, the Hong Kong dollar crash of 1982, the political reality of 1997 when Hong Kong reverts to Chinese control, the need for Hong Kong to reassure the world community as it strove to become a leading financial center, and the aftermath of the October 19 stock market crash.

The role Hong Kong plays in the world financial markets is vastly disproportionate to the size of its population (5.51 million) or its geographic area (2,916 square kilometers, of which only 1,045 kilometers are land). Its exports increased by HK$117 billion in 1987 alone. Its gross domestic product grew by 12 percent in 1988 to $53 billion. Today, Hong Kong stands as the third largest financial center in the world in terms of the number of deposit-taking institutions. In 1987, Hong Kong emerged as the biggest syndicated loan taker in Asia (Exhibit 6.1) and the second largest foreign exchange trading center in Asia after Tokyo.

The responsibility for structuring, regulating, and monitoring the financial system of Hong Kong in the late 1980s is not centralized in a single agency, ministry, or office. It is sufficiently streamlined with clear lines of demarcation, but with still a considerable amount of self-regulation.

The banking sector of Hong Kong has had three tiers since 1981. Each tier is authorized for a certain type and level of activity, but considerable overlap exists, as explained below. The first tier consists of licensed banks, the second tier of licensed deposit-taking companies (DTCs), and the third tier of registered DTCs. The governor in council grants banking licenses, the financial secretary grants the licensed DTC status, and the Commissioner of Banking grants the registered DTC status. The Hong Kong Association of Banks (to which all licensed banks must belong) also plays a regulatory role in setting terms and conditions, such as deposit rates, etc., on interbank and bank/customer deals.

Hong Kong does not have its own version of Glass–Steagall. Consequently, its banks are free to diversify into investment banking, investment management, and insurance—and they did just that with increasing vigor during the 1980s.

Exhibit 6.1

Hong Kong Emerges as the Biggest Syndicated Loan Taker, 1985–1987 (Volumes in US$ million)

Country	Volume	1987 Rank	Deals	Volume	1986 Rank	Deals	Volume	1985 Rank	Deals
HONG KONG	2226	1	19	1543	4	11	1072	4	16
CHINA	1900	2	27	1877	2	23	2196	3	5
SOUTH KOREA	1059	3	14	1707	3	15	3912	1	41
INDIA	1042	4	16	911	7	9	99	10	4
INDONESIA	760	5	6	933	6	3	84	11	3
THAILAND	314	6	8	1395	5	6	619	6	6
NEW ZEALAND	290	7	5	466	10	6	99	9	1
AUSTRALIA	239	8	4	3521	1	11	3315	2	12
JAPAN	181	9	2	791	9	4			
SINGAPORE	137	10	1	41	12	2	130	8	5
PAKISTAN	125	11	1	100	11	1	150	7	1
MALAYSIA	90	12	3	806	8	5	61	12	4
TAIWAN				100	11	1			
MACAU				21	13	1			
PHILIPPINES							925	5	1
DRG							52	13	2
OTHERS							45		3
TOTAL	8363		106	14212		98	12759		104

Source: Asian Finance (15 January 1988): 15.

The securities industry is regulated by the Office of the Commissioner for Securities and Commodities Trading. The commissioner's office registers dealers in securities and commodities and investment advisors and their representatives, and supervises the securities, financial management, and futures industries under the Securities Ordinance, the Protection of Investors Ordinance, and the Commodities Trading Ordinance. The entire insurance industry (all classes) is covered by the Insurance Companies Ordinance, which is administered by the Registrar General (Insurance Authority).

The peculiarities of the Hong Kong regulatory system are already apparent. What is most interesting, however, is how Hong Kong conducts its monetary policy and defends its currency. No country in the world does it in quite the same way.

Hong Kong has no central bank. The functions of this institution are performed by the Monetary Affairs Branch of the Government Secretariat, the Exchange Fund which dates back to 1935, and, yes, two commercial banks. The Exchange Fund holds the territory's foreign currency assets, defends the parity of the Hong Kong dollar through spot market intervention, and provides backing for the notes issued by the designated commercial banks. Two commercial banks in Hong Kong—the Hong Kong and Shanghai Bank and the Chartered Bank—are authorized to issue notes. Their note issues are backed by the Exchange Fund through the issuance of certificates of indebtedness (CIs). These certificates are backed by gold, silver, foreign exchange reserves, and foreign currency securities. The two banks are required to purchase the certificates as a cover for their notes in circulation. The CIs are issued and redeemed at a fixed exchange rate: HK$7.80 = US$1. The fixity of the exchange rate is transmitted by the two note-issuing banks in their transactions with other banking institutions in Hong Kong. This maintains the stability of the exchange rate of the Hong Kong dollar vis-à-vis the U.S. dollar—a policy objective of the Hong Kong government.

Under this institutional arrangement, only three instruments of monetary policy exist:

- Intervention in the foreign exchange market maintains the par value of the H.K. dollar with respect to the U.S. dollar. The maintenance of this par value means the maintenance of interest rates comparable to those of the United States.

- The required purchase of CIs against note issuance by the two banks means a reduction of U.S. dollar holdings of the banks as new notes are issued.

- In addition to the issuance of notes, the two designated commercial banks, the preeminent banking institutions in Hong Kong, hold the government demand and fixed (time) deposits and serve as a central clearinghouse for banking transactions. The Exchange Fund can therefore exercise some control by adding to or withdrawing its deposits held by the two banks.

All these measures are of limited effectiveness. The fact remains that "there have not been any restrictions on the growth of the money supply in Hong Kong, and it can be expanded at will by the banks."[1]

The Hong Kong regulatory structure discussed above was born, not unlike that of the United States, out of financial crises and economic setbacks. Interestingly, it took shape during a period when financial centers throughout the world were being deregulated. Hong Kong had to move in the opposite direction from the rest of the world to put itself at par with the leading financial centers. A structure had to be provided for the Hong Kong financial system that would reassure investors and depositors and that would ensure the stability of the Hong Kong banking system and economy.

The Genesis of the Hong Kong Banking Regulatory System

The period preceding 1964 could be characterized as the "Wild West" banking era of Hong Kong. The banking industry was completely self-regulated, and market "discipline" was the sole constraining force.

During 1964, the Banking Ordinance was enacted. Because it declared all banking licenses issued under previous legislation null and void, all existing banks had to apply for a new license from the Banking Commissioner. In 1965, a banking crisis hit Hong Kong, leading to a freeze on the issuance of new banking licenses which lasted until March 19, 1978.

The 1965 Banking Crisis

The banking crisis of 1965 saw the failure of two banks and the voluntary suspension of one bank. Thousands of depositors lost their savings, and hundreds of firms went bankrupt in the wake of the liquidity scramble. This crisis clearly exposed the serious deficiencies of the Hong Kong banking system.

The 1965 crisis, which consisted of a series of runs on a substantial number of banks, actually occurred in four phases over a period of more than a year. The first phase involved only the Ming Tak Bank, a small, unincorporated bank heavily involved in real estate dealings. In mid-January, rumors circulated that the bank was in financial difficulties. On January 23, 1965, U.S. checks issued by the bank were not honored, and on January 26, the foreign bank that acted as the Ming Tak's clearing agent announced its intention to stop clearing checks. The next day, crowds gathered at the offices of the bank to withdraw their deposits, and the banking commissioner took control of the bank at noon the same day. The bank was found to be illiquid and insolvent.

The second phase began on February 6, when a run started on the Aberdeen branch of the Canton Trust and Commercial Bank. After the failure of the Ming Tak, the banking situation was tense, and all kinds of rumors were circulating. Because public confidence was low and depositors were nervous, the number of runs steadily increased. As the situation seemed out of control, the government announced emergency regulations to limit cash withdrawals.

The third phase started in mid-March and involved only the Hang Seng Bank. The Hang Seng Bank was also heavily involved in real estate loans and investments. In March, rumors began to circulate regarding the bank and certain members of its board. Few big depositors removed their accounts. The next morning the bank announced that with the approval of the government, the Hong Kong and Shanghai Banking Corporation had acquired controlling interest in the Hang Seng. The merger was seen as the best method of averting a greater disaster.

The fourth phase of the crisis involved two small banks, the Far East Bank Ltd. and the Yau Yue Bank Ltd., both of which were heavily involved with real estate loans and investments. There was no apparent massive run in this phase, but the banks sustained a loss of deposits through the clearing to an extent that if outside help had not been available, they would have collapsed. Authorities took action quickly to keep the situation under control, primarily because they feared another outbreak of bank failures.

The main cause for the crisis was the weak real estate sector to which banks were heavily committed. (Some of the later regulatory reforms reflect this fact.) In early 1965, there were indications of a recession in the real estate sector, and that recession developed into a serious slump which directly affected the liquidity and solvency of some banks. The banks that sustained runs were suspected by the public to be heavily involved in the property business. Another reason for the crisis was the gross mismanagement within some of the more irresponsible banks. Irregularities also compounded the mismanagement of two banks, the Ming Tak and the Canton Trust. The quality of loans and investments of certain banks was steadily deteriorating, and real estate loans were not properly administered. The deterioration in the quality of the asset structure of these banks allowed liquid reserves to fall to a dangerously low level, and this low liquidity was a poor defense against the massive cash withdrawals. Also, structural deficiencies helped to cause the banking crisis: the absence of a central bank, the lack of a built-in stabilizer (e.g., deposit insurance), and the lack of asset diversification.

Interestingly, the crisis of 1965 did not result in a massive introduction of regulations. The reaction was subdued and consisted of a ban on new banking licenses, allowing banking activity to become more concentrated. The banking commissioner's office found safety in size and was willing to see the Hong Kong bank garner as much as two-thirds of the deposits and assets of the licensed banking sector.[2]

In 1972, however, the banking commissioner allowed some overseas and local banks to set up deposit-taking companies (DTCs) to compete with licensed banks for deposits and banking services. Foreign banks took advantage of this opportunity to set up merchant banks to offer syndicated loans, corporate financial advice, investment management, leasing, etc. The new entrants, especially the local ones, did not have the necessary experience and funding to compete effectively, resulting in a large number of DTC failures during 1973 and 1974. The "remedy" was the DTC Ordinance of 1975, which tightened capital and liquidity requirements, but only temporarily solved the banking problem.

On March 15, 1978, public pressure and hospitable economic conditions led

Financial Secretary Phillip Haddon to end the ban on issuing banking licenses. This took place while Hong Kong still did not have a regulatory structure, even after two major crises.

Further restructuring of the banking sector occurred in 1981. The banking industry was moving from a two-tier system to a three-tier system, and by 1983, the financial institutions of Hong Kong belonged to one of three tiers: licensed banks (commercial banks), licensed deposit-taking companies (DTCs), and registered DTCs. These DTCs grew initially at very high rates because they were completely unregulated prior to 1976 and were able to offer more competitive rates and narrower spreads than commercial banks were.

Local licensed banks are required to have a majority beneficial ownership by Hong Kong citizens, a paid-up capital of HK$100 million or more, and minimum assets and deposits by the public of HK$2,500 million and HK$1,750 million, respectively. A minimum of 10 years' experience is also required. A foreign bank must ordinarily meet tougher standards. It must be in good standing, be subject to adequate supervision, and have minimum assets of HK$14,000 million. However, these requirements did not discourage foreign banks from seeking a foothold in Hong Kong, and by the end of 1987, there were 154 licensed banks in Hong Kong, 120 of which were foreign. Together, the licensed banks had HK$642 billion in deposits at the end of 1987. Only licensed banks are permitted to accept demand and time deposits, regardless of size or maturity.

Licensed DTCs, (now able to call themselves banks), on the other hand, are required to have a minimum issued capital of HK$100 million and to meet other criteria regarding size and quality of management. They may accept only those deposits that exceed HK$500,000 for any maturity. By the end of 1987, 35 licensed DTCs were in operation, with deposits equal to $28 billion. These DTCs are also referred to as merchant banks.

Registered DTCs (now simply referred to as DTCs) must have a minimum capital of HK$25 million, and at least half of their ownership, like the licensed DTCs, must be by a banking institution. DTCs may accept deposits of HK$100,000 and more with a minimum maturity of three months. By the end of 1987, 232 registered DTCs were in operation, with deposits of HK$34 billion.

Unfortunately, the veritable (but limited) regulatory reforms of the Hong Kong market had to await another banking crisis.

The Banking Crisis of 1983–1986

The regulatory structure of the Hong Kong banking industry was feeble prior to 1983. The government showed clear preference for a laissez faire approach to the banking system. This attitude began to change as evidence of mismanagement, fraud, and financial irregularities began to emerge. The government intervened to restore stability and confidence.

Between 1983 and 1986, the government had to rescue seven banks from financial difficulties. The first bank was the Hang Lung Bank, rescued in September 1983. The bank became insolvent allegedly due to fraud, and faltered only days after the Hong Kong dollar dropped to a record low amidst heightened concerns about the political future of Hong Kong. Sir John Bremridge, the financial secretary, used the money from the government's Exchange Fund to rescue the bank.

In June 1985, the Overseas Trust Bank and its subsidiary, the Hong Kong Industrial and Commercial Bank, became the next two banks to be rescued. The rescue of the Overseas Trust Bank was necessitated by alleged insider fraud. Once again, the government used capital in the Exchange Fund to rescue the banks. For the first three of the problem banks, government help came in the form of a takeover. However, authorities attempted to reduce their takeover role as public opposition to the use of government funds to bail out banks grew.

The government arranged the rescue of the Ka Wah Bank in July 1985. The bank's capital and reserves had been wiped out because of loose lending practices in Malaysia and Singapore. Private-sector interests took over the bank on the condition that the government would shoulder any uncollectible bank loans. In December 1985, Wing On Bank was also taken over by private-sector interests on the same condition as was attached to the Ka Wah acquisition.

In March 1986, the government opened another line of credit to rescue the sixth bank, the Union Bank of Hong Kong. Authorities took temporary control of the bank until a buyer was found in July. The government then took control of the Hong Nin Bank on September 8, 1986. A prolonged period of withdrawals had left the bank with a serious liquidity problem. The bank's public deposits were falling, and loans could not be called in as fast as deposits were withdrawn. The government intervened to stop the deterioration in liquidity, and the Exchange Fund was again used to honor any obligations that the bank could not meet. This left the government as a leading local banker as well as a bank regulator because at this time the government was still engaged in helping in the recovery of four banks (Hang Lung, Hong Kong Industrial and Commercial, Overseas Trust, and Hong Nin).

These failures and other problems in the banking sector led to sweeping changes in banking regulations in the form of the 1986 banking ordinance. The banking ordinance of 1982 had not done the job, although it did lay the foundation for the 1986 ordinance. This foundation included the licensing requirements discussed earlier and allowed an avenue for regulating interest rates.

The interest rate on deposits under HK$500,000 is regulated by the Hong Kong Association of Banks (HKAB), which was established in 1981 to replace Hong Kong Exchange Banks. All licensed banks, including nonauthorized banks, must become members. The HKAB is a statutory body, the rules and regulations of which are binding on its members. It regulates exchange transactions and supervises the interest rate agreement. Furthermore, the HKAB also operates the Bankers Clearing House.[3]

A bank must maintain liquid assets at least equal to 25 percent of its deposit liabilities. In addition, 15 percent of its deposit liabilities must be held in "highly liquid assets." Liquid assets are defined as assets that are due on demand or on 24 hours' notice. This liquidity ratio is designed to ensure that the banking system has adequate liquidity to meet withdrawal demands. The average liquidity of all licensed banks during 1982 was 49.6 percent, which was well above the 25 percent requirement.[4] The excess liquidity acts as a buffer to unexpected economic changes.

Loans to directors and employees are also regulated. The amount of advances is limited to 10 percent of the paid-up capital. The object of these rules is to reduce the risk to depositors.

DTCs were dealt with in a 1983 ordinance. Under this ordinance, registered DTCs cannot accept deposits from the public of less than HK$100,000 or for a period of less than three months; licensed DTCs cannot accept deposits from the public (for any term) of less than HK$500,000. The purpose of this ordinance is to protect the small depositor; it is reasoned that anyone with high deposits should be able to look after himself. In addition, the ordinance also ensures the effectiveness of the interest rates agreement of the HKAB as an instrument of macromonetary policy. DTCs intending to engage in the securities business or to provide investment advisory services must register (or gain exemption) under the Hong Kong Securities Ordinance.

The real reform, however, followed the 1983–1986 crisis in the form of the Banking Ordinance Amendments, which became effective September 1, 1986. They called for the merging of the past commissioner of DTC and the commissioner of banking. The new commissioner of banking would be responsible for regulating all financial institutions, with reporting requirements to the territory's Executive Council. All publicly owned financial institutions would henceforth have to publish a list of their shareholders with 10 percent or more of equity shares, and these shareholders would have voting rights only if the commissioner approves. The commissioner can require banks to diversify. He must also approve all new licenses, allowing him to control the number of banks and thus avoid overbanking. In 1987, Hong Kong had 154 licensed banks maintaining around 1,400 offices.

Under the 1986 amendments, banks are prevented from acquiring or holding more than 25 percent of the equity of a company, unless the equity is held as security or collateral for debt due, or the bank has written approval from the commissioner. This has had wide-ranging effects on many Hong Kong banks because they are family controlled, with the families involved in substantial nonbanking activities. Banks are also prevented from holding or acquiring any interest in real estate exceeding 25 percent of their own paid-up capital.

The 1986 legislation called for new capital adequacy requirements. Financial institutions have to satisfy a minimum capital adequacy ratio of not less than 5 percent of assets. This can be raised to 8 percent for banks and 10 percent for DTCs at the commissioner's discretion. The capital adequacy ratio is the ratio of capital base to risky assets. Also imposed are liquidity requirements (setting liquid assets as a percentage of qualifying liabilities) for banks and DTCs, and restrictions on bank lending to a single borrower connected by shareholdings or directorship. Exhibit 6.2 summarizes the regulation of banks and DTCs.

The 1987 banking ordinance, which took effect on September 1, 1987, is another regulatory step worth noting. It replaced the old three-tier system with

Exhibit 6.2
A Comparison between Banks and DTCs: Regulatory Perspective

	Banks		DTCs	
	Local	Foreign	Licensed	Registered
Issued Share Capital	HK$100mn	HK$100mn	HK$100mn	HK$10mn
Paid-Up Capital	HK$100mn	HK$100mn	HK$75mn	HK$10mn
Deposit base	HK$1.75bn	n/r	n/r	n/r
Total Assets	HK$2.5bn	US$1+bn	n/r	n/r
Deposit Minimums	None	None	HK$500,000	HK$100,000
Experience	10 years as a DTC	Negotiable	Negotiable	Negotiable
Interest Rates Allowed	HKAB rates	HKAB rates	Any	Any
Liquid	25%	25%	25%	25%

n/r: no restrictions
n/a: not applicable
*not enforced until 1988.

Source: Baring Securities Inc., *Hong Kong Banking Sector,* 1989.

both banks and deposit-taking companies (collectively known as authorized institutions) and placed them under a unified regulatory structure.

The Regulation of the Securities Markets in Hong Kong

Not unlike in the banking case, the regulation of the securities markets in Hong Kong came late and after a series of market jitters. Until 1985, the only regulation affecting the securities markets was that passed in 1974. This ordinance, patterned along the New South Wales Securities Industry Act of 1970, was enacted following the market jitters of the early 1970s. It provided a framework within which securities were traded and stock exchanges operated. It required the licensing of stockbrokers, dealers, and investment advisors with the mandated office of commissioner for securities. Members of the exchange were required to contribute to a fund which compensates clients for any defaulting broker. The ordinance prohibited short selling, option dealing, and forward trading, and it provided for regulatory oversight through the Securities Advisory Board and for investigation of suspect activities. The ordinance did not make insider trading an offense, but it included provisions for inquiry by the Insider

Trading Tribunal. The lax treatment of insider trading turned out to be one of its major failings. The ordinance obviously did not go as far as U.S. securities legislation did as early as the 1930s.

Aware of the abuses against investors, the government enacted the Protection of Investors Ordinance on February 13, 1974. Also of interest is an emergency ordinance enacted one year earlier: the Stock Exchange Ordinance. This ordinance was intended to prohibit the creation of any more exchanges. By then, five exchanges were in operation under different structures and rules; some used Chinese as the trading language, the others English.

The next important development in the securities markets was the permission granted in 1979 by three exchanges—the Far East Exchange (the first to do so), the Hong Kong Exchange, and the Kam Ngan Stock Exchange—to overseas institutions to trade directly on the exchange as *full* members. The next year, 1980, witnessed the enactment on August 7 of another emergency ordinance: the Stock Exchange Unification Ordinance. Under this ordinance, the Stock Exchange of Hong Kong (later incorporated on July 7, 1986) was empowered as the only exchange. This ordinance disqualified banks, DTCs, corporations, and firms from membership, but the disqualification of corporations was reversed in an amendment to the ordinance enacted in August 1985. The distribution of membership between individuals and corporations is shown in Exhibit 6.3.

The other major set of ordinances dealt with commodities trading. In 1976, the Commodities Trading Ordinance permitted the establishment of a commodity exchange and set trading rules for commodity futures contracts. The first exchange operated under the name Hong Kong Commodities Exchange Limited. In 1984, the license was renewed under a new name: the Hong Kong Futures Exchange Limited (HKFE). The 1984 ordinance also required the registration of brokers, dealers, and advisors; specified acceptable trading practices; and provided for compensation of investors who have been deceived by brokers.

The major purpose of the ordinance was to allow Hong Kong to enter a major market segment so it could be at a competitive par with U.S. and British markets, and to compete effectively with Singapore, which had taken the lead in derivative products. The Singapore International Monetary Exchange Ltd. (SIMEX) was the first financial futures exchange in Asia and the first to link up with a U.S. exchange, the Chicago Mercantile Exchange, with the right of offset.

The Hong Kong Futures Exchange Ltd. introduced the Hang Seng Index (HSI) futures contract. The HK dollar worth of this contract was HK$50 times the value of the index, which is made up of 33 major stocks. The contract thereon, like all futures contracts, is used for hedging, price discovery, and speculative purposes.

The index mentioned above was constructed at a time when the Hong Kong stock market was in a bull trend. By year end 1986, the Hang Seng Index had passed the 2,500 mark, 46 percent over its level at the end of 1985. The index broke the 3,000 level by early June 1987 and passed the 3,500 mark by August 1987. By October 1, the index had reached the 3,950 point, its highest ever. Turnover during the first 10 months of 1987 reached HK$333 billion, 273 percent

Exhibit 6.3
The Stock Exchange of Hong Kong: Number of Individual and Corporate Members, April 1986–April 1988

Date (end of month)	Individual Members	Corporate Members	Total
2nd April 1986 *	892	8	900
June 1986	860	22	882
September 1986	832	34	866
December 1986	788	51	839
March 1987	760	58	818
June 1987	736	68	804
September 1987	714	75	789
December 1987	688	85	773
March 1988	669	96	765
April 1988	664	98	762

* Unified Exchange commenced trading

Source: The Stock Exchange of Hong Kong Limited, September 1988.

higher than in the first 10 months of 1986. The HSI futures followed suit. Between May 1986 (the date of introduction) and September 1987, the turnover grew by 2,000 percent. Then came the October 19, 1987, crash (Exhibit 6.4).

The 1987 crash was a financial earthquake which shook the entire Hong Kong financial structure, woke up many financial leaders to the fragility of the market, and pointed out the interdependence between the Hong Kong market and the rest of the world. On that historic day, the index fell by 421 points. Trading was suspended for four days—the HKFE was the only exchange to opt for this drastic measure. The intent was to clear the confusion in the market and put an end to panic selling. Unfortunately, the exchange miscalculated badly. When the market reopened on October 26, 1987, the index lost 1,121 points, an all-time record. A third of the value of the stock market was wiped out in one day. The overwhelming majority of opinion in Hong Kong and elsewhere is that the closure was not necessary and that the international standing of Hong Kong was seriously damaged.

Simultaneously, the developments in the futures markets were equally dramatic. Trading was suspended for the same period, and those with losses defaulted on their contracts. The Guarantee Corporation, which interposes itself between every buyer and every seller, did not have sufficient resources to cope with the enormity of the problem. As a result, the government had to come to the rescue and to provide $4 billion in credit facilities to the corporation. A few banks and some members of the exchange also contributed in order to salvage the credibility of the futures market. By the end of 1987, the market closed at 2,303, down from the 2,568 level at the end of 1986. The overall performance for 1987

Exhibit 6.4
Monthly Trading Volumes (in Lots) of Various Contracts on the HKFE, January 1986–April 1988

	Hang Seng Index	Soybeans	Sugar	Gold
1986 (monthly average	103160	27544	22817	531
1987 Jan	185380	26311	33030	488
Feb	222859	51468	27608	522
Mar	323361	26332	28850	574
Apr	276529	38228	23420	520
May	293001	63969	22894	546
Jun	340994	48885	18097	520
Jul	420505	49419	20247	600
Aug	483389	47683	14910	518
Sep	601005	67619	22193	574
Oct	399606	85279	22764	492
Nov	47194	71674	17371	168
Dec	17486	59108	20853	170
1988 Jan	15471	34160	20226	160
Feb	12130	25163	18552	144
Mar	14388	36899	15372	184
Apr	16247	29047	11559	144

Source: Hong Kong Futures Exchange Ltd., 1988.

was not bad because $44.1 billion of capital was raised in the stock market during the year and 150 listing proposals by listed companies were received, compared with 69 in 1986.

The HKFE has yet to recover from its near collapse amid a wave of defaults. The number of futures contracts traded has plummeted to a daily average of 1,000, compared with the 4,000 a day needed to cover operating costs and the 30,000 a day during the bull run prior to Black Monday. The HKFE was by then trading the most successful index futures contract behind the United States. By the end of 1988, the Hang Seng Index has recovered to 2,696.44, and index futures had an open interest of 1923 contracts.

However, share prices and the Hang Seng Index are both buoyant again, although at levels sharply below those prior to the October crash. Although average daily trading volume on the Hong Kong Stock Exchange deteriorated to HK$810.2 million in the first quarter of 1988, compared with HK$1,509.8 million in 1987, it was still well above the levels of the years up to 1986. In March 1988, the Hang Seng Index rallied, rising 10 percent to around 2,600 points, supported by renewed post-crash confidence in the domestic economy as companies reported annual profit growth averaging 37 percent and as the property boom continued unabated. The Hang Seng Index hit 2,772 in July 1988 and then slid back to 2,500 amidst news of the interest rate rise, slower domestic export growth, and the first quarter HK$1.8 billion deficit on visible trade.

The reverberations from the huge drop and the decision to close the market for four days were still being heard long after the crash. It was natural that an investigation be launched. The Davidson Commission, appointed to conduct an inquiry into the futures equity market, discovered that the exchange was an "insider coterie" operating "without any regard to proper and adequate surveillance." The entire exchange was run as a private club, and speculators built up huge leverage positions that could not possibly be met in a significant market downturn. As to the stock exchange, the situation was not much better. Insider trading was rampant, disclosures were incomplete or false, and brokers were dealing in their accounts at the expense of the public.

The Davidson Commission proposed many changes, among them a statutory body with strong reserve provisions, independent of the government and paid for by the market; a new body called the Stock Exchange Council; an extension to three days (from one day) of the settlement period; and a new, computerized central clearing system.

The Impact of the Regulatory Changes

The Hong Kong market is a most interesting market. The "colony" is getting rich at an astounding rate. Total deposits in the domestic banking system grew by 28 percent in 1987 alone to US$90 billion. About 56 percent of the deposits were denominated in foreign currencies and 44 percent in the Hong Kong dollar. Total assets in the banking system grew by 50 percent in 1987 to $413 billion.

All this clearly suggests a very positive vote of confidence in the future of the island, despite the ever-present political uncertainty. How much of this phenomenon can be attributed to "regulation" is very hard to discern in a country that has very stable prices (5.5 inflation), a real GDP growth of 13.6 percent in 1987 (11.2 percent in 1986), and a growth of 11 percent in exports, and that is much less concerned about its political future because it has secured at least 50 years of capitalism, even as part of Communist China. It is worth noting that Chinese-owned banks in Hong Kong experienced the fastest growth rate in deposits in 1987 (36 percent). This was recently reversed after the crackdown on the movement to democratize China.

Regulation appears to have had a stabilizing effect on the financial markets in a country with a fast-increasing middle class that is concerned with the safety of their new affluence, a culture that thrives on gambling but is anxious to know the rules of the game and to secure equal opportunity for all participants, and an economy that has repeatedly been racked by financial scandals and setbacks like the real estate crisis which brought on the 1965 banking and securities crisis. The completely free market system served Hong Kong well after World War II, but the weaknesses of a completely unconstrained system became all too apparent. The foreign financial institutions that were attracted to Hong Kong because of the unlimited freedom it provided finally realized that a system that allows insider trading, that allows contracts with minimal or no guarantees to be leveraged and heavily traded, and that tolerates mediocrity and unethical conduct, etc., is inherently unstable and could hurt everyone in the process. The minimal regulatory structure provided through the various ordinances was correct and sound. Major protection mechanisms are still missing, however. Some form of deposit insurance is needed, especially for the smaller investors, because Hong Kong banks are no less leveraged (no better capitalized) than their counterparts anywhere else.

One of the most interesting observations about the crises Hong Kong experienced is that none, no matter how major it was, threatened the existence of the banking system as a whole. This empirical evidence is a powerful rebuttal to those who argue that the deposit insurance system in the United States is absolutely necessary to prevent a contagion effect and to protect the banking system. It seems quite clear that government action, both quick and properly measured, coupled with a lean and dynamic economy, can weather a storm.

The issue with respect to regulation is, because of the Hong Kong experience, more focused than ever. The issue is not "to regulate or not to regulate"; it is the appropriate level of regulation in a specific market, given the tradition and the economic setting.

Reassured politically and financially through a regulatory structure that is reasonable, although still in need of fine tuning,[5] Hong Kong managed to reach several milestones simultaneously. A few will now be discussed.

Debt Markets

The Hong Kong government is in the enviable position of having garnered a huge surplus. Consequently, it issues no debt, and, hence, there is no government securities market. The major debt instruments traded on the Hong Kong market are certificates of deposit (CDs), commercial paper (CP), and floating-rate notes (FRNs). Their distribution for 1984–1987 is shown in Exhibit 6.5. Clearly, the dominant instrument is the fixed-rate CD.

Recent innovations include a gold-linked CD launched by Citicorp International. This CD allows for a higher return the higher gold prices are, in exchange for a lower initial rate of 5.25 percent. Another innovation is the "mismatched" FRN launched by Sun Hung Kai Properties (Financial Services) Ltd. This issue carries a rate of 0.0625 percent over the three-month Hong Kong Interbank Offer Rate (HIBOR). The payment rate is to be adjusted monthly, and the cost of funds for banks that buy the notes is one-month HIBOR. These innovations, while interesting for Hong Kong, are copied from a much wider and more innovative market: the Euromarket.

On the foreign exchange side, Hong Kong plays a very vital role. Local brokers who specialize in trades involving the HK dollar and international brokers who specialize in trades involving the HK dollar and international brokers who trade every major currency (about 100 banks) realized a daily turnover of $20 billion. The market is deep and wide. The lion's share of non–HK dollar trading (40 percent) is dollar/DM followed by dollar/yen (30 percent). An active

Exhibit 6.5
HK$ Capital Markets: Total Issues, 1984–1987 (Volume in HK$ million)

Year	Fixed rate CDs		Floating rate CDs		CPs/Bond		Floating rate notes		RUF		TOTAL	
	No. of Issues	Volume	No. of Issues	Volume	No. of Issues	Volume	No. of Issues	Volume	No. of Issues	Volume	No. of Issues	Volume
1984	3	260	13	1.950	6	2,100	1	500	—	—	23	4,810
1985	47	5,410	11	1.510	15	8,100	4	1,760	—	—	77	16,780
1986	78	10,101	6	1.200	9	3,755	7	3,850	9	4,485	109	23,391
1987	32	3,856	6	1.299	4	1,740	1	400	4	3,450	47	10,745
TOTAL	160	19,627	36	5,959	34	15,695	13	6,510	13	7,935	256	55,726

Source: ASIAN Finance, March 1988.

forward market exists in the HK$ with maturities of up to five years. Non–HK dollar futures currency contracts are also traded on the HKFE. The currency swap market is active and is the most accepted form for hedging currency risk after asset/liability management through maturity/duration matching.

The Equity Market

The equity market is strong with surprisingly low P/E ratios (9.3), compared with 68.5 for Japan (Exhibit 6.6). These ratios are nominal and must be adjusted for differing accounting rules and risk before comparison can be made. Nonetheless, the performance of the Hong Kong stock market in 1988 was most impressive, indicating strong confidence on the part of the world financial community in the future of the island. The Hang Seng Index closed at 2,696.44 on December 31, 1988, up from 1,750 a year earlier.

Based on these developments, one can conclude that Hong Kong is becoming a more important financial center by the year. This writer contends that the regulation of the markets helped pave the way. Hong Kong's future appears

Exhibit 6.6
Stock Market Capitalization as a Percentage of GNP and P/E Ratios

	Capitalization % of GNP	PE ratios	Per capita income
Hong Kong	159.7	9.3	8,227
Japan	143.6	68.5	21,100
Taiwan	128.2	25.0	5,936
Singapore	114.9	22.0	7,495
United Kingdom	85.6	11.1	11,605
Malaysia	85.0	20.0	1,809
Australia	55.8	13.1	12,032
South Korea	44.8	26.6	2,826
US	42.2	11.8	18,565
Thailand	21.4	12.2	962
India	9.8	10.7	310
Indonesia	0.1	4.0	500

Source: Asian Finance, 15 May 1988.

secure unless another cultural revolution or a significant form of revisionism befalls mainland China.

Conclusions

The Hong Kong financial markets remain the freest of markets with all the mystery, dynamism, and abuse associated with such markets. The economy was operating according to the prescription and spirit of Adam Smith. Balance of payments surpluses reflected themselves in an increased money supply which produced inflation and ultimately eliminated the surplus. The government did not have the necessary structure for an interventionist policy. Furthermore, the existing system had an inherent flaw in that it allowed commercial banks to act as lenders of last resort (to self-insure) at a time when Hong Kong did not have (and still does not have) a deposit insurance scheme like the FDIC. Also, banks are allowed to maintain "inner reserves," which are never disclosed to the public. These reserves allow banks to manipulate their profits by transferring funds in and out of the reserve account. Therefore, technically, a bank can report profits when in fact it has incurred a loss. This does not do much to increase the confidence of depositors or shareholders and allows for manipulations by insiders for their private gain.

The changes in the financial markets have been in the right direction. More will be made in the future and are likely to be in the direction of more regulation. The key issue occupying the people of Hong Kong today is not financial in nature but political. The agreement between China and Britain with respect to the return of Hong Kong to Chinese rule has resolved only one issue: Hong Kong will be Chinese in 1997. The major question still outstanding is this: Will it remain a dynamic member of the world free-market-oriented community? The lack of clarity on this continues to haunt many of Hong Kong's residents as they stand in long lines in front of certain embassies trying to buy an insurance policy: another passport.

All the regulatory changes have had a salutary effect on the financial markets. They have provided for a more stable economic environment amidst political uncertainty. How responsible they have been for Hong Kong's economic performance in 1988 is not known for certain.

THE DEREGULATION OF THE AUSTRALIAN FINANCIAL MARKETS

The deregulation of the Australian markets represents both a sharp contrast to the Hong Kong case and a political contradiction because it evolved and matured under a government that gained office promising strict regulation in the grand old tradition of socialist governments.

Australia is an island continent the size of the continental U.S. with a population of only 16.2 million and a 1988 GDP of $193.2 billion. Its trade and current account deficits have persisted since 1985. During 1988, the current account deficit was averaging $1.2 billion a month despite fiscal and monetary restraints and a depreciated Australian dollar. This deficit combined with local net investment needs to produce a huge external debt of $60 billion.

The political structure in Australia is particularly relevant to this analysis. The reason is that in 1983, Australia appeared to be on its way to becoming more insular and protectionist. The Australian Labor Party (ALP) led by Robert Hawke was swept into power in 1983 on a platform pledging "to control wages, reduce unemployment and stimulate output through expansionary budget deficit and rapid monetary growth." The country was in serious economic difficulty: real wages and commodity (export) prices in the world markets were falling, while unemployment (10.4 percent), budget and trade deficits, and foreign debt were rising. The resolution of these problems required, it turned out, a drastic change in the proposed economic program. Hawke began, out of necessity, to speak and act as if he were a leader of the Liberal Party, not the ALP. The opening of the Australian financial markets became an integral part of the economic revitalization plan and a natural continuation of a worldwide trend which started in the United States.

The major reforms of the Australian financial markets were triggered by the Campbell Report in 1979, followed by the Martin Report in 1983. Both reports recommended the dismantling of the country's traditional protectionist policies. The latest deregulation focused on the banking industry, and primarily on the entry of foreign banks since February 1985.

This analysis will concentrate on the deregulation of the banking sector, the securities market, and the currency markets, and on the impact of this deregulation.

The Australian Banking System

There are currently 29 authorized trading banks (authorized commercial banks). The rest of the banking system is comprised of the Reserve Bank (the Australian central bank), 16 savings banks, and 2 specialized banks: the Commonwealth Development Bank and the Australian Resource Development Bank (Exhibit 6.7).

As seen in Exhibit 6.7, the trading banks are the most important of Australia's financial institutions. Their total assets amounted to 57.8 percent of the assets of all financial institutions. In addition to commercial banking, most trading banks conduct a wide range of other activities through subsidiary and affiliated companies, such as savings banks, merchant banks, finance companies, insurance companies, unit trusts, stockbrokers, futures and bullion dealers, and trustee companies. It is obvious from this that there is no Glass–Steagall Act in Australia and that the reach of banks into all forms of financial services is wide indeed.

The four major trading banks (the so-called "Big Four") with their nationwide

Exhibit 6.7
Australian Banks by Type and Total Assets

%		A$m
11.2	Reserve Bank (1)	25,552.0
57.8	Trading Banks (29)	131,323.4
30.0	Savings Banks (16)	68,039.9
1.0	Special Banks (2)	2,073.7
100.0	Total (48)	226,989.0

Source: Commonwealth of Australia Gazette, 25 May 1988.

branch networks have dominated the commercial banking industry in Australia. The Big Four's assets accounted for 73.4 percent of the assets of the financial sector and for 88 percent of the industry's 5,268 domestic branch offices in 1987.

These and other banks are regulated and supervised by the Reserve Bank of Australia, established in 1960. In addition, the central bank is, unlike in Hong Kong where no central bank exists, in charge of the conduct of monetary policy, is the banker for the government and for other banks and authorized money market dealers, manages foreign exchange holdings, and exercises whatever control the government wishes to exercise over the foreign exchange market. Trading banks are required to hold reserves against deposits and to report regularly to the Reserve Bank, which also regulates savings banks.

Other financial institutions play a significant role in the Australian economy. They include special purpose banks which are largely government owned, merchant banks, finance companies, building societies, pension funds, insurance companies, credit unions, and unit trusts.

The rest of the banking sector can be divided into five groups:

- The general banking divisions of three state trading banks, which operate primarily within their own states

- The three smaller Australian banks

- The three foreign banks that had branch representation in Australia prior to the postwar period and operate as direct branch offices of their foreign parents

- The 15 foreign-controlled trading banks, approved on February 27, 1985 (J. P. Morgan & Co., though approved, had not commenced business.)

- The newest trading bank, the Primary Industry Bank of Australia, which must still hold at least 50 percent of its assets in agriculture and the agricultural industry

The Australian Financial Market Structure
before Deregulation

The banking industry in Australia before deregulation was characterized by heavy government control of interest rates and protection from foreign bank entry. Government control of interest rates and the willingness of bank depositors to use noninterest-bearing demand deposit accounts helped the trading banks in offering corporate borrowers the lowest-cost funds in Australia. While government controls kept bank loan charges artificially low, they also limited the ability of banks to fund their assets by attracting deposits through higher rates.[6]

The protection from foreign competition allowed the four-member oligopoly—Westpac, National Australia, ANZ, and Commonwealth Banking Corporation (government owned)—to dominate the market and become some of the most profitable banks in the world.

The Deregulation Process

The deregulation of the Australian financial markets was initiated with the establishment of the Campbell Committee on January 18, 1979. The committee was asked to examine the operations and regulation of Australia's financial system and to make recommendations to improve its effectiveness. The main theme of the committee's report, issued on September 29, 1981, was that government involvement in the financial markets should be minimized and, where possible, removed. The major recommendations of the committee are listed in Exhibit 6.8. They focus on three areas: decontrolling interest and exchange rates, allowing foreign competition on a "level playing field," and protecting investors.

Not to be outdone by the previous government, the Hawke Labor government commissioned a new group—the Martin Review Group—to further study the financial markets of Australia and make recommendations. The main results are

Exhibit 6.8
Selected Campbell Committee Recommendations

- Remove direct interest rate controls from the Banking Act and Financial Corporations Act.

- Remove exchange controls.

- License domestic institutions as trading banks so long as they are of sound standing.

- Restrict new foreign participation Australian banking only by the number of licenses granted.

- Banking licenses issued to non-residents should carry no different requirements than those held by residents.

- No direct controls on size or growth of lending nor any restrictions on deposit-taking by banks, building societies, credit unions and other deposit-takers.

- Allow exchange rates to be determined by market forces.

- Remove captive market arrangements for financial institutions to hold Government securities or to provide funds to Federal Government or its agencies at less than market rates of interest.

- Provide greater protection for investors and depositors with financial institutions.

Source: Michael Skully, *Financial Institutions and Markets in the Southwest Pacific* (London: Macmillan Press, 1985).

Exhibit 6.9
Selected Martin Review Group Recommendations

- Remove the 14- and 30-day rule restriction on bank deposits.

- Remove the 60 per cent limit on trading bank ownership of merchant banks.

- Give non-bank financial institutions access to the cheque clearing system.

- Do not proclaim Part IV of the Financial Corporations Act.

- Remove all interest rate controls on banks.

- Develop a secondary mortgage market.

- Grant four to six banking licenses through a one-off tender.

- Consider the possibility of additional foreign exchange dealers.

- Abolish remaining captive market requirements for financial institutions to hold government securities.

- Adopt a more flexible approach to foreign investment particularly for restructuring present ownership.

Source: Australian Financial System: Report of the Review Group (Canberra: Australian Government Publishing Service, 1984).

shown in Exhibit 6.9. They call for further liberalization of the financial markets, more competition in the banking industry, and complete decontrol of interest rates.

Following the recommendations of the Campbell Committee and the Martin Review Group, the government lifted the restrictions on foreign bank entry in Australia. By February 27, 1985, 16 foreign banks had been granted licenses to compete in the Australian banking market. The American banks involved in this effort were predictable: Citibank, Chase Manhattan Bank, Bank of America, J. P. Morgan, and Bankers Trust. Other significant changes took place before 1985, as Exhibit 6.10 shows.

The deregulation momentum continued, yet the Reserve Bank continued to exercise considerable powers, albeit with considerable changes in the regulation or the approach to implementation. Statutory reserve deposits are a case in point.

The statutory reserve deposit (SRD) system has been in existence since 1960. In December 1983, the reserve requirement stood at 7 percent. This sum is kept with the Reserve Bank in a special account. The utilization of the SRD system became optional so long as the banks honored the liquid assets and government securities convention which called for trading banks to hold a certain percentage (23 percent lately) of their assets in specific liquid assets made up largely of government securities. This restricts the composition of the asset portfolio, but, unlike the Fed requirements in the United States, the restricted assets earn market rates of interest. Should these restrictions prove insufficient for the government to effect policy objectives, direct controls of all forms can be used. During 1987,

Exhibit 6.10
Regulatory Changes in Australia

January 1979 - The Committee of Inquiry into the Australian Financial System was established. The "Campbell Committee" issued its Interim Report in May 1980, and its Final Report in September 1981. The Committee's findings provided a major impetus to the deregulation of the financial system which occurred in the 1980s.

December 1979 - Treasury notes were offered at tender for the first time.

December 1980 - Ceilings on interest rates paid on bank deposits were removed. While movement in the direction of freer markets had been under way for a number of years, this was one of the first big steps in the deregulatory process which took place in the first half of the 1980s.

June 1982 - The Loan council agreed to the introduction of a tender system for Treasury bonds. The first tender was announced in July 1982. This together with the tender arrangements for Treasury notes, improved the processes of debt and liquidity management.

Source: Michael Skully, *Financial Institutions and Markets in the Southwest Pacific* (London: Macmillan, 1985).

the government announced that the SRD requirement of 7 percent of deposits will be replaced by a non-callable deposit requirement equal to 1 percent of total liabilities. This applied to commercial as well as savings banks; the latter institutions were not required to hold SRDs.

Another potent regulatory measure is the capital adequacy requirement. Until recently, this ratio was 6 percent for banks established before 1981 and 6.5 percent for those banks established later. Late in 1988, a minimum 8 percent ratio of equity to weighted risky assets was adopted, putting Australia at par with the rest of the world banking community which was trying to cope with the huge expansion of off-balance-sheet banking activities and the riskiness they bring to the banking sector.

Australia, again learning from developments elsewhere, introduced offshore banking units (OBU). Any trading bank or merchant bank registered as a foreign exchange dealer in Australia may be licensed to operate an OBU. The interest on deposits in OBUs is exempt from withholding taxes.

These and other changes helped Australia achieve a competitive position in the world banking community.

Developments in the Securities Markets

The developments in the securities markets paralleled in many ways those of Hong Kong. On April 1, 1987, the six regional exchanges at Adelaide, Brisbane, Hobart, Melbourne, Perth, and Sydney merged into a new national exchange known as the Australian Stock Exchange (ASE). This new exchange allowed Australia to compete regionally and internationally. The ASE continued the listing of foreign firms, and American, New Zealand, and other foreign companies have listed. This is similar to the situation in which Australian companies trade on the New York Stock Exchange in the form of American Depository Receipts (ADRs). The ASE has also set up international linkages with exchanges in Canada and the Netherlands.

The centralization of securities trading allowed for predictable and necessary technological changes. A new electronic trading system, referred to as SEATS (Stock Exchange Automated Trading System), was set up. This system was later supplemented by CENSAS (Central Scrip and Settlement System) to allow for a larger trade volume and for international trading.

The regulation of this industry was almost nonexistent until 1979. Prior to that date, securities regulations were only state regulations and were ineffectual for all practical purposes. In 1979, a new national regulatory system was agreed to by the states and the commonwealth (the government of Australia). The National Companies and Securities Commission (NCSC) was created to coordinate state regulatory functions and oversee securities firms. Despite this step, the Australian market is underregulated when compared with any other major financial center. In 1990 the NCSC was replaced by the Australian Securities Commission.

Another major development in the Australian securities markets was the expansion of the Sydney Futures Exchange, Ltd. (SFE). This exchange, established in 1960, traded commodities futures initially and moved into financial futures in the 1980s. Today, it trades a stock index futures contract under the unusual name of All Ordinaries Share Price Index futures, a 90-day bank bills contract, and 10-year and 3-year Australian Treasury bonds and Australian dollar contracts. At the end of 1986, the SFE linked up with the COMEX of New York for gold futures trading and with the LIFFE of London for U.S. Treasury bonds and Eurodollar futures contracts trading. Traders may deal on either exchange with a right of offset. This effectively links the exchanges in time and contributes to making the futures market a 24-hour market.

Today, the SFE ranks as the tenth largest futures exchange, with an average daily turnover of 25,000 contracts. The SFE allows for individual and corporate membership, and associate memberships are also available.

On the foreign exchange front, the Australian currency system was changed from a fixed to a floating exchange rate regime in December 1983, almost 10 years after the U.S. dollar experienced a similar change. The Reserve Bank continued to "manage" the currency through interventions in the spot market. The preceding October, it had withdrawn from the forward market and granted permission to the banks to hold foreign exchange balances. Later, the Australian government was to remove most constraints on foreign exchange dealings so that the movement of capital across its borders would be largely unrestricted.

The Impetus for Deregulation

The impetus for the regulatory changes in Australia was partially discussed earlier. We now consider it in greater detail.

The economic conditions in Australia in the early 1980s were poor. The balance on current account was experiencing substantial and persistent deficits as was the trade account. To discourage imports and encourage exports, the Australian dollar was devalued. Capital inflows came largely in the form of net borrowing. To increase investment (direct and portfolio) capital flows, the government had little choice but to deregulate the financial and foreign exchange markets in order to improve return and decrease special types of risk, such as blockage of funds conversion risk, etc. Thus, deregulation was born partially out of economic necessity.

The competition with Hong Kong and Singapore for funds inflows has required that Australia keep pace with the developments in those two dynamic and very aggressive markets. To be insular means the acceptance of a suboptimal solution.

The appointments of the two committees by two governments at different ends of the political spectrum suggested that the well-educated, well-traveled, and technologically sophisticated Australians were ready for a change. That is in fact why the recommendations of the committees were enthusiastically endorsed and implemented.

The lessons from the other continents were very encouraging. Many experimentations with freer markets in other countries appeared to be working, with handsome dividends to the citizenry. The world was moving toward integration, as evidenced by increased trade, investment flows, and the expected economic integration of Europe in 1992.

The four major Australian banks were well heeled and well situated to compete aggressively in an international market. Like their American counterparts, they welcomed foreign banks and managed to outmaneuver them in practically all areas.

The increased risks, financial and otherwise, resulting from trade and foreign investments had to be hedged. Thus, the introduction of futures contracts and currency swaps involving the Australian dollar was inevitable. The Australian regulators owed it to the citizenry. Even developing countries such as the Philippines had created a futures market.

The Impact of Deregulation

The granting of banking licenses to foreign banks provided for added competition. The intensity grew, but the Big Four trade banks maintained their leadership position, although their net profits were not uniformly impressive in 1987, as Exhibit 6.11 shows.

Yet the results for the first half of 1988 were very impressive, as the Australian economy and the Australian dollar recovered. Westpac's profits increased by 67 percent, ANZ's by 32.5 percent, and NAB's by 72.6 percent.

The share of total banking assets held by local banks was at 90 percent at the end of 1987, well after the foreign bank invasion. One explanation for the failure of foreign banks to penetrate the Australian market is the extensive time Australian banks had to prepare to meet foreign competition head on. They were equipped and ready for competition. New products were introduced, the number of branches was increased, and the quality of the service was improved. Additionally, the four major trading banks were extremely profitable and could meet any challenge from internal or external sources. Furthermore, these four banks were no strangers to competition, having competed successfully in many foreign

Exhibit 6.11
How the Major Banks Fared in 1987

	Westpac	National	ANZ	Commonwealth
Net Profit	A$409m**	A$328m	A$385m	A$192m
	+3.6%	+8%	+22.1%	-33%
Bad and doubtful debts				
	A$309.9m	A$200.3m	A$332m*	
	+30.8%	+91.3%	+69%	+121%
Taxation	A$397.6m	A$276.5m	A$427m	A$180.8m
	+48%	+41.4%	+73.8%	+15.6%
Group assets	A$70.3bn	A$47bn	A$65.3bn	A$43.9bn
	+15.8%	+11%	+15.3%	+10.5%
Return	14.8%	12.5%	13.1%	NA
Previous	18.8%	13%	13.1%	NA
Annual Div	28.5c	24.75c	21c	NA
Previous	28c	24.1c	20.6c	NA

Source: Asian Finance, 15 May 1988.

markets. ANZ, the most international of the four, had been particularly aggressive internationally. In 1984, it purchased London-based Grindlays Bank. Its 1986 profits in the Canadian market, for example, increased by 230.9 percent. Collectively, the Big Four's overseas assets as a percentage of total assets had increased from 24 to 31 percent between 1983 and 1987.[7]

Their lack of success in Australia was doubly disappointing to foreign banks because their initial expectations were particularly high. They had expected to capture 20 percent of the Australian banking market in five years and ended up with about 10 percent. Some banks succeeded; others experienced disappointment. Citibank Australia met success in an aggressive pursuit of consumer banking. Bankers Trust was profitable as a result of concentrating on the expansion of its merchant banking network. Bank of Tokyo and Mitsubishi Bank were successful as a result of their concentration on corporate accounts and money market finance. The Hong Kong Bank was not as fortunate: Its results were not as expected, and it had to close two branches.[8]

Foreign banks also failed to realize their objective because

• Australia is overbanked, especially for a country of only 16 million people. There is one branch for every 2,500 Australians, compared with countries that are apparently not overbanked, the U.K. with 1:3,800 and France with 1:5,500. In Australia today, there are 29 trading banks, 15 savings banks, 145 finance companies, 65 building societies,

105 merchant banking groups, 300 credit unions, 95 foreign banks, and 2 development banks. In a country with only 16 million people, it is little wonder that the big bankers themselves say Australia is overbanked. Australia has become one of the toughest banking environments in the world.[9]

- Too many foreign banks were granted licenses. Many had expected 6 to 8 foreign banks to be admitted, rather than 15. Also, the economy has slowed from a growth rate of more than 6 percent in late 1984, when foreign banks were invited to apply, to 2.5 percent in 1987.[10]

- The Big Four have deposit bases of which up to 30 percent is virtually interest-free because of long-established trading bank activities.[11]

- Competition is strong from other financial institutions, notably merchant banks, building societies, credit unions, and finance companies which are trying intensively to lend money to many of the same customers. As a result, lending margins to the corporate sector are at record lows in Australia. For example, margins on lending instruments like bill finance have dropped from a range of 0.5–0.7 percent in 1985 to 0.2–0.3 percent in 1987.[12]

The net results of all these maneuvers are shown in Exhibit 6.12.

The other change of significance was the removal of the statutory reserve deposit by the Reserve Bank. This change would affect the corporate bond market and foreign bank operations in Australia. The advantages of raising money offshore disappeared under the change, the purpose of which was to get commercial banks to lower interest rates.

Exhibit 6.12
Who's Got the Money? A Breakdown of Bank Assets in Australia

NATIONAL	
Commonwealth	17.4%
National	17.3%
Westpac	17.1%
State Bank	17.0%
ANZ	16.0%
New Local	3.7%
FOREIGN	
North America	4.9%
British	1.7%
New Zealand	1.4%
Europe	0.9%
Hongkong Bank	0.8%
Chartered	0.7%
IB	0.4%
Bank of Tokyo	0.2%
Mitsubishi	0.2%
Singapore	0.2%
Bank of China	0.1%

Source: Asia Week (3 June 1988).

Exhibit 6.13
Volume of EuroAustralian Dollar Bonds Launched since January 1987

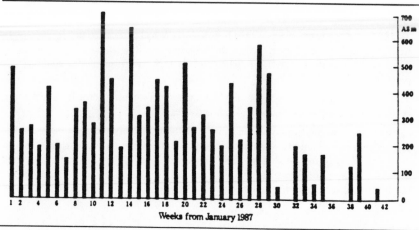

Weeks from January 1987

Source: Hambros Bank.

The securities and foreign exchange markets of Australia were also impacted by deregulation and market liberalization. The adoption of the floating exchange rate system in December 1983 led to very active trading in the Australian dollar, making it the fifth most heavily traded currency in the world. Consequently, EuroAustralian dollar issues began to appear. In 1986, $2 billion worth of these bonds were issued. By the middle of 1987, the market mushroomed by $6 billion. The enthusiasm seemed to wither by the end of 1987, however (Exhibit 6.13). The causes were the market crash and the weakening Australian dollar. The EuroAustralian dollar market was to recover later.

The debt of the commonwealth was A$50.6 billion. The turnover in common-wealth debt was A$874.9 million on February 20, 1989. Approximately A$1 billion of commonwealth debt and A$1 billion of semigovernment debt are traded daily. The debt futures contracts trade approximately A$1 billion daily. New government issues dropped from A$8,740 million in 1986–87 to A$5,936 million in 1987–88. The primary reason was a budget surplus. In terms of performance, the total return (coupon income plus capital growth) measured by the Commonwealth Bank Bond Index was 18.6 percent in 1987 and 9.6 percent in 1988.

The equity markets performed admirably after the merger of the various ex-changes. However, new highs were set only to come crashing down in October, 1987, and the market crash in Australia was perhaps the worst of all. Values on the Sydney exchange dropped 43 percent or $82 billion. This cataclysm called for dramatic action by the government. Budgets were tightened, monetary policy was adjusted, and securities firms came under closer scrutiny. The stock market recovered in 1988.

The changes in market capitalization are shown in Exhibit 6.14. The liquidity of the market as a percentage of average market capitalization was 42.2 percent

Exhibit 6.14
Market Capitalization of the Australian Equity Markets

	31/12/87 $M	31/12/88 $M	Change on Year
Domestic Companies	140,691	156,570	+11.3
Overseas based companies	44,271	52,730	+19.1
	184,962	209,300	+13.2
Options & Convertibles	5,163	4,322	-16.3
Total Value	190,125	213,622	+12.4
Total No. of companies listed	1,453	1,417	-36

Source: John Nolan & Associates, Australia, 1989.

in 1986, 40.2 percent in 1987, and 29.6 percent in 1988 and the early part of 1989. The daily average turnover of stocks was A$305 million in 1987 and A$188.3 million in 1988.

The Australian Stock Exchange introduced stock indices on December 31, 1979. Two types of indices are currently published: price indices with a base of 500 and accumulation indices (price plus dividends) with a base of 1,000. Both types have a December 31, 1979, base period. The distribution of the indices across industries is shown in Exhibit 6.15.

Conclusions

The transformation of the Australian financial markets has been dramatic and has had considerable impact. Except for a few peculiarities, the Australians copied the other markets and proved to themselves in the process that their banking sector was mature enough to handle a deregulated financial environment.

THE DEREGULATION OF THE CANADIAN FINANCIAL MARKETS

The experience of Canada with deregulation places it somewhere between the Big Bang of London and the slow-moving reforms of Japan, but certainly ahead of the United States. The Canadian experience is best described as a series of "small bangs," which effectively blurred, if not eliminated, the walls separating the "four pillars" of its financial system: banks, trust and mortgage loan institutions, insurance companies, and securities dealers.

Any discussion of the regulatory changes in Canada must be prefaced by a comment on the legal (jurisdictional) structure within which the Canadian system functions. The Canadian legal system has recently begun to consider financial institutions as natural persons. Consequently, any legislation can only specify what they cannot do.

The other legal issue deals with the jurisdiction of the province vis-à-vis the federal government in Ottawa. The province has jurisdiction over civil rights and property matters, and because stocks and bonds come under the definition of

Exhibit 6.15
Australian Equity Indices, December 31, 1988

	Index Group	Price Indices	Accumulation Indices	the AOI
1	Gold	1468.4	3738.0	5.4
2	Other Metals	837.9	2044.6	12.2
3	Solid Fuels	505.9	1472.3	1.3
27	ALL MINING	676.8	1712.7	18.9
4	Oil & Gas	546.8	1199.4	3.5
5	Diversified Resources	1057.5	3017.6	8.8
28	ALL RESOURCES	746.5	1926.5	31.2
6	Developers & Contractors	2876.7	8673.1	3.0
7	Building Materials	2064.5	6703.6	5.7
8	Alcohol & Tobacco	5844.1	18644.7	0.9
9	Food H/Hold Goods	3283.2	10566.6	3.8
10	Chemicals	2136.1	7330.1	1.9
11	Engineering	1323.7	4423.4	3.6
12	Paper & Packaging	1843.1	6517.5	3.6
13	Retail	2608.5	8387.2	4.1
14	Transport	2894.6	8896.4	3.6
15	Media	5605.2	1549.2	2.8
16	Banks & Finance	2219.0	7882.0	10.7
17	Insurance	4122.0	11974.4	0.8
18	Entrepreneurial Investors	4716.4	13972.1	3.8
19	Investment, Finance Ser.	2216.5	6800.4	2.0
20	Property Trusts	1023.7	4276.2	3.5
21	Miscellaneous Services	1089.6	3268.8	2.1
22	Miscellaneous Services	1288.4	3899.7	14.6
23	Diversified Resources	3575.0	11869.6	13.0
29	All Industrials	2477.7	7983.6	68.8
30	All Ordinaries	1487.4	4334.9	100.0
26	Twenty Leaders	706.8	4163.5	47.9
31	Fifty Leaders	1385.5	4051.2	71.5

Source: Collins Associates, Newport Beach, Calif., 21 February 1989.

AOI is index number 30—the "All Ordinaries Index."

property, they become subject to provincial laws and regulations. This makes it particularly difficult to have a uniform, coherent national policy, and even more difficult to negotiate agreements with other countries. Banks, trust companies, and insurance companies come under federal jurisdiction, by contrast.

The conflicts between the jurisdictional powers of the provinces were evident in a recent case in which the province of Ontario would have exclusive jurisdiction over securities firms operating in the province while Ottawa would have jurisdiction over foreign bank entry into Ontario. A similar deal could not be struck between Ottawa and Quebec, for example.

The Old Regulatory Structure

The old Canadian system of financial regulation was strict in terms of permissible activities for specific financial institutions and in terms of the definition of a bank, an insurance company, etc. All financial institutions had restricted domains.

Insurance companies were regulated by a law dating back to the early 1900s. The restrictions imposed dealt primarily with the type of business allowed and the investments that could be undertaken.

Trust companies were a late nineteenth century introduction. They specialized in providing executor, administrator, and trustee services and in booking mortgages. Trust companies were prohibited from issuing debentures, taking deposits, and making commercial loans, and their asset portfolios were limited to certain investments and loan categories.

The bank structure dates back to 1822. Banks were subject to interest rate ceilings, were unable to book consumer or mortgage loans (until 1967), and were not permitted any incursion into the securities dealing industry. There were more Canadian operations overseas and more across provinces. All this had to change, and it did as Canada decided to become a major force in the international financial markets. The internal conditions were simply too restrictive.

The securities industry was initially the domain of banks. It began, as in the United States, with the underwriting of government securities. The early 1900s marked the emergence of investment dealers as issuers of corporate and government securities. These firms were barred from accepting deposits and generally from entering the domains of the three other categories of financial institution.

For many reasons, today's Canadian institutions do not resemble their predecessors in several major ways.

The Impetus for Change

There is little that is particularly Canadian in the transformation of the Canadian financial markets. The developments therein parallel those in many markets. The differences lie in the speed and level of the adjustments and in the political and economic circumstances.

The Canadian economic environment played a major role in the deregulation of the financial markets. During the 1960s and 1970s, the volatility of interest rates, the changing needs of Canadian corporations, and the need for flexibility within banks to be responsive to client needs played a major role in the generation of pressure for change. Volatile interest rates meant less stable portfolios, requiring much more flexible asset and liability structures in order to develop natural hedges. Corporations wanting to ride the yield curve or to test their expectations about yield curves shifted out of necessity during that period into short-term maturities. Banks were not sufficiently free to respond and consequently had to watch their traditional loan business slip away into securities issued by corporations desperate for short-term funds. This new business opportunity propelled many nonbanking firms into seeking ways to capitalize on it, thus providing more competition for banks and putting greater pressure on regulators.

The second factor, related to the one just mentioned, was the need to diversify the bank portfolio in order to arrive at a higher efficiency frontier. Diversification was to take different forms: geographic, industry (client), input (sources of funds), and asset/investment structure. The constraints were almost purely regulatory because the major Canadian banks possessed the resources—financial and human—to achieve whatever level of diversification they desired.

As in all deregulation cases we have examined in this study, technology played a major role. The cost of technology was becoming more and more reasonable, the power greater and greater, and the reach wider and wider. In addition, Canada had the trained work force necessary to make technology work in improving the performance of its banks, at both the domestic and the international levels.

The financial services industry was becoming, at that time, more competitive and more international. The domestic securities industry needed a strong injection of capital and expertise in order to meet world standards. The deregulation of the financial markets was a necessary ingredient in this process.

Also, the emergence in Canada of financial conglomerates which were aggressively pursuing traditional banking business produced a situation that necessitated a radical change in the banking industry, lest the payment system and the adequate financing of Canada's economic growth be placed in jeopardy. Adding to the pressures was the acquisition of major trust companies by commercial entities. One glaring example is the acquisition of Canada Trust (Can$64 billion in assets) by Imasco—a huge conglomerate.

Two additional factors made deregulation quite necessary: The first is bank and trust failures. Crown Trust, two western Canadian banks, and several smaller banks failed. One reason for these failures was the insufficient flexibility of the regulatory system. The second reason for deregulation was the need for reciprocal treatment. Canadian banks were setting up overseas operations in large numbers. They could not continue to do so unless they allowed foreign banks into their market to do essentially the same business permitted Canadian banks in the host markets. American banks were putting pressure on Canada with the hope that a successful experimentation in a neighboring country might produce, for example, a repeal of the Glass–Steagall Act. As it turned out, the Canadian

Parliament was much more flexible than the U.S. Congress, which still believed that everything of value flows north, not south.

These major factors and others of lesser importance combined to produce the changes we discuss below.

The New Era

The regulatory changes dramatically affected each of the pillars of the financial system, causing the walls separating them to crumble. As in the U.S. case, many of the changes were brought about by the banks' endless ability to find ways to circumvent regulation, and others by the changes in laws and regulations produced by economic reality and by a built-in legal exigency: Canadian banking laws have a 10-year sunset provision.

Three major regulatory changes transformed the Canadian financial markets: the first occurred in 1967, the second in 1980, and the third in 1986.

The Bank Act was revised in 1967. The revision did away with interest rate ceilings (about 20 years before this occurred the United States) and granted banks more freedom to compete with trust companies. Banks were allowed to provide consumer and mortgage loans under the new law.

By 1980, Canadian banks consisted of six large national banks, referred to as Schedule A banks, and two regional banks. Closely held ownership was not permitted at Schedule A banks. These banks had 3,500 branches in Canada and offices in 40 countries. Canadian banks were protected by law from foreign competition in their home country. However, all this changed in 1980, as foreign banks were allowed entry into the lucrative Canadian market. Within five years, 59 foreign banks had set up subsidiaries in Canada. These subsidiaries are referred to as Schedule B banks, as are Canadian Banks where one party holds more than 10 percent of outstanding shares.

Under the act permitting foreign banks, the definition of bank was very broad indeed. Reciprocity between the home country and Canada was paramount. The acquisition of more than 10 percent of the voting shares of any financial institution would require the consent of the Cabinet prior to the commitment of funds. The acquisition of 100 percent of a Canadian securities dealer was made possible in 1986. This initially presented a problem to American banks as the U.S. government does not reciprocate. However, this was overcome.

The foreign banks operating in Canada multiplied—and prospered. However, Canadian regulation does place a ceiling on the market share they can hold (currently 16 percent). This is so because Canada is intent on preserving a fundamentally Canadian character for its banking industry.

The third "mini-bang" was the outcome of the Commission of Inquiry set up after the failure of the Canadian Commercial and Northland Banks in 1985. The commission, chaired by Justice Willard Z. Estey, issued its report, "New Directions for the Financial Sector," on December 16, 1986. The commission intended to integrate the financial services sector, to check the growth of commercial and financial institutions' linkages, and to provide for a new framework for prudential regulation and supervision. The report contained 46 recommendations for strengthening bank supervision, and most were adopted. The 1986 bills that followed the report allowed for the following occurrences.

The Office of Superintendent of Financial Institutions was created to replace the Department of Superintendent of Insurance and the Office of Inspector General of Banks. The new agency had much greater regulatory authority than its predecessors did.

Trust companies, insurance companies, and banks were granted permission to acquire securities dealers. However, banks, including foreign banks, are not permitted to underwrite securities or insurance directly or indirectly. They may, however, own securities dealers and insurance and trust companies. They may also set up holding companies that can own different financial institutions, provided they are adequately controlled so all dealings are at arm's length. In November 1986, the province of Quebec was the first to grant a bank, the Bank of Nova Scotia, permission to open such a holding company, Scotia Securities. The snowball rolled fast thereafter. But these changes did not put all institutions on a level playing field, and trust companies and financial conglomerates may still have an edge.

Trust companies evolved and learned to circumvent regulations prohibiting deposit taking. They took in funds initially as guaranteed investment certificates and were finally allowed to accept deposits, even without reserve requirements. They were allowed, in addition, to make unsecured loans, restricted commercial loans, and an expanded set of permissible investments.

The securities industry's horizons and possibilities were also expanded. It became less narrow and specialized, began to pay interest on clients' credit balances (copying the American experience), and even offered checking account services.

Insurance companies were no longer restricted to life and other insurance activities. They began to compete aggressively with deposit-taking institutions through the administration of group pension contracts, the sale of life insurance with savings features, and the sale of deferred annuities. Their investment opportunity set was also enlarged significantly.

In conclusion, the changes reduced markedly the distinctions among the different "pillars" and allowed them to compete aggressively, domestically and internationally, under the sharper, more watchful eyes of a more streamlined and powerful supervisory agency.

The Impact of Deregulation

The deregulation of the Canadian financial markets produced a greater sentiment for the separation of financial services and commerce. The concerns were with self-dealing and abusive practices and with the undue concentration of economic power. The lines of demarcation between banking and investment banking disappeared in most cases. This rapprochement, while sanctioned, had to be controlled effectively. Consequently, new "regulations" emerged as the markets were being deregulated:

- A new requirement for a minimum number of independent directors
- More stringent rules on transactions with related parties: officers, directors, auditors, and anyone owning more than 10 percent of any class of shares

Deregulation also brought about increased competition in most markets. Financial firms of all types became "leaner and meaner," and margins dropped on most lines of business. The system suddenly was in need of better warning signals and better risk-measuring devices. Regulators were hard at work developing precisely those tools. The risk-adjusted capital base requirements were an example of the outcome.

The acquisition of financial firms from within the industry and by nonfinancial conglomerates was very prevalent. Hundreds of cases can be cited; among them are the more recent ones reported in *Euromoney:*

- Canadian Imperial Bank of Commerce purchased 63 percent of Wood Gundy at 2.1 times book value for a package of cash and stock valued at Can$190 million (US$157 million).
- Bank of Montreal bought 75 percent of Nesbitt Thompson for Can$280 million (US$232 million) or 2.75 times book value.
- Bank of Nova Scotia acquired McLeod Young Weir for Can$419 million (US$347 million) or 2.1 times book value.
- Royal Bank of Canada had 67.2 percent of Dominion Securities as of November 1988 and will be increasing this stake to 75 percent over the next 3 years, the total price being Can$385 million (US$319 million).
- National Bank of Canada acquired 73 percent of Levesque Beaubien, the largest French-speaking dealer, for a package valued at Can$100 million (US$83 million).
- The California-based Security Pacific Bank acquired 30 percent of Burns Fry for US$75.8 million in the summer of 1988. This was the only non-Canadian acquisition.[13]

Foreign banks, especially U.S. banks, were very active in the Canadian market. By 1988, 18 U.S. banks had established Schedule B banks in Canada. The most profitable was Citibank Canada, with total net profits equal to more than four times those of its nearest American rival: Morgan Bank. The Japanese banks are also heavily involved. Their strongest representation has come from Sumitomo Bank, the second largest in Japan.

The mergers and the influx of foreign financial institutions into Canada brought huge capital inflows. The resulting institutions were better capitalized, enjoyed a wider product range, and were more competitive internationally. A smaller number of independent Canadian dealers did not turn out to be the disaster some had predicted. In fact, several institutions, Canadian and foreign, operating in Canada were showing record profits despite increased competition. The profits of U.S. Mellon Bank and Australian ANZ Bank increased by 275.2 percent and 230 percent, respectively, in 1986 alone.

The Canadian dollar was generally allowed the freedom of the marketplace. A strong Canadian dollar Eurobond market developed, as shown in Exhibit 6.16.

Exhibit 6.16
Canadian $ Eurobond Issues, January 1980–March 31, 1987

(C$ million)	Sovereign/Govt Amount	Issues	Authorities Amount	Issues	Supranational Amount	Issues	Other public Amount	Issues	Other private Amount	Issues	Total Amount	Issues
Fixed rate	350.00	3	3,512.60	63	718.00	8	3,112.90	46	12,008.00	170	19,701.50	290
Fixed rate extendable		0	150.00	1		0		0		0	150.00	1
Fixed rate zero coupon		0		0		0		0	45.00	1	45.00	1
Fixed rate + warrants for debt		0		0		0		0	75.00	1	75.00	1
Fixed rate adjustable		0	220.00	3		0	70.00	1	285.00	5	575.00	9
Fixed Rate:	350.00	3	3,882.60	67	718.00	8	3,182.90	47	12,413.00	177	20,546.50	302
Convertible:		0		0		0		0	120.00	3	120.00	3
Floating Rate:		0	75.00	1		0		0		0	75.00	1
Total of issues used (C$):	350.00	3	3,957.60	68	718.00	8	3,182.90	47	12,533.00	180	20,741.50	306

Source: "Special Survey," *Euromoney* (May 1987). Reprinted with permission.

The Export Development Corporation of Canada has been a very active participant in the Euromarket: "It is the most significant Euro, CD borrower. Its offerings are known as treasury notes (those with less than one year to maturity) and Swiss investors own 70% of the more than U.S. $300 million outstanding."[14]

The equities markets, domestic (Canadian) and international, were active with Canadian issues. Bell Canada Enterprises was the early issuer of international equities back in 1983. It was also the first Canadian company to raise capital in Japan. In 1986, "it sold 5 million shares and raised $191.8 million. The issue was priced in Canadian dollars at 1% discount to the closing price on the Toronto Stock Exchange on the pricing date."[15] This confirms, once again, the international character of the financial markets and the desire of Canada to be a major player and beneficiary.

The domestic Canadian equity markets also reflect the new vibrancy of the Canadian economy. The October 19 crash did not spare Canada, as we discuss below.

Canada has three major stock exchanges and one futures exchange: the Montreal Exchange, the Toronto Stock Exchange, the Vancouver Stock Exchange, and the Toronto Futures Exchange. The Toronto Stock Exchange is dominant.

All the exchanges are placing considerable emphasis on technology and product development, reflecting developments in the United States and other financial markets. The Toronto Stock Exchange developed a Computer Assisted Trading System (CATS) through which more than half of the 1,700 listed stocks are traded (not without resistance from floor traders). These stocks tend to be the less active ones. The Vancouver Stock Exchange is also well computerized and is connected internationally with the Montreal, Sydney, and Amsterdam exchanges via the International Options Clearing Corporation.

The value of shares listed on the Toronto Stock Exchange was Can$608.9 billion in 1986, Can$737 billion in 1987, and Can$727.5 billion in 1988. The decrease in 1988 was due to several factors: the lasting effects of the October 19 crash, the competition from the other exchanges, and the less than rosy predictions for the Canadian economy. New issues on the exchange totaled 175, 190, and 89 for 1986, 1987, and 1988, respectively. Supplementary issues by already listed companies were 67, 68, and 25 for 1986, 1987, and 1988, respectively.

The Toronto Stock Exchange Composite Index showed steady growth between 1985 and 1988:

1985	2900.60
1986	3066.18
1987	3160.05
1988	3389.99

The October 19 crash brought the index down by 400.4 points (less than the drop in the United States) from an all-time high of 3,598.6 on the Friday preceding the crash.

The Montreal Stock Exchange, the second largest in Canada and Canada's leading futures and options market, also benefited from increased economic activity in Canada. Its Canadian market portfolio index (25 stocks) closed at 1,533.46 in 1986, 1,589.61 in 1987, and 1,698 in 1988. The market crash was a bit less severe on the Montreal Stock Exchange than on the Toronto Stock Exchange. The index fell 167.88 points on that day, from a high of 1,762.03.

The Vancouver Stock Exchange is an exchange with a different character. It is primarily a vehicle for raising venture capital. Its 2,300 listed companies are primary-resource-based, with a large percentage from the technology sector.

The futures and options markets are active but well behind their American counterparts. Stock index futures contracts were introduced in 1984 but were not very successful. The first contract covered 300 stocks, and the results were as follows:

	Total Cumulative Volume	Open Interest at Year End
1984	19014	315
1985	25050	382
1986	51491	0

The index futures contract on 35 shares was introduced in early 1987. Within 2 years it proved to be much more successful than its predecessors were. The results for 1987 and 1988 were 367 and 800, respectively, in open interest. This is a far cry from the open interest in many other index futures contracts such as those on the S&P 500 (120,212 as of March 1989).

These and other products that are more successful, such as equity options traded on the Montreal Stock Exchange (and introduced on the Toronto Stock Exchange in 1989), are steps in the right direction as they offer Canadian and foreign portfolio managers a larger set of choices in dealing with portfolio risk and other risks present in various markets and instruments.

Conclusions

The transformation of the Canadian financial markets has been deep and wide. It has touched every segment of the Canadian economy and every Canadian, directly or indirectly. The impetus, nature, and impact of this transformation are not much different from those of Australia except for the fact that Canada is next door to a financial, economic, and military giant and spans different time zones. The political and competitive structure within which Canada operates is radically different from that of Australia, although both are part of the British Commonwealth and of the world financial system. The integration of Canada's (and Australia's) financial markets has not and is not likely to completely decimate the national character of those markets. The financial markets of Canada and Australia will continue to evolve, as will those of Hong Kong, albeit from a different direction.

NOTES

1. The Economist, *Intelligence Unit Country Profile: Hong Kong, Macau* (London: Economist Publications Ltd., 1986).

2. See David G. Lethbridge, *The Business Environment in Hong Kong* (Oxford, England: Oxford University Press, 1980): 159–99.

3. Maximillian J. B. Hall, "The Reform of Banking Supervision in Hong Kong," *Hong Kong Economic Papers* 16 (1988): 74–96.

4. Monetary Statistics Ordinance, November–December 1988, 13.

5. See Hong Kong Securities Review Committee, "The Operation and Regulation of the Hong Kong Securities Industry: Report of the Securities Review Committee" (Hong Kong, 1988).

6. See Michael T. Skully, "Australian Banking, Its Regulation and Internationalization," paper presented at Pacific Asian Management Institution, University of Hawaii, 1988.

7. See Skully, "Australian Banking."

8. See *Asian Business* (July 1988).

9. "The Invasion That Fizzled," *Asia Week* (3 June 1988): 48–49.

10. Franklin R. Edwards, "Can Regulatory Reform Prevent the Impending Disaster in Financial Markets?" *Economic Review* 73, no. 1 (January 1988).

11. Stephen Hughes, "A Place in the Sun," *Banker* (November 1987): 24.

12. Edwards, "Can Regulatory Reform Prevent the Impending Disaster in Financial Markets?"

13. Beth McGiddrick, "Little Bang Brings Down Barriers," *Euromoney* (November 1988): 159–62.

14. Ibid.

15. Barry Critchley, "Canada: Europe Comes up with the Goods," *Euromoney* (May 1987): 48–52.

7

The Impact of U.S. Deregulation

The deregulation of the U.S. financial markets began in the 1960s with the introduction of the certificate of deposit by Citicorp. The fundamental objective of this new instrument was the circumvention of Regulation Q, which placed a ceiling on the interest banks were allowed to pay on time deposits. This bold and historic step by Citicorp was mandated neither by law nor by any regulatory agency. Market conditions and competitive pressures produced this first link in the deregulation chain.

The deregulatory cycle accelerated during the 1980s as the financial markets of the world became more mature, as the philosophical orientation of the United States came to be more in tune with the spirit of freer markets under the determined leadership of Ronald Reagan, and as this philosophy became infectious worldwide with Margaret Thatcher of Britain declaring herself as the first disciple.

The economic conditions in the United States and in most developed countries aided the process of deregulation. The United States had begun what turned out to be the longest peacetime expansion in its history (Exhibit 7.1). This expansion continued in 1989 at a robust pace. Good economic times encourage experimentation with new ideas, risky and unconventional as they may be. Regulators and legislators are more apt to look the other way or to accommodate the changes with new legislation or with the elimination of existing legislation during economic prosperity.

The deregulatory process is very dynamic and cumulative. The successful introduction of one instrument encourages the introduction of another in the same country or in a different country. Financial futures contracts encouraged financial

Exhibit 7.1
U.S. Economic Cycles, 1949–Present

	Periods of Growth	Periods of Recession
Oct.'49 - July'53	45*	0
July'53 - May'54	0	10
May'54 - Aug.'57	39	0
Aug.'57 - April'58	0	8
April'58 - April'60	24	0
April'60 - Feb'61	0	10
Feb.'61 - Dec.'69	106**	0
Dec.'69 - Nov.'70	0	11
Nov.'70 - Nov.'73	36	0
Nov.'73 - March'75	0	16
March'75 - Jan.'80	58	0
Jan.'80 - July'80	0	6
July'80 - July'81	12	0
July'81 - Nov.'82	0	16
Nov.'82 - Present	64+***	0

* Korean War
** Vietnam War
*** With the exception of wartime, this is the longest period of economic growth in U.S. history.

Source: Time (21 March 1988).

options contracts in the United States and a large set of strategies culminating in a fertile set of "portfolio insurance" schemes, which ebbed and flowed as portfolio managers learned more about them and as stock market conditions changed.

The fundamental proposition here is that regulation begets circumvention. Once proved successful, it produces an information set which expands nationally and then internationally (often vice versa), culminating in a general acceptance of the product and/or strategy. This can lead to expansion in derivative areas or to reregulation of the market or to development of new regulations to establish boundaries on the market, allowing for the necessary comfort zone for regulators. The cycle is thus established:

Regulation → Circumvention → Deregulation → Innovation →
Market acceptance through information →
Internationalism → More deregulation → Innovation of different types →
Possible reregulation or new forms of regulation

Innovations like the CD are generally a product of the regulatory environment, the economic environment, technology, and competitive forces. The interaction among these different and frequently converging forces produces a new product and strategy mosaic, at times totally different from the initial expectations. It appears that when market forces are set in motion, there is no telling how far they will go and what new character they will mold for the market. This unpredictability, romantic and full of opportunities as it may be, is precisely the wrong medicine for regulatory zeal—thus the tendency for reversion in the deregulatory process.

DEREGULATION AND ECONOMIC POLICY

The conduct of monetary policy and the interest of regulators in protecting the solvency of the banking system place constraints on the operations of banks, some of which are very restrictive and costly. In fact, many of the new instruments and channels of intermediation were designed to circumvent regulatory restrictions. The history of banking (international and domestic) is replete with evidence to this effect. A few examples should suffice.

Major implements to the growth of the Eurodollar market were Regulations Q and I. Regulation Q sets ceilings on the interest rates banks pay on deposits, and Regulation I sets the reserve requirements on U.S. bank deposits. The extent to which banks are able to circumvent these regulations by, for example, internationalizing their operations weakens the ability of the Fed to conduct monetary policy effectively and exposes the banking system to a risk level considered unacceptable by regulators. The monetary policy referred to here is the one intended primarily to deal with economic cycles.

The interest equalization tax, introduced in 1953, was intended to reduce the effective yield on foreign bonds issued in the United States, thereby reducing the incentives for Americans to purchase foreign bonds and, in the process, reducing capital outflows. This then provided incentives to develop alternative markets for dollar-denominated bonds and marked the birth of the Eurobond market and a switch by foreigners from bond financing to bank financing. To deal with the latter problem, the Voluntary Foreign Credit Restraint (VFCR) Act was initiated in 1964 and made mandatory on January 1, 1968. These actions simply induced U.S. banks to go overseas and foreign banks to come to the United States, without achieving their goal: the reduction of the U.S. balance of payment deficit.

The capital requirements set by the Fed have also produced a long list of off-balance-sheet items such as notes issuance facilities, swaps, options, etc. Once again, these make regulators fret with anxiety. This predictably led to the new proposal for a risk-adjusted capital base advanced by the Fed and the Bank of England (see Chapter 2).

The above examples suggest that the higher the interest rates are and the more restrictive the monetary policy is, the more innovative bankers become. Therefore, because deregulation means the abolition of or a significant change in regulations, or the development of mechanisms to circumvent existing regulations, the new products and strategies can only serve to upset the calculations of the monetary authorities.

Deregulation has also served to integrate the financial markets and, in so doing, has increased the interdependence among them and, by necessity, the interdependence among the monetary policies of different countries. The latter implies that it is harder today to conduct an independent monetary policy, and this has led many economists to argue for a coordinated monetary policy among the Western Allies and for a steady growth rate in the money supply to avoid worldwide inflation. The European monetary system is one example of effective coordination of monetary policy. The threshold of divergence is a method for calculating the departure from the expected norm of monetary policy. A member country violating this threshold must adjust its monetary policy to reduce inflationary pressures. It is a matter of time before this is done on the OECD level. This writer's observation is that this is already taking place informally, and quite frequently on a formal basis, through economic summits and consultations among central bankers, foreign ministers, and finance ministers.

The globalization of financial markets has produced a high interest elasticity for capital flows. The net arbitrage margin—the interest differential adjusted for the forward premium or discount—is playing a major role in capital flows. Many countries are adjusting their discount rates—Britain in the early 1980s and Germany, the United States, and Japan in 1988—in order to influence capital flows and their exchange rate. As a consequence:

The exchange rate takes on a greater role in the transmission of monetary policy impulses, since actual or perceived shifts in relative monetary conditions in major markets lead rapidly to exchange rate changes. The external sector thus becomes more important in determining the effects of monetary policy on actual and expected inflation, relative prices, and the level and composition of output. On the other hand, the different adjustment speeds of the real and monetary "sector" of the economy imply a tendency for the exchange rate to overshoot. Thus, there is an increased danger that active use of monetary policy may destabilize exchange rates and, through this channel, the real economy. The increased sensitivity of exchange rates to individual countries' policies also implies that there will tend to be larger spill-over effects on other economies, particularly when the major countries are involved.[1]

The recent behavior of the U.S. stock market confirms this. Any weakness in the U.S. dollar produces concern that the Fed will tighten monetary policy by raising the discount rate, and higher rates will increase capital inflows. This is easier to achieve in the short run than is a dramatic increase in exports. The new technology allows the transfers to be effected almost instantaneously. The problem, however, is that high interest rates are bearish because of their negative effects on investments and, through the multiplier effect, on general economic performance.

The difficulty of conducting monetary policy in a deregulated environment is further compounded by the ability of borrowers to source capital from institutions not subject to the same constraints as banks. The increased reliance on securities issuance, pension fund assets, and private placement with insurance companies is a case in point. Securitization is becoming easier as loan stripping and credit rating companies have become widespread.

The quantum jumps in technology are also troublesome in the conduct of monetary policy. The need for transaction balances is eroding, and with it the demand for the monetary base. This reduces the effectiveness of monetary policy that has the control of the growth in the monetary base as one of its cornerstones. As the definition of "money" becomes more and more malleable, so does the extent of control by the monetary authorities. The control of monetary aggregates becomes a less desirable policy tool than the control of interest rates is.

The other side of the above argument is partially reassuring:

In principle, wider recourse to variable rate financing and to the new risk management techniques makes the financial system more responsive to the actions of the monetary authorities. Changes in the interest rates under the authorities' control are reflected more rapidly and fully in the whole structure of interest rates.[2]

However,

Some of the effects of financial innovation tend to weaken the interest link between monetary policy and the real economy. The greater flexibility of the new financial instruments has made it possible for an increasing number of non-financial enterprises to engage in liquidity management. Debtors may thus be partially shielded against rising interest rates. Moreover, monetary policy can rely less on locking-in effects: in the past, when interest rates were "high" and thought likely to remain so only temporarily, the private sector was induced to postpone its borrowing decisions for fear of being locked-in at the higher interest rates. Extensive recourse to floating rates makes the behavior less common.[3]

The empirical evidence on all the issues relating to deregulation and monetary policy is scattered and frequently contradictory. A study by the Federal Reserve Bank of San Francisco attempts to gauge the effect of deregulation on the behavior of M1. While earlier studies suggested an increased response of M1 to changes in interest rates, this study concludes that

Any tendency for the interest sensitivity of M1 to increase in recent years represents an intermediate rather than a lasting effect of deposit deregulation. In this regard, we think that the behavior of M2, which has undergone more complete deregulation, gives us a view of what deposit deregulation may mean for M1. The behavior of M2 suggests that, with complete deregulation, the long-run response of M1 to changes in interest rates may actually be smaller. In the short run, by contrast, sluggish rate adjustment by banks will result in an exaggerated response of M1 changes in market rates.[4]

The effects of deregulation on fiscal policy are also significant. The twin towers of the federal and the balance of payments deficits could only be financed in one of three ways:

• Monetization of the debt

• Domestic savings

• Foreign savings and accumulated dollars overseas produced by a balance of payments surplus with the United States

The first option was not acceptable because it represented a form of taxation. The second was not possible because U.S. domestic savings were barely sufficient to meet the domestic investment requirements of the business sector. The third option was the only one that made sense under the circumstances. The presence of Japanese investment firms at Treasury auctions is real and, some argue, alarming. The wishes of these firms and their collective bargaining power may have forced the federal government to pay higher rates of interest than it would have under different circumstances.

The effects of deregulation are even more visible in the secondary markets for U.S. government securities. These markets are deeper and more international than ever. The innovations therein are truly historic with bond stripping (Tigers, etc.) and swaps expanding the financial vocabulary and possibilities.

The effects on the fiscal side are also visible in the bailouts of the savings and loans and in the huge write-offs of sovereign debt and real estate loans (in Texas and Oklahoma especially) which have a powerful impact on the tax revenue side. And to the extent that deregulation increased the instability of the financial system, the contingent liability of the U.S. government and consequently the expected tax liability of the U.S. taxpayers have also increased.

The other side of this is that the U.S. government is in a better position to buy time and postpone inflation, and may in fact have succeeded in paying lower rates of interest on its new issues as a result of stiff international competition for default-free, high yielding, and highly liquid investments. The empirical evidence on this issue is lacking. It appears that the net effects on fiscal policy are mixed at best.

The deregulation of financial markets has increased the transmission effects across national borders. A given policy is immediately copied or counteracted in another country. A boom or a bust is immediately transmitted from the United States to other countries, requiring occasional monetary and/or fiscal action. The October 19, 1987, crash was quickly reflected in the stock markets of Japan, Hong Kong, and Europe, compounding the financial cataclysm and requiring immediate action by the central banks. Indeed, a series of articles in *The Wall Street Journal* following the crash documented in painful detail the dramatic actions by the Fed to ensure the liquidity of the financial system. Were it not for these and similar actions overseas, an economic catastrophe would have befallen the world economy. The leadership of the United States in the world, in both good and bad economic times, has been repeatedly documented. The U.S. stock market leads the world stock markets—but that lead is barely a day.[5] This makes the transmission effects practically instantaneous.

DEREGULATION—NEW REGULATION

The changes brought about by deregulation have been widespread and very fundamental in certain cases. The savings and loan industry was severely impacted by deregulation, and its problems were compounded by inept and, in some cases, corrupt management.

The first major deregulation act to pass the U.S. Congress in the 1980s was the Depository Institutions Deregulation and Monetary Control Act. The act began as the Monetary Control Act of 1979 (HR 3864) and three different Senate bills. It was finally passed on March 31, 1980, and signed by President Carter on the same day. The act contained eight titles in total. Title I established uniform reserve requirements across all depository institutions (whether they are Fed members or nonmembers) and effectively reduced the absolute amount of reserves they were supposed to hold. Also, the Federal Reserve System was given control over the reserves of all depository institutions. Title II mandated the phasing out of Regulation Q over a six-year period. All depository institutions were permitted to offer market-determined rates of interest to depositors. Title III allowed savings and loan institutions to diversify their portfolios by investing up to 20 percent of their assets in commercial paper, consumer loans, and corporate debt securities. This put the S&Ls in direct competition with commercial banks for the first time in their long history. The other titles of the act dealt with usury laws and amendments to national banking laws.

The impact of DIDMCA on the market value and risk of depository institutions was studied by Paul R. Allen and William J. Wilhelm,[6] using evidence from the capital markets as suggested by G. William Schwert.[7] Allen and Wilhelm used intervention analysis "to measure the market's reaction to news concerning the evaluation of DIDMCA."[8] Three portfolios of different depository institutions—FRS banks, non-FRS banks, and S&Ls—were investigated:

Taken as a whole the results of this study suggest that DIDMCA had a significant impact on the competitive structure of the depository institutions industry. In particular, FRS banks appeared to have profited at the expense of other parties in the industry.[9]

The study also found "no significant alteration in the systematic risk of any portfolio. Thus, DIDMCA does not appear to have had the risk altering effect suggested by Peltzman."[10]

The results are not surprising because DIDMCA, while liberalizing the portfolio mix of S&Ls, forced them to pay market rates and simultaneously to hold noninterest-bearing reserves. The systematic risk did not change significantly because portfolio diversification simply reduced the unsystematic portion of total risk.

The second major legislative act dealing with depository institutions was Public Law No. 97-326 signed into law by President Reagan on November 15, 1982. This law puts thrift institutions more at par with commercial banks. However, it could have served the nation better if it had abolished S&Ls altogether by giving them (the healthy ones at least) a federal bank charter. There is no potent argument this writer is aware of in favor of maintaining S&Ls as a separate industry with its own FSLIC (now defunct) and supervisory agency.

The 1982 Monetary Control Act, also known as the Garn–St. Germain Depository Institutions Act, amended the Homeowners Loan Act of 1933. It set limits on the aggregate amount of loans to a borrower from an S&L as a percentage of capital, and it specifically authorized lease financing and commercial lending activities. Direct deposit relationships were permitted only with those "persons or organizations that have a business, corporate, commercial or agricultural loan relationship with the association." An S&L may not, however, accept demand deposits from a business entity for "the sole purpose of effectuating payments thereto by a nonbusiness customer."

The act also addressed the form of assistance to thrift institutions, emergency thrift acquisitions, net worth certificates, conversion to federal charters, etc. All these provisions were sought by the S&L industry. The interesting thing, however, is that these provisions did not rescue the industry. The hemorrhaging continued. In early 1989, the S&L industry was losing about $12 billion annually while President Bush and the new Congress were scurrying for solutions.

A study by the Federal Reserve Bank of San Francisco found that most of the S&Ls created their own problems as they "chose not to exercise their asset powers mainly because of the tax advantages associated with residential mortgage lending."[11] Also:

nonmortgage loans account for only a small portion of the rise in the ratio of nonmortgage assets to total assets in recent years. Second, special factors account for the change in "other assets," . . . . For example, included in "other assets" is "good-will and other intangible assets." The value of this asset category was boosted considerably through the purchase accounting procedures used in savings and loan mergers. The rise in the ratio of "other assets" to total assets also reflected savings and loans' investments in their service corporation subsidiaries, a power they already held before MCA [Monetary Control Act].[12]

It is clear, therefore, that the payoffs from the regulatory revisions did not match the initial legislative intent.

Another major change in the banking laws dealt with interstate branching. This change was regressive by design, however. It plugged a loophole in the Bank Holding Company Act of 1956. Under that act, bank holding companies were able to introduce the limited service bank (LSB) concept to expand across state lines. LSBs offered all banking services except deposit taking or commercial loans. Commercial banks were prohibited from engaging in these activities across state lines under the McFadden Act of 1927. The change lasted seven years:

After a long Battle, Congress decided in July 1987 to ban new LSBs and to limit the expansion of the existing 170 LSBs to 7 percent per year. A major defeat of Reagan's deregulation efforts, this ban on LSBs also closed a loophole through which industrial firms, such as Sears or Gulf & Western, had entered the banking business and thereby circumvented the separation of commerce and banking.[13]

Sears Roebuck ended up selling Sears Savings to Citicorp Savings in 1987.

Other recent major changes in regulations contributed to the redefinition of the character of banks. The Office of the Comptroller of Currency (OCC) granted approval in March 1988 for Chase Manhattan Bank to *underwrite* pools of its commercial real estate loans. This was the first time banks were granted approval to underwrite asset-backed securities through their subsidiaries.

In May 1988, the OCC permitted First National Bank of Chicago to operate an arbitrage business in interest rate instruments through FNCB, a futures brokerage subsidiary. This subsidiary was consequently capable of making markets and arbitraging T-bills, CDs GNMAs, and Eurodollar time deposits. The OCC was promised that the bank would not be responsible for any liabilities emanating from exchange membership.

The Federal Reserve Board, in August 1988, approved final risk-based capital standards after a long period of comments by member institutions. The approved standards were endorsed by 12 countries so that risk-based capital rules would be uniform among the signatories to this agreement. The adopted standards were, incidentally, quite different from those initially proposed by the Fed and the Bank of England. The changes were in the assignment of some assets to the various risk categories.

In May 1988, the Federal Reserve Board approved the acquisition of Fairhaven Savings Bank and its real estate investment and development subsidiary by Citizens Financial Group. The real estate subsidiary was to continue operating as a direct subsidiary of the bank. A bank holding company was not required to issue the approval.

The Security Pacific case, also occurring in May 1988, allowed its bank holding subsidiaries to join forces and underwrite $15 million in equity securities from a single issuer, busting the $2 million limit set by law. Also, the subsidiaries were allowed on a trial basis to make subordinate loans to one another to cover their underwriting commitments.

The changes on the state level mirrored the developments at the federal level. In Indiana, for example, nonmember state-chartered banks were allowed to underwrite municipal revenue bonds and to sell mutual funds and mortgage-backed securities. In Minnesota, state banks were given leasing authority similar to that of national banks. Arkansas passed a law permitting interstate banking with 16 other states. In Texas, the court ruled that national banks may branch anywhere in the state. In Mississippi, state-chartered banks were put at par with national banks. In Florida, national banks were permitted to branch statewide, as were thrift institutions.

The above documentation makes clear that one deregulation at one level in one geographic or product area is very likely to produce more deregulation in the financial sector. Occasionally, deregulation begets regulation, which typically stops attempts by financial institutions to circumvent an existing law or regulation. The regulatory process continues with battles fought in the courtroom, the boardroom, or the regulators' towers. There is nothing like success (or the absence of failure), actual or perceived, to encourage regulators to go the extra step.

DEREGULATION AND FINANCIAL INNOVATION

The evidence presented thus far is ample: Deregulation begets innovation (almost by necessity), which begets more deregulation and innovations of different types. The deregulatory and innovation processes are also dependent on the economic environment, technology, and level of competition, the last being a measure of the extent of deregulation.

Competitive pressures in the banking sector forced the disappearance of Regulation Q. They also produced what became known as *unbundling:* the breaking up of the banking service into its component parts and pricing the parts separately, frequently in totally different markets. Interest rate risk produced swaps, interest caps and collars, interest options, futures-like instruments, and a host of strategies (immunization, dedication, etc.) designed to reduce, if not eliminate, it. The income and the risk associated with these activities became of strategic concern to the bank management and to the regulators, and these points of view did not always converge, as the previous sections have demonstrated.

One of the more interesting consequences of these developments is the new reliance of banks on innovative ideas to compete and improve earnings instead of merely increasing their size by increasing their loan portfolio. The value of human capital became, almost surreptitiously, so magnified as to overwhelm the physical and financial resource considerations. A new age has dawned with "quant types" running departments they were previously banned from or ridiculed in.

The unbundling of services and products produced a large array of securities and a host of methods for underwriting and placing them. The financial dictionary had to be expanded markedly to include collar swap, circus, delayed cap FRN, mini-max FRN, Startrek, etc. The underwriting industry added tender acceptance facility, swingline, stop-out bid, grantor underwritten note (GUN), multioption facility (MOF), revolving underwriting facility, and others to their list of underwriting mechanisms. And the revolution continues.

Herbert L. Baer and Christine A. Pavel argue that deregulation has produced a shift in the role of banks "from funding loans to issuing guarantees."[14] The data are clear on this: "'depository institutions' share of total intermediated assets held by households has declined more or less steadily since 1975. [Also,] banks have clearly become less important suppliers of short-term debt." Securitization has allowed the banks to "continue originating and servicing loans while others supply funding and bear at least a portion of the credit risk."

The securitization of bank assets became a necessity as banks attempted to overcome their disadvantage in warehousing loans:

This disadvantage stems from the "regulatory taxes" banks must pay in the form of deposit insurance premiums that do not vary with risk, required reserves that do not bear interest, and mandatory capital requirements that exceed those that banks would maintain in the absence of regulation.

The securitization is evidenced on both the liability and the asset sides of the banks' balance sheets. On the liability side, securitization is reflected in banks' borrowing more intensively in the international bond markets. On the asset side, banks hold more long-term marketable securities than ever before, sell participation, undertake loan swaps and loan sales, and use traditional assets such as mortgages, auto loans, etc., as backing for marketable securities.

The "regulatory taxes" are a major ingredient in financial innovation according to Judd,[15] Pavel and Phillis,[16] Benveniste and Berger,[17] Koppenhaven,[18] and Baer and Pavel.[19] The findings of Baer and Pavel suggest

that many of the problems currently faced by banks result not from fundamental changes in the relative efficiency of bank intermediation but rather from a policy that requires banks to increase their equity to asset ratios without regard for the risk of the underlying assets. The additional funding disadvantage created by double taxation of equity income reduces bank competitiveness in the market for low-risk assets.[20]

While the early 1980s were characterized by unbundling, the 1985–1988 period could be characterized by *rebundling,* which is "the combination of a specific new instrument either with another new instrument or with a security to produce a new product."[21] An example of this is the range forward, which is a combination of two options.

The period of 1985 and beyond saw the following:

- Notes issuance facilities gave way to Eurocommercial paper (ECP).
- Interest swap activities doubled, especially at U.S. branches of foreign banks.
- Securities with embedded options increased markedly.
- The trend continued toward more reliance on the capital markets and less on bank financing.
- Competition intensified in practically all segments of the financial markets.
- Dependence increased on fixed-rate borrowing to lock in the low rates prevalent in most markets.
- Use of swaps to transform liability structures at the time of new financing dominated.
- The institutionalization of saving and the use of professional money managers to manage pools of funds continued.
- Sensitivity to investors' needs increased, as reflected in the design of securities and portfolios.
- A new program began that swaps securities on an "ongoing basis."
- Better models emerged to price swap risk and the risk of warehousing swaps.
- Exchange-traded futures and options grew rapidly all over the world (even Japan allowed its financial institutions to trade options on physical currencies as of March 22, 1988).
- Bonds with embedded forwards (principal redemption linked to an index of commodity price) grew in popularity.

- There was a huge increase in the issuance of bonds with detachable equity warrants (the Japanese use the warrants to circumvent restrictions on the issuance of new equities).
- New risk management tools such as range forwards and collars were introduced.
- There were openings of new exchanges—The Paris Financial Futures Exchange (the MATIF) in February 1987 and the German Options Exchange in 1990.
- A new index for a futures contract (the Nikkei index) was introduced in 1987.
- Trading of U.S. Treasury bond futures contracts began in Sydney and in Singapore.
- New futures markets were launched in Hong Kong and Rio de Janeiro.

All these developments are byproducts of an era in which the regulator opted to oversee the market as it evolved instead of setting its tone and direction. The evolution of the financial markets was predictable in its unpredictability and wide reaching into every segment of the market product, institution, and geographic location. The newly found freedom was exercised in a generally responsible manner. Many ideas and products came and went. Only those that met with a genuine demand stayed in a market with low tolerance for ineffective tools and strategies.

One can only conclude, based on the above, that innovation was driven by the genius (in many cases) and the creativity of the new breed of financial managers. Deregulation provided the playing field—the proper environment in which imagination could be exercised on a rather long leash.

One of the side effects, if not the original intent, is to make the balance sheet of banks more risky because most of these transactions were booked below the line [off the balance sheet (OBS)]. A 1988 report by the U.S. General Accounting Office expressed concern over the trend and attributed it to the following factors:

. . . The absence of certain regulatory costs. OBS activities are not assets nor liabilities, so banks are not routinely required to maintain capital or hold funds in reserve against them.

. . . Increased competition from non-banking institutions. . . .

. . . Fluctuations in interest rates and exchange rates. Banks can use some OBS activities to insulate against potential losses arising from volatile rates.

. . . Technological advances that have facilitated the use of certain automated services, such as electronic payment systems. These have, in turn, given rise to certain types of OBS contingencies.[22]

The size of the activities is staggering. The GAO study calculates, based on the Call Report data, that "OBS activities rose from $1.4 trillion at year-end 1984 to $2 trillion at year-end 1986 . . . 54 and 67 percent of industry assets and 8.8 and 10.8 times the amount of industry equity capital, respectively. In mid-1987, these OBS activities totaled $2.6 trillion."[23] The growth continued through 1988.

The off-balance-sheet activities of commercial banks can be placed into three categories:

- Commitments—e.g., revolving underwriting facilities
- Guarantees—e.g., standby letters of credit
- Market-related transactions—e.g., option contracts, interest and currency swaps, etc.

All OBS activities allow the bank to earn income without having to source funds or set aside capital or reserves. It is, therefore, more lucrative than the typical loan. The problem, however, is that there is no free lunch. The attending risks are many and serious, as noted below.

- *Liquidity Risk.* A banking institution is not able to predict the size and timing of the funding of, for example, a revolving underwriting facility (RUF) commitment. It may have to borrow, if it can, at less than desirable rates.
- *Credit Risk.* An RUF, for example, is exposed in a significant way to credit risk. Since an RUF is a bank commitment to purchase at a specified price the notes its customer cannot sell at or below some predetermined interest cost, the commitment may be exposing the bank to credit risk. A change in the credit quality of the borrower could take place between the time the commitment is made and the time the bank has to purchase the notes. Similarly, the bank is exposed to credit risk in a swap position where it acts as one of the counterparties. In the event of a default by the counterparty, the bank stands to lose a significant sum if the swap is out-of-the-money at the time of default.
- *Settlement Risk.* This risk stems from electronic funds transfers where a bank is making payments throughout the day before securing the funds to cover them. These overdrafts are offset by borrowing in the interbank market or from the Fed. Their daily size is estimated at $120 billion for the entire banking system.
- *Information Risk.* This risk results from the lack of maturity and experience of market participants in adequately pricing a new instrument or the unavailability or inadequacy of information. The inexperience may lead to systematic underpricing of risk, as does the lack of information. Several banks made major mistakes in pricing swaps, and practically all major U.S. banks made a mistake in booking sovereign loans without adequate information; almost universally they based their judgments on antiquated country risk assessment models.
- *Market Liquidity Risk.* The trend toward securitization was hailed as a positive development because it increased the flexibility and liquidity of the bank balance sheet. All is not well in this paradise, however, if everyone attempts to exit the market at the same time. Witness October 19, 1987, and the huge discounts banks were willing to accept on their sovereign debt (sold in whatever form) to simply wipe it off the books.
- *Peculiar Risks.* These risks are specific to certain instruments and represent a major concern to regulators. Currency and interest options are a case in point.

Both the market and credit risk patterns are asymmetrical between writers and buyers of options. With respect to market risk, the buyer has the possibility of unlimited profits if price moves in his favor but this loss is limited to the amount of premium paid (option price) if price moves adversely. Conversely, the writer is limited in his income to the amount of the premium earned, while in principle he is exposed to unlimited loss. With respect to credit risk, the writer of the option is exposed to the buyer for the amount of the premium between the transaction date and the payment of premium. Thereafter, and through the life of the contract, the buyer must take the risk that the writer will fail to meet his obligations, while the writer has no credit risk since the buyer has no obligations to perform.[24]

The concern with the market risk side is understandable, especially for those banks that have a net short option position. Banks with such exposure typically set up delta hedges and/or limits on the size of the trading position. It is worrisome, however, that 8 years after the introduction of swaps, many major banks still have not figured out a satisfactory model for measuring the size of their position exposure. Also troublesome is the practice of *blind* application of the Black-Scholes models, despite many restrictive assumptions and the peculiarities of certain contracts.

All these developments have, some argue, been addressed by the new risk-adjusted capital base regulation adopted by the Fed. This rule serves to increase the capital requirements of the bank but does not change the inherent riskiness of the activities. An enlarged capital base is a small defense against major difficulties in any one market. More vigilant supervision remains a requirement, no matter the bank capital, because even under the new rules, the banking industry remains the most leveraged of industries. The safety net provided by the Fed, while desirable, may end up costing the taxpayers untold sums, as the S&L experiences indicate.

THE OTHER MAJOR SIDE EFFECTS

The deregulation of the financial markets increased the trend to multinationalize commercial and financial firms. The view from the corporate boardroom became decidedly geocentric. The linkages between the foreign exchange markets and the money markets became stronger as instruments containing equity or bond features with foreign exchange option features began to proliferate. The effects are also seen in greater conversion between domestic and Eurorates. Central bankers can no longer ignore developments in the Euromarkets as they go about setting their monetary policy.

The investment portfolio observed in the late 1980s is markedly different from that of the early 1980s. The most dramatic changes are the following:

- The type of individual running the fund, and even his nationality, has changed. The labor market of portfolio managers has also become international.

- The type of securities and their geographic origin have become more diverse and more international.

- The currency composition has also changed. The use of ECU-denominated securities has become more widespread than anyone predicted only a few years ago. The dollar has been downgraded from king to prince, and if the trend continues, it may be overtaken by the yen by the year 2000. The type of strategy has also changed. More than ever, sound analysis and international arbitrage (including tax arbitrage, computerized trading, complex hedging strategies, and other features) count heavily in quality portfolio performance.

- The education of bankers and portfolio managers is more universal and also more rigorous and quantitative than ever before. The spread of business schools in Europe and the Far East, to include mainland China, is not a historical coincidence. A cadre of financial managers must be developed if any country aspires to compete in the international markets. The classrooms are becoming more international, as are the professors and the curricula. The various cultures of the world appear to have done more to join students and scholars than to separate them.

Another major effect of deregulation is the increased concentration in the delivery of financial services.

The carnage can be seen in looking at the corporate genealogy of, say, Shearson Lehman, which is today a subsidiary of American Express. More than 30 firms, once proudly independent names in the business, went into its making—among them Spencer Trask, Shearson Hayden Stone, Hemphell Noyes, Faulkner Dawkins & Sullivan, Hornblower and Weeks, Joeb Rhoades, Lehman Brothers, and Kuhn Loeb.[25]

The increased concentration did not hurt the industry, nor did it reduce the intensity of competition. Stronger competition makes for a healthier industry as industry sales, profits, and employment levels rise.

The ten biggest firms' share of total revenues has increased from 48.7% in 1979 to 57.5% and their shares of the industry's total capital from 45.8 to 63.2. The heavyweights are seeking growth in profits by becoming financial supermarkets and by taking on more investment banking business.[26]

One source for the increased profits is the huge increase in the volume of stocks traded. The annual average daily volume increased from 16,487,000 in 1972 to 188,938,000 shares in 1987. Institutions accounted for 51.2 percent of this volume, as Exhibit 7.2 shows. This participation is up from 3.1 percent of total volume in 1965 and from 16.6 percent of total volume in 1975. Institutions have become a dominant market force as securitization continues and as the institutionalization of the savings function becomes more pervasive. Institutions are also a great source of profits. Some argue that this fact has led investment firms to ignore the small investor.

Where is the small investor? In many cases, he is standing in front of a machine receiving a standardized service and having to pay a premium for talking to a live teller or advisor. The spread of discount brokers has lowered transactions costs (some by as much as 70 percent) but may have eliminated occasionally valuable advice and the ability to develop a sense of trust between the investor and his broker. When an investor calls a discount brokerage firm, he talks to the firm (to anyone) and not to a recognizable person whose judgment and trustworthiness he has been able to measure and appreciate.

The small investor, however, seems to be quite willing still to participate in the stock market measured by odd-lot volume (a traditional indicator of participation by small investors). Small investor participation increased from 209 million

Exhibit 7.2
NYSE Large Block Transactions, 1965–1987

	Transactions		Shares	% of Reported
	Total	Daily average	(thousands)	volume
1965	2,171	9	48,262	3.1%
1970	17,217	68	450,908	15.4
1971	26,941	106	692,536	17.8
1972	31,207	124	766,406	18.5
1973	29,233	116	721,356	17.8
1974	23,200	92	549,387	15.6
1975	34,420	136	778,540	16.6
1976	47,632	188	1,001,254	18.7
1977	54,275	215	1,183,924	22.4
1978	75,036	298	1,646,905	22.9
1979	97,509	385	2,164,726	26.5
1980	133,597	528	3,311,132	29.2
1981	145,564	575	3,771,442	31.8
1982	254,707	1,007	6,742,481	41.0
1983	363,415	1,436	9,842,080	45.6
1984	433,427	1,713	11,492,091	49.8
1985	539,039	2,139	14,222,272	51.7
1986	665,587	2,631	17,811,335	49.9
1987	920,679	3,639	24,497,241	51.2

Source: New York Stock Exchange, *Fact Book 1988* (New York: NYSE, 1989), 75.

shares in 1986 to 341.5 million shares in 1987, and there were more individual investors in the United States. Thus, the quantity factor is significant and reassuring. The quality factor—quality of service to small investors—is not so clear or reassuring.

Then came the October 19 crash, which shook the foundations of everyone's belief in the stock market. The financial earthquake reverberated throughout the world and bankrupted poorly capitalized and highly leveraged firms.

Total NYSE share volume for the week of October 19th was 2.3 billion shares—almost as much business as was done in all of 1967. On October 19th, NYSE volume was 604 million shares, more than three times the average daily volume experienced for the year up to that point. The very next day—Tuesday, October 20th—NYSE volume hit 608 million shares and followed with three more days of extraordinarily high volume. From January to September 1987, the average number of trades each day was 87,000. In contrast, on October 19th and 20th, there were more than 200,000 trades per day. The average number of orders received by the NYSE's Designated Order Turnaround System (known as Super-DOT) from January to September 1987 was just under 144,000 or 6.1 orders per second. On October 19th, the Exchange received 470,000 orders, or 20.1 orders per second, through SuperDOT. And on October 20th, those numbers were 585,000 orders received at a rate of 25 orders per second, or four times the previous daily average during 1987.[27]

The causes of these unprecedented developments are many. The culprits that have been cited are numerous and especially institutional in character:

- Computer-assisted trading
- Portfolio "insurance" schemes
- The archaic system of specialists
- Concurrent trading in stock index futures (computerized arbitrage)
- Margin rules
- The absence of "circuit breakers," such as trading suspensions and limitations on price movements
- The overleveraged U.S. economy operating in a nervous stock market concerned about budget deficits and trade deficits
- The increased volatility of stock prices

Richard Roll found little support for any of the institutional arguments and for the theory that the U.S. stock market dragged the rest of the world on that day: "The overall pattern of intertemporal price movements in the various markets suggests the presence of an underlying fundamental factor, but it debunks the notion that an institutional defect in the U.S. market is the cause and it also seems inconsistent with a U.S.-specific macroeconomic event."[28]

Professor Roll ran various statistical tests and found that none of the institutional variables explained the crash convincingly.

A world market index was constructed and found to be statistically related to monthly returns in every country during the period from the beginning of 1981 up until the month before the crash. The magnitude of marked response differs materially across countries. The response coefficient, or "beta", was *by far* the most statistically significant explanatory variable in the October Crash. It swamped the influences of the institutional market characteristic.[29]

This evidence confirms the new reality in the international markets: There are effects well beyond the domestic fiscal monetary policy. Their exact nature, extent, and predictability are not very clear, however. This is one major by-product of deregulation.

Not all studies agree fully with Professor Roll, however. A Securities and Exchange Commission study concluded that the index arbitrage "may have accelerated the steepest portion of the market decline." Program selling on October 19 accounted for more than "35 percent of Big Board Volume in the S&P 500." The initial decline was caused, according to the SEC study, by "mixed economic news."

The interesting fact, however, is that virtually none of the recommendations of the various commissions that studied the crash, including those of the Brady Commission, was implemented. Program trading is better watched by the NYSE, and action aimed at stopping it is much more likely to be taken as price changes move beyond acceptable limits. Margins on index futures contracts did not change, nor should they have.

DEREGULATION AND BANK PROFITABILITY

Isolating the effects of deregulation on bank profitability is not an easy matter because profits could rise or decline as a result of many factors other than deregulation. This, however, did not discourage many from trying.

As noted earlier, a 1984 study at the Federal Reserve Bank of San Francisco attempted to measure the effects of the gradual disappearance of Regulation Q. The study found that the way banks competed for deposits and not the degree of competition changed. As to profitability:

The deregulation of interest rate ceilings appears to have had only minor effects on profits. Western banks' profitability, whether measured by return on assets (ROA) or return on equity (ROE), has declined by over 50 percent over the last two years. However, the falloff appears more directly related to the serious asset quality problems experienced by a limited number of large banks than to the accelerated trend toward deposit rate deregulation.[30]

Usually, it is most difficult to isolate the effects of specific legislation on the performance of a given market. An alternative method of analysis of deregulatory effects entails a statistical test of the equality of the rates of return on equity and on assets, and of the stability of those returns during two distinct time periods (eras) characterized by significantly different regulatory environments. It can be said, based on Chapter 3, that the 1980s have witnessed the most dramatic changes in U.S. financial history—the passage of DIDMCA, the almost total breakdown of Glass–Steagall, the introduction of futures index contracts, the freeing of foreign exchange markets (especially from 1980 to 1984), etc.—and consequently may be considered significantly different from the 1970s in terms of the regulatory environment.

The test conducted here utilizes data from 1967 to 1988 on 10 U.S. banks: 5 regional and 5 international. The regional banks are the Bank of New York, NBD Bancorp, Firstar, NCNB, and Security Pacific. The international banks are Bankers Trust, Citicorp, Manufacturers Hanover, J. P. Morgan, and First Interstate.

The returns on equity and on assets (for each bank for each year) and their mean values and standard deviations (per bank across years and per year across banks) are shown in Exhibits 7.3 and 7.4.

Our null hypotheses are

1. H_0: $\bar{\mu}_{1970s} = \bar{\mu}_{1980s}$
   H_1: $\bar{\mu}_{1970s} < \bar{\mu}_{1980s}$

where $\bar{\mu}$ is the mean of the means across years and across banks.

2. H_0: $\sigma^2_{1970s} = \sigma^2_{1980s}$
   H_1: $\sigma^2_{1970s} < \sigma^2_{1980s}$

where σ^2 is the variance of the means across years and across banks.

Exhibit 7.3
Rate of Return on Assets, 1967–1988

YEAR	BANKERS TRUST	CITICORP	MANNY HANNY	JP MORGAN	FIRST INTERSTAT	BANK NY	NBD BANCORP	FIRSTAR	NCNB	SECURITY PACIFIC
1967	0.69	0.61	0.64	0.76	0.60	0.84	0.68	0.65	0.70	0.71
1968	0.62	0.58	0.62	0.66	0.52	0.84	0.63	0.75	0.56	0.76
1969	0.42	0.52	0.58	0.61	0.61	0.69	0.72	0.77	0.76	0.79
1970	0.56	0.54	0.62	0.71	0.66	0.72	0.71	0.76	0.81	0.69
1971	0.48	0.58	0.56	0.84	0.52	0.78	0.66	0.59	0.78	0.54
1972	0.45	0.59	0.48	0.74	0.46	0.71	0.57	0.59	0.73	0.49
1973	0.33	0.58	0.50	0.70	0.43	0.74	0.60	0.55	0.63	0.45
1974	0.35	0.54	0.50	0.64	0.46	0.82	0.59	0.13	0.45	0.37
1975	0.30	0.61	0.50	0.71	0.42	0.74	0.70	0.33	0.46	0.45
1976	0.25	0.63	0.46	0.70	0.45	0.64	0.68	0.33	0.46	0.48
1977	0.26	0.49	0.44	0.69	0.53	0.46	0.69	0.31	0.51	0.55
1978	0.32	0.55	0.45	0.67	0.64	0.51	0.72	0.38	0.69	0.62
1979	0.37	0.51	0.44	0.66	0.72	0.49	0.80	0.45	0.70	0.66
1980	0.63	0.44	0.41	0.71	0.73	0.48	0.69	0.65	0.66	0.65
1981	0.56	0.47	0.43	0.70	0.67	0.51	0.54	0.60	0.77	0.63
1982	0.57	0.56	0.46	0.75	0.53	0.58	0.66	0.62	0.67	0.63
1983	0.64	0.62	0.52	0.79	0.56	0.71	0.62	0.66	0.68	0.65
1984	0.61	0.59	0.47	0.81	0.61	0.71	0.67	0.58	0.76	0.63
1985	0.73	0.57	0.53	1.02	0.60	0.70	0.71	0.61	0.83	0.60
1986	0.76	0.54	0.55	1.15	0.61	0.85	0.69	0.74	0.72	0.62
1987	0.00	0.00	0.00	0.11	0.00	0.45	0.69	0.00	0.58	0.00
1988	1.50	1.70	0.65	1.20	0.10	0.60	0.95	1.70	0.85	0.80

MEAN	0.497727	0.544090	0.491363	0.742272	0.519545	0.662272	0.680464	0.579545	0.670909	0.580454
STD	0.218900	0.141667	0.127966	0127966	0.172744	0.129331	0.081546	0.315601	0.118394	0.167344

MEAN ACROSS BANKS EACH YEAR		STD ACROSS BANKS EACH YEAR	
1967	0.688	1967	0.68234
1968	0.654	1968	0.94994
1969	0.647	1969	0.114197
1970	0.678	1970	0.080473
1971	0.633	1971	0.119
1972	0.581	1972	0.107093
1973	0.551	1973	0.119870
1974	0.485	1974	0.176025
1975	0.522	1975	0.151115
1976	0.508	1976	0.143443
1977	0.493	1977	0.131988
1978	0.555	1978	0.130019
1979	0.58	1979	0.137404
1980	0.605	1980	0.110657
1981	0.588	1981	0.101173
1982	0.603	1982	0.077207
1983	0.645	1983	0.071309
1984	0.644	1984	0.092649
1985	0.69	1985	0.138996
1986	0.723	1986	0.169708
1987	0.183	1987	0.263098
1988	0.875	1988	0.394493

1967 TO 1979 ROA	
MEAN OF MEANS ACROSS BANKS	0.582692
STD DEVIATION OF MEANS	0.068251
1980 TO 1988 ROA	
MEAN OF MEANS ACROSS BANKS	0.671625
STD DEVIATION OF MEANS	0.087999

Exhibit 7.4
Rate of Return on Equity, 1967–1988

YEAR	BANKERS TRUST	CITICORP	MANNY HANNY	JP MORGAN	FIRST INTERSTAT	BANK NY	NBD BANCORP	FIRSTAR	NCNB	SECURITY PACIFIC
1967	12.38	9.90	10.19	10.42	10.77	11.60	10.11	9.79	11.47	10.42
1968	11.74	10.04	10.70	9.90	10.34	12.80	9.71	10.57	10.47	11.25
1969	9.38	10.12	10.93	9.74	10.59	13.13	12.48	11.90	13.60	11.31
1970	12.15	11.29	11.70	11.52	13.13	13.60	12.46	12.47	15.25	10.50
1971	10.92	12.65	11.47	14.02	11.40	14.23	11.74	10.69	16.08	10.10
1972	11.92	12.94	10.40	13.75	10.90	13.12	10.38	11.25	13.51	10.45
1973	11.21	13.87	12.51	15.02	11.03	13.37	11.15	11.64	14.38	10.86
1974	12.28	15.05	14.77	15.94	11.57	14.40	11.52	2.72	9.14	9.55
1975	8.94	14.80	14.26	15.06	9.42	12.85	11.85	6.97	9.00	9.94
1976	7.80	15.08	13.16	13.92	10.14	11.86	10.86	7.50	9.38	10.70
1977	7.47	13.05	12.27	13.59	12.30	10.07	11.47	7.54	10.31	12.83
1978	9.70	15.10	13.00	15.20	15.60	12.30	11.00	9.90	13.50	14.50
1979	12.30	15.10	13.60	14.80	17.60	12.20	13.50	11.70	14.80	15.80
1980	18.50	12.90	13.50	16.90	16.70	12.80	14.40	14.20	13.60	15.50
1981	14.40	12.80	13.50	15.50	15.40	13.10	16.20	12.30	13.80	15.70
1982	14.70	14.90	12.00	16.30	12.10	14.70	11.80	12.00	14.50	15.70
1983	14.20	14.40	12.60	13.90	11.80	13.70	13.00	11.40	14.20	14.80
1984	13.00	13.80	10.70	13.90	12.10	14.10	14.10	10.10	14.80	14.80
1985	14.90	12.80	11.50	16.10	11.70	14.10	15.40	10.60	15.80	13.20
1986	15.70	11.60	10.90	17.00	12.30	14.80	14.90	11.30	15.20	13.40
1987	0.00	0.00	0.00	1.70	0.00	8.50	9.60	0.00	11.00	0.50
1988	18.00	19.00	14.50	17.00	2.50	9.00	17.50	26.50	13.00	16.50
MEAN	11.89045	12.78136	11.73454	13.69	11.33590	12.7965	12.50590	10.59272	13.03590	12.22090
STD	3.842671	3.459327	2.890193	3.369146	3.832830	1.725541	2.099300	4.708115	2.185977	3.832830

MEAN ACROSS BANKS EACH YEAR	STD ACROSS BANKS EACH YEAR
1967 10.60555	1967 0.786908
1968 10.52444	1968 0.611175
1969 11.318	1969 1.361673
1970 12.462	1970 1.201955
1971 12.33	1971 1.795388
1972 11.862	1972 1.290579
1973 12.504	1973 1.469531
1974 11.694	1974 3.716407
1975 11.309	1975 2.698997
1976 11.04	1976 2.377511
1977 11.09	1977 2.085085
1978 12.98	1978 2.085569
1979 14.14	1979 1.741378
1980 14.9	1980 1.826472
1981 14.27	1981 1.296186
1982 13.87	1982 1.627912
1983 13.4	1983 1.092703
1984 13.14	1984 1.570477
1985 13.61	1985 1.84632
1986 13.71	1986 1.996221
1987 3.13	1987 4.365558
1988 15.35	1988 6.041729

1967 TO 1979 ROE	
MEAN OF MEANS	
ACROSS BANKS	11.83526
STD DEVIATION	
OF MEANS	0.988077
1980 TO 1988 ROE	
MEAN OF MEANS	
ACROSS BANKS	14.03125
STD DEVIATION	
OF MEANS	.711537

The variance test was run first in order to determine (1) whether a significant difference exists between the stability measures for the different eras and (2) whether the t test can be used for the mean equality test.

The critical region of size σ (0.5 percent, in our case) for testing the null hypothesis $\sigma^2_{1970s} = \sigma^2_{1980s}$ against the one-sided alternative $\sigma^2_{1970s} < \sigma^2_{1980s}$ is

$$\frac{S^2_{1980s}}{S^2_{1970s}} \geq F_{\alpha, n_2-1, n_1-1}$$

For the rates of return on assets,

$$\frac{S^2_{1980s}}{S^2_{1970s}} = \frac{.087999}{.068251} = 1.289344$$

For the rates of return on equity,

$$\frac{S^2_{1980s}}{S^2_{1970s}} = \frac{.711537}{.988077} = .720123$$

The table value of $F_{\alpha, n_2-1, n_1-1} = F_{.05,6,12} = 3.00$.

Therefore, the null hypothesis of equality of variance (equal stability) cannot be rejected because calculated Fs (1.289344 and .720123, respectively) are lower than the tabled F value (3.00). It must be pointed out that 1987 was dropped from these calculations because it was an unusual year in which banks, especially the international ones, took huge write-offs against their profits because of their sovereign debt exposure and losses. This problem is not specifically related to deregulation. Rather, it started with the oil crisis in 1973–1974 and culminated in 1987. It has yet to be fully resolved.

To test the equality of means, we use a t test of the following form:

$$t = \frac{\bar{x}_{1970s} - \bar{x}_{1980s}}{\sqrt{\dfrac{(n_1 - 1) S^2_{1970s} + (n_2 - 1) S^2_{1980s}}{n_1 + n_2 - 2}} \sqrt{\dfrac{1}{n_1} + \dfrac{1}{n_2}}}$$

For ROA,

$$t = \frac{0.582692 - 0.671625}{\sqrt{\dfrac{(12)(.068251) + (6)(0.087999)}{13 + 7 - 2}} \sqrt{\dfrac{1}{13} + \dfrac{1}{7}}}$$

$$= \frac{-.0088933}{(.27331)(.37650)} = \frac{-.008890}{.10292} = -.08643$$

Thus, the null hypothesis can not be rejected.

For ROE:

$$t = \frac{11.83526 - 14.03125}{\sqrt{\dfrac{(12)(0.988077) + (6)(.711537)}{18}}\ \sqrt{.1418}}$$

$$= \frac{-2.19599}{.3564} = -6.16$$

Therefore, the null hypothesis can be rejected.

It appears that the ROE for banks (in our sample) improved significantly during the 1980s—a period of more deregulation than was the 1970s. This improvement was realized with no corresponding increase in the variance of the returns. These U.S. banks were prospering in a more competitive environment.

We now look at the impact of financial deregulation in the United States on interest rates, foreign exchange rates, and returns on bank stocks.

Effects on Interest Rates

The study of the effects of deregulation on U.S. interest rates covered the period of January 1973 through June 1988. Monthly data were broken down for testing purposes into four subperiods corresponding to major changes[31] in the financial markets:

Jan. 1976   Introduction of futures contracts on Treasury bills

June 1978   Authorization of banks and thrifts to issue money market certificates

Oct. 1979   Switch of monetary policy from controlling interest rates to controlling commentary aggregates and passage of DIDMCA

Sept. 1985   Reversal to controlling interest rates as a result of the Venice Agreement

The test used to determine the effects of deregulation was the Chow Test, which allows us to test whether two samples (from two different subperiods) are drawn from the same population. The application of this test requires that an interest determination model be developed. Three interest rate models were used:

• Carr and Smith model[32]

• Distributed lag model[33]

• Liquidity preference model[34]

Carr and Smith Model

This model has an interest rate (i) that is a function of the following independent variables:

$$i_t = b_0 + b_1 \left[\left(\frac{\Delta M}{M} \right)_t - \left(\frac{\Delta M}{M} \right)^e_{t-1} \right] + b_2 \left(\frac{\Delta P}{P} \right)^e_t + b_3 G + \epsilon_t$$

where

M = Money supply, M_2

P = Consumer price index

$\left(\dfrac{\Delta M}{M} \right)_t$ = Actual monthly percentage change in money supply (M_2) from $t - 1$ to t

$\left(\dfrac{\Delta M}{M} \right)^e_{t-1}$ = Expected monthly percentage change in money supply from $t - 1$ to t, where expectations are formed at time $t - 1$.

$\left(\dfrac{\Delta P}{P} \right)^e_t$ = Expectations of inflation, weighting past values of inflation

G = Changes in net government bonds held by the Federal Reserve Bank

The variable $(\Delta M/M)^e_{t-1}$ is constructed using a geometrically declining weighting method:

$$\left(\frac{\Delta M}{M} \right)^e_{t-1} = \sum_{i=0}^{\infty} \lambda(1 - \lambda)^i \left(\frac{\Delta M}{M} \right)_t$$

Previous empirical tests show that this lag pattern works best with $1 - \lambda = 7$.

The variable $(\Delta P/P)^e_t$ is constructed using the Almon interpolation technique. In this test, a second-degree polynomial was found to be the most satisfactory.

The coefficients of b_0 and b_1 are expected to be positive and b_2 to be negative.

Another variable was added to the model to measure the intensity of the Fed's intervention in the bond markets through open market operations. This variable was the change in Federal Reserve System net holdings of government bonds (G). The Carr and Smith model was run with and without this variable, and the results were practically the same. The "intensity" variable proved to be insignificant across all three models.

The regression results were disturbing and interesting because the signs of the coefficients were different from those outlined by Carr and Smith for b_1 (consistently) and b_2 (in some subperiods).

The Chow Test is:

$$H_0: \ \beta_0^{\text{period 1}} = \beta_0^{\text{period 2}}, \ \beta_1^{\text{period 1}} = \beta_1^{\text{period 2}}$$
$$H_1: \ \beta_0^{\text{period 1}} \neq \beta_0^{\text{period 2}}, \ \beta_1^{\text{period 1}} \neq \beta_1^{\text{period 2}}$$

and similarly for other periods. The results, shown in Exhibit 7.5, suggest that only in the last period comparison is the test significant. This, however, cannot

Exhibit 7.5
The Chow Test Results: Carr & Smith Model, 1973–1988

Period A	Period B	Chow Test	F*(α = 0.05)
Jan '73 - Dec '75	Jan '76 - May '78	0.15722	1.831705
Jan '76 - May '78	June '78 - Sep '79	0.42700	2.2355
June '78 - Sep '79	Oct '79 - Aug '85	1.3763	1.815154
Oct '79 - Aug '85	Sep '85 - June '88	4.9907	1.789662

be attributed solely to a specific regulatory change because there was none that could have had this much effect, but rather it results from a combination of a change in monetary policy and the fiscal deficits that had major effects on interest rates.

Distributed Lag Model

The distributed lag model has the following form:

$$R_t = \alpha_0 + \sum_{i=0}^{K} \beta_i R_{t-1} + \sum_{i=0}^{M} C_J \dot{P}_{t-J} + dG + \epsilon_t$$

where

$R_t =$ Nominal interest rate at time t

$\dot{P} =$ Inflation rate $\left(\dfrac{\Delta P}{P} \right)$

$G =$ Change in net holdings of government bonds by the Fed

$t =$ Time

The coefficients α, β, and C are expected to be greater than zero. The Chow Test results, shown in Exhibit 7.6, indicate structural stability across all periods, suggesting, once again, that deregulation and changes in monetary policy direction did not have a major effect on interest rates.

Exhibit 7.6
The Chow Test Results: Distributed Lag Model, 1973–1988

Period A	Period B	Chow Test	F* (α = 0.05)
Jan '73 - Dec '75	Jan '76 - May '78	0.031856	1.831705
Jan '76 - May '78	June '78 - Sep '79	0.020196	2.2355
June '78 - Sep '79	Oct '79 - Aug '85	0.017432	1.815154
Oct '79 - Aug '85	Sep '85 - June '88	0.32003	1.739552

Liquidity Preference Model

This model consists of the following equation:

$$R_t = C_0 + C_1 ln\ M_t^R + C_2 ln\ Y_t^R + \sum_{i=0}^{K} b_i \dot{P}_{t-1} + d(R_{t-1} - R_{t-2}) + eG + \epsilon_i$$

where

$$R_t = \text{Nominal interest rate in question at period } t$$
$$Y^R, M^R = \text{Real industrial productivity and real money balances}$$
$$\dot{P}_t = \text{Inflation rate at period } t$$

The expected signs of the coefficients are

$$C_1 < 0,\ C_2,\ b_i,\ d > 0, \text{ and } e = ?.$$

Once again the test did not produce consistently "correct" signs as reported in the original study. This is an interesting revelation about the potency of the liquidity preference model across time periods. The Chow Test results across the time periods are shown in Exhibit 7.7.

These results, except for the third comparison, do not allow the rejection of the null hypothesis. The structural instability in the third test indicates a significant effect due to DIDMCA.

A close examination of all the results across the various time periods and the different models inevitably leads to the conclusions that either

- Deregulation and changes in monetary policy have had no significant effect on interest rates, or
- The effects of deregulation, if any, were cancelled out by other factors, such as fiscal policy.

Exhibit 7.7
The Chow Test Results: Liquidity Preference Model, 1973–1988

Period A	Period B	Chow Test	$F^*\ \alpha=.05$
Jan '73 - Dec '75	Jan '76 - May '78	0.063334	1.831705
Jan '76 - May '78	June '78 - Sep '79	0.22168	2.2355
June '78 - Sep '79	Oct '79 - Aug '85	2.7862	1.815154
Oct '79 - Aug '85	Sep '85 - June '88	0.14504	1.739552

One can safely say, however, that the negative effects are nonexistent or minimal at best.

Effects on Foreign Exchange Rates

The procedure used to test the effects of deregulation on the foreign exchange market is similar to that used above for interest rates. The model used here is Bilson's.[35]

$$ln(S_t) = \beta_0 + \beta_1 ln(M) + \beta_2 ln(M^*) + \beta_3(i - i^*) + \beta_4 ln(Y) +$$
$$\beta_5 ln(Y^*) + \beta_6 t + \beta_7 ln(S_{t-1}) + \beta_8 IFX + \epsilon_1$$

where

$$S_t = \text{Spot rate at time } t(\text{US\$/¥})$$
$$S_{t-1} = \text{Spot rate at time } t - 1$$
$$M, M^* = \text{M2 for U.S. and Japan, respectively}$$
$$i - i^* = \text{Inflation rate } \left(\frac{\Delta P}{P}\right) \text{ for U.S. and Japan, respectively}$$
$$Y, Y^* = \text{Industrial productivity for U.S. and Japan, respectively}$$
(instead of national income used by Bilson) (Monthly data were needed.)
$$t = \text{Time } t$$
$$IFX = \text{Intervention fund index } l$$

The reader should note that the word "regulation" is used loosely in the case of foreign exchange markets. What is being examined here are the effects of different foreign exchange "regimes" (intervention levels) on the exchange rates. The government "regulates" exchange markets through intervention.

The Bilson model was run as initially specified by its author and as shown above with the intervention variable. The variable IFX was a 0, 1, 2, 3, or 4 variable, with 0 for no intervention and 4 for heavy intervention.

Size of Intervention[36]	Index
0–49 million	0
50–99 million	1
100–149 million	2
150–199 million	3
200 million	4

The *Federal Reserve Bulletin* quarterly reports on foreign exchange intervention were read carefully in order to assign the "correct" index number—and it was an onerous task. The cutoff points were

Jan. 1973–Jan. 1981	President Reagan assumes office; new philosophy on intervention at the White House.
Feb. 1981–Sep. 1985	The Plaza Agreement: Western countries and Japan agreed on September 20, 1985, to intervene to lower the value of the dollar; a major turning point in U.S. foreign exchange policy.
Oct. 1985–June 1988	The present.

The Chow Test results, shown in Exhibit 7.8, suggest that different exchange rate regimes do influence exchange rates. The calculated F values exceed the tabled F values. Incidentally, the intervention variable was significant for the entire period (186 observations). It is wise, henceforth, to include it in foreign exchange forecasting models.

The results are tentative because of serious data problems. The exact size of the intervention for each month is not disclosed to the public. Every attempt was made to obtain the data, but without success. Thus, the index was developed with the best approximation possible.

These results, tentative as they may be, do contradict those obtained by Owen F. Humpage in a series of studies at the Federal Reserve Bank of Cleveland.[37] A summary of his studies shows that there is no "systematic relationship between intervention and exchange rate movements."[38] His data and methodology are considerably different from what is presented here.

Effects on Returns on Bank Stocks

This section was inspired by the study of G. William Schwert,[39] who argued convincingly for the use of financial data to measure the effects of deregulation.

The model tested was the standard CAPM, using CRSP daily data files on regional and international banks. The regional banks are the Bank of New York, Financial Corporation of America, First Wisconsin Corporation, and NDB Bank-Corp. The international banks are Bankers Trust, Citicorp, First Interstate Ban-Corp, Manufacturers Hanover, and J. P. Morgan.

Exhibit 7.8
The Chow Test Results: Bilson Model, 1973–1988

Period A	Period B	Chow Test	F* ($\alpha = 0.05$)
Jan '73 - Jan '81	Feb '81 - Sept '85	4.2192	1.53
Feb '81 - Sept '85	Oct '85 - June '88	4.0388	2.31

The data commenced on May 15, 1975, and ended on June 30, 1988. The subperiods were

May 15, 1975–April 15, 1982	The introduction of stock index futures (April 1982)
April 16, 1982–Oct. 15, 1987	Market crash
Oct. 16, 1987–June 30, 1988	Present

The results of the regression analysis are presented in Exhibits 7.9 and 7.10.

The results for the regional banks are not of value. The R^2s are not significantly different from zero. Their returns seem to be affected more by regional factors than by the behavior of the overall stock market.

The international banks had significant t values, and the R^2s were more than acceptable. The Chow Test indicates that the null hypothesis can be rejected, confirming a structural instability in the relationship between market rates of returns and bank rates of return. This, however, suggests that the different time periods and the specific events chosen to separate them have important effects on stock returns, but in no way rule out other effects: political, economic, financial, and others.

The Other Effects

What was referred to as the "Reagan Revolution" was based on lower taxes, more deregulated markets, and less intervention in the financial markets by the

Exhibit 7.9
Regional Bank Returns: Stocks

	(1) t=1-534	(2) t=535-2276	(3) t=2277-3658	(4) t=1-3658
n	534	1742	1382	3658
R-Square	0.2013	0.0006	0.0003	0
β	0.63809 (11.580)	1.8582 (0.98400)	-1.8592 (-0.66867)	0.50182 (0.41066)
Constant	-0.00052921 (-0.85210)	-0.015119 (-1.0545)	-0.014768 (-0.81327)	-0.013148 (-1.3653)
Chow Test		0.1309 <————————————————>		
			0.65088 <————————————————>	

Exhibit 7.10
National/International Bank Returns: Stocks

	(1) t=1-534	(2) t=535-2276	(3) t=2277-3658
n	534	1742	1382
R-Square	0.4740	0.3932	0.4364
β	0.97198 (21.893)	0.86681 (33.580)	1.3081 (32.690)
Constant	0.00018538 (0.374047)	-0.00039083 (-1.994)	-0.00038437 (-1.4708)
Chow Test		5.4077 <------------------------>	
			94.354 <------------------------>

federal government. The results of this revolution are impressive, as Exhibit 7.11 shows. The world took notice as U.S. economic policy prescriptions began to be copied everywhere, even in most communist countries. The economists will never cease to argue over whether this was indeed a revolution and whether deregulation, whatever its form and extent, did indeed produce this economic prosperity. Many have been arguing that the prosperity of the Reagan years was achieved through huge budgetary deficits—old-fashioned Keynesian prescriptions—and would have obtained with or without deregulation. To settle this argument in this book is not possible.

The other effects are observed in the huge successes of interest futures and options contracts, currency futures and options contracts, and index futures and options contracts. In many cases, these contracts have achieved open interest exceeding 100,000 contracts. *The Wall Street Journal* reported that the S&P 100 Index Option traded on the Chicago Board of Trade (CBT) had an open interest of over 360,000 contracts, the Treasury bond futures contract on the CBT had over 112,000 contracts in open interest, and the Eurodollar futures contract trading on the International Monetary Market in Chicago had over 137,000 contracts.[40] The underlying value of the volume in derivative products swamps that of the cash market.

These numbers suggest that the volatility of the deregulated financial markets is being successfully hedged in these deep and liquid derivative markets and that market participants have become mature in the use of these markets, a condition reflected in the marketplace.

Exhibit 7.11
Gross National Product and Unemployment Rates, 1980–1988

Gross National Product ($Bn)

1980	2673.0	2672.2	2734.0	2848.6
1981	2978.8	3017.7	3099.6	3114.4
1982	3112.6	3159.5	3179.4	3212.5
1983	3265.8	3367.4	3443.9	3545.8
1984	3674.9	3754.2	3807.9	3851.8
1985	3925.6	3979.0	4047.0	4107.9
1986	4180.4	4207.6	4268.4	4304.6
1987	4391.8	4484.2	4568.0	4662.8
1988	4724.5	4823.8	4906.7	4992.9

Unemployment rate (Percent of civilian labor force)

1980	6.3	6.3	6.3	6.9	7.5	7.6	7.8	7.7	7.5	7.5	7.5	7.2
1981	7.5	7.4	7.4	7.2	7.5	7.5	7.2	7.4	7.6	7.9	8.3	8.5
1982	8.6	8.9	9.0	9.3	9.4	9.6	9.8	9.8	10.1	10.4	10.8	10.8
1983	10.4	10.4	10.3	10.2	10.1	10.1	9.4	9.5	9.2	8.8	8.5	8.3
1984	8.0	7.8	7.8	7.7	7.4	7.2	7.5	7.5	7.3	7.4	7.2	7.3
1985	7.4	7.2	7.2	7.3	7.2	7.3	7.4	7.1	7.1	7.1	7.0	7.0
1986	6.7	7.2	7.1	7.1	7.2	7.1	7.0	6.9	7.0	6.9	6.9	6.7
1987	6.7	6.6	6.5	6.3	6.3	6.1	6.0	6.0	5.9	6.0	5.9	5.8
1988	5.8	5.7	5.6	5.4	5.6	5.3	5.4	5.6	5.4	5.5	5.5	5.5

Source: Data Disk, 1989.

CONCLUSIONS

This chapter is the most ambitious and the most demanding of all the chapters in this book. The tests were conducted with care, but their results were not as robust as was expected. Isolating the effects of a given environmental or regulatory change is most difficult, even under the best of circumstances. A multitude of factors are always operating in the marketplace with varying degrees of effects which are often not independent.

This writer trusts that the reader will focus on the value of the small steps taken here and will forgive the absence of keen prophetic powers.

NOTES

1. Lamberto Dini, *Financial Innovation, International Markets, and the Conduct of Monetary Policy* (Geneva: Center for International Monetary and Banking Studies, 1986).

2. Ibid.

3. Ibid.

4. *FRBSF Weekly Letter,* 11 October 1985.

5. See Sarkis J. Khoury and Alo Ghosh, eds., *Recent Developments in International Banking and Finance,* (Lexington, Mass.: D. C. Heath, 1987).

6. Paul R. Allen and William J. Wilhelm, "The Impact of the 1980 Depository Institutions Deregulation and Monetary Control Act on Market Value and Risk: Evidence from the Capital Markets," *Journal of Money, Credit, and Banking* 20, no. 3 (August 1988): 364.

7. G. William Schwert, "Using Financial Data to Measure Effects of Regulation," *Journal of Law and Economics* 24 (April 1981): 121–58.

8. Ibid.

9. Ibid., 376.

10. Ibid., 375–76.

11. *FRBSF Weekly Letter,* 2 August 1985.

12. Ibid.

13. Robert Guttman, "Changing the Guard at the Fed," *Challenge* 30, no. 5 (November–December 1987): 9.

14. Herbert L. Baer and Christine A. Pavel, "Does Deregulation Drive Innovation?" *Economic Perspectives* (Federal Reserve Bank of Chicago) (March/April 1988).

15. John Judd, "Competition between the Commercial Paper Market and Commercial Banks," *Economic Review* (Federal Reserve Bank of San Francisco) (Winter 1979): 39–53.

16. Christine A. Pavel and David Phillis, "Why Commercial Banks Sell Loans: An Empirical Analysis," *Economic Perspectives* (Federal Reserve Bank of Chicago) 2 (May–June 1987): 3–14.

17. Lawrence Benveniste and Allen N. Berger, "An Empirical Analysis of Standby Letters of Credit," in *Proceedings of a Conference on Bank Structure and Competition, 1986* (Chicago: Federal Reserve Bank of Chicago, 1986).

18. Gary Koppenhaven, "The Effects of Regulation on Bank Participation in the Guarantee Market," Staff memoranda SM87-6 (Chicago: Federal Reserve Bank of Chicago, February 1987).

19. Baer and Pavel, "Does Regulation Drive Innovation?"

20. Ibid., 14.

21. "Recent Trends in Innovations and International Capital Markets," Federal Reserve Bank of New York, April 1987.

22. U.S. General Accounting Office, *Banking: Off-Balance Sheet Activities* (Washington, D.C.: U.S. Government Printing Office, 1988), 3.

23. Ibid., 4.

24. *Recent Innovations in International Banking* (Bank for International Settlements, 1986), 11.

25. *Economist* (16 August 1986).

26. Ibid.

27. New York Stock Exchange, *Fact Book 1988* (New York, NYSE, 1989).

28. Richard Roll, "The International Crash of October 1987," UCLA Working Paper Series, April 1988, 6.

29. Ibid., 20.

30. *FRBSF Weekly Letter,* 13 July 1984, 1.

31. Deregulation and change in intervention policy are used interchangeably. One can think of regulation as the ultimate form of intervention.

32. Jack Carr and Lawrence B. Smith, "Money Supply, Interest Rate, and the Yield Curve," *Journal of Money, Credit, and Banking* 4, no. 3 (1972): 583–94.

33. F. Modigliani and R. Shiller, "Inflation, Rational Expectations and the Term Structure of Interest Rates," *Economica* (1973).

34. M. Feldstein and O. Eckstein, "The Fundamental Determinants of the Interest Rates," *Review of Economics and Statistics* (Nov. 1970).

35. John F. O. Bilson, "The Monetary Approach to the Exchange Rate: Some Empirical Evidence," *International Monetary Fund Staff Papers,* 19.

36. Data are from the *Federal Reserve Bulletin,* January 1973 through June 1988.

37. See, for example, Owen F. Humpage, "Intervention and the Dollar Decline," *Economic Review* (Federal Reserve Bank of Cleveland, 1988 Quarter): 2–17.

38. *Economic Commentary* (1 September 1988).

39. Schwert, "Using Financial Data to Measure Effects of Regulation."

40. *Wall Street Journal,* 3 March 1989.

8

The Future of Deregulation

The preceding chapters confirm some of the publicly held beliefs about financial markets and institutions, and deny many others. Also, we have explored the similarities and dissimilarities among the deregulations of the various markets. The purpose here is to further accentuate the legitimacy of the concerns, understandings, and theories; to look at the most likely scenarios for the evolution of the financial markets, financial institutions, and their regulations; and to offer concluding comments.

It is clear from the preceding analysis that the regulations and banking laws of many countries are still antiquated. Some of the unrevised laws and regulations are being circumvented without penalty. Governments have taken a proactive strategy, as in the case of London, Australia, and Canada, to deregulate their financial markets in order to stimulate their sluggish economies. The liberalization of some markets was implemented at a faster pace and on a more comprehensive basis once the experiments in other markets proved successful. All markets went the liberalization route, while Hong Kong had to constrain its openness. All experiments, thus far, have been rather successful. The permanency of the changes is still in doubt. The real test would lie in the reaction of governments and financial institutions to a severe worldwide economic setback.

The international financial environment of the 1960s, 1970s, and 1980s, developed partially by design, but largely as a result of the dynamic market forces that produced more competitive markets all over the world and "leaner and meaner" financial institutions. The consolidation through mergers and acquisitions that took place reduced the number of firms to be sure, but the competition among the remaining firms increased dramatically as spreads shrank and a larger set of financial firms offered a given product. The breakdown in Glass–Steagall contributed to this as banks, investment banks, and insurance companies began to invade each other's domain.

This competition will continue to increase as markets become more global and as new, aggressive entities come into the market. The Japanese firms which were once nowhere on the list of prominent financial institutions are now dominant in the world of finance. The Korean and the Chinese will also become major players and, in so doing, will wrestle some business from existing players, especially those who are lethargic and suffer from a shortage of human capital—the critical ingredient for success in the 1990s and beyond. The economic unification of Europe in 1992 becomes a major factor in this regard. European financial institutions are hard at work acquiring footholds in the various markets in Europe, streamlining their operations, and improving their product mix and their resource base in order to better compete in a united Europe. The concern here is with regulating foreign competition out of existence. The new laws dealing with goods flows and agricultural commodities are not very encouraging, and they may well spill over into the financial sector.

Barring restrictions on capital flows and barriers to entry, it is quite logical to assume that we will witness further redistribution of the international pie, away from perhaps the Japanese and more likely the American financial institutions. The American firms are particularly vulnerable unless the regulatory changes in the United States are accelerated, especially with respect to Glass–Steagall, and unless U.S. policymakers prove more cerebral in their negotiations with other countries in terms of obtaining a more level playing field.

The competition among financial institutions will be in three areas: price (mainly), quality of service, and product innovation. The innovations, however, will not necessarily always emanate from the private sector. Swaps were introduced by the World Bank, the government of Sweden introduced a large array of new financial instruments, occasionally with complex terms, and Islamic nations showed considerable innovation in borrowing internationally while remaining true to the prescriptions of their faith. The European market and the futures market in Japan had to await official sanctioning by the Japanese government, despite the fact that Japanese financial institutions were already using futures outside Japan and possessed the needed technology to commence trading these contracts in Japan. The restructuring of the S&L asset portfolio had to await DIDMCA. Thus, innovation can be induced or stifled (if only temporarily) by government action. That is why a good portion of this chapter is devoted to the dynamics of regulation and the relationship between the private sector and government as the character of the financial markets is remolded.

Again, it must be emphasized that regulation is as cyclical as the market itself and the economy are, and that what some called deregulation was nothing more than the substitution of one regulation for another. In any case, whatever "progress" has been achieved thus far can be easily reversed. A large number of economists and government officials staunchly believe in regulated markets and would regain considerable if not instantaneous credibility the minute economic conditions worsen. A reoccurrence of the October 19 crash coupled with a soft economy will undoubtedly produce a reversal in the regulatory process. The yin and the yang of regulation are a historical constant and are not independent of the economic cycles.

With this in mind, one must still consider the future because trends, and the ability to observe and react to them, are an essential ingredient in the management of both portfolios and banking/investment banking institutions.

THE EQUITY AND BOND MARKETS AND THEIR DERIVATIVE MARKETS

Three key words set the tone for the future of all these markets: "Watch the Japanese."

The almost complete control Japanese securities firms have been able to exercise over certain markets (e.g., Euroyen, Samurai, and domestic yen bonds) is not likely to diminish anytime in the near future, nor is their leadership in the Eurobond market (including the Eurodollar bonds), as documented in Chapter 1.

The Japanese firms have the necessary technology (hardware and human) and the huge accumulated resources, especially dollar-denominated assets, to be very potent competitors with any firm of any nationality, particularly in the placement of issues they underwrite. Furthermore, the relationship Japanese financial institutions have with their government is a peculiar one indeed because they are provided the needed support for continued expansion of their international activities while still, to a considerable extent, protecting their domestic market from foreign competition. The concentration of economic power in banking (top six) and investment banking (top four) also helps significantly in international competition because huge resources are available to meet any challenge in the marketplace. Also, Japanese financial institutions' attitude toward long-run profits and long-term customer relationships and their disposition toward (and patience in) cultivating a client who has long-run potential allow them to accept low margins. Japanese banks are backed by a regulatory financial structure that has much stronger safety nets, extending philosophically and operationally to all types of corporations, than those of almost any country in the world.

Japanese firms' power in the world financial markets, their desire to appropriate to themselves the greatest possible market share, and their intention to have as much business activity as possible flow through Japan are best illustrated in the latest developments in the options and futures markets.

The Japanese are currently building options and futures exchanges in Tokyo and Osaka to compete with the Chicago exchanges, which currently account for about 70 percent of the world transactions in these instruments. Two fundamental issues arise in this regard: The first is the need for such exchanges, and the second deals with how the Japanese plan to compete, given the current structure of the industry.

The Linkages

The trend in the world equity markets, as pointed out in Chapter 1, is toward increased globalization, in both the primary and the secondary markets. Cross-listing is pervasive across exchanges and is growing.

Another trend is toward more linkages and agreements for mutual right offset trades across futures exchanges. This effectively allows for around-the-clock trading because an investor can purchase a contract on one exchange and offset it on another in a foreign country. While this has worked well in many cases, a notable exception is the linkage between the American Stock Exchange (AMEX) and the Toronto Stock Exchange. This linkage was cut after Toronto realized that the order flow was unidirectional—toward the AMEX—and that the trading, given the time zones, was done on the AMEX at the expense of the Toronto Stock Exchange. The preservation of the integrity of the Toronto Stock Exchange required the rupture of the linkage.

The Need for a New Exchange

Consider, in light of the above, the following scenario:

- All major Japanese stocks become cross-listed on a U.S. exchange.
- A U.S. exchange trades options on all stocks that are cross-listed.
- Options are traded on the U.S. exchange on a 24-hour basis.

Or, better yet, assume that the underlying is a currency, and consider that the Philadelphia Stock Exchange (PHLX) establishes 24-hour trading, further extending its current expanded trading hours as a result of early morning and evening sessions. Then, on what economic grounds would any other exchange trade currency options, given that the PHLX is already very liquid? These are a few possibilities:

- The monopoly rent, if any, that accrues from trading current options can be shared. This rent can be realized simply by buying a seat on the PHLX. This seat has a market price and can be purchased in the open market by anyone.
- The absence of economies of scale in one market makes the duplication of exchanges a reasonable economic event. However, exchanges that have considerable depth and breadth have by definition achieved considerable economies of scale; otherwise, any newcomer could wrestle business away from them. The PHLX has apparently achieved that, because those that have tried to take business away have thus far failed. The cost curve is not declining throughout until transaction costs are zero, however. Therefore, any newcomer that can switch business from an existing exchange to itself on a scale large enough to quickly achieve prevailing or superior scales would be wise to do so on purely economic grounds. Why this would happen now in violation of all historical precedents is puzzling indeed unless something other than pure economic considerations is motivating the switch. This is discussed further below.

- The old, well-established exchanges have not been consistently the most innovative. Financial futures contracts, for example, were not introduced by the Chicago Board of Trade. A new exchange with a better "mousetrap" or an entirely new contract could succeed as the Chicago Board Options Exchange, the Chicago Mercantile Exchange, and the PHLX have. The extent to which synergy in product development on the exchanges exists and the liquidity of various contracts are not independent. A new exchange may be able to justify its existence if it is more dynamic and enterprising than an existing exchange.

- A new exchange may trade an existing contract on a new underlying instrument—an option on a new currency or an option on lesser known Japanese stocks that are not cross-listed. In this scenario, there would be one truly international exchange for a given contract and satellite exchanges for variations on existing contracts or for the same contract on a lesser known underlying instrument. Satellite exchanges are not what the Japanese have in mind, however.

The exclusion of the above possibilities, which are justifiable on purely economic grounds, leaves one rationale for the building of Japanese exchanges that trade futures on T-bonds, futures and options on currencies, and other contracts that are reproductions of existing contracts on U.S. exchanges: economic control. This, in effect, is a very subtle way of reversing the progress made toward more international markets. Or it may, optimistically speaking, be the interim step in the development of truly global markets. If the Japanese desire an international market, they will work for its realization only if Tokyo is at its center. Exchanges could also proliferate as one country copies the developments in another country, and the exchange with the most resiliency and sophistication in a fair and open system will prevail. The fairness and openness of markets are of critical concern. *Euromoney* suggests that the new Japanese exchanges may achieve competitiveness or even domination of the derivative markets through procedures that are not altogether fair:

- Making "wash sales"—carrying on fictitious trading (buy/sell orders) to produce the illusion of liquidity.
- Setting unreasonably low margins with the express purpose of putting the Chicago exchanges at a disadvantage.
- Channeling business to Japanese exchanges, regardless of their competitiveness internationally. The lessons on the product side of Japanese trade are perhaps relevant here.[1]

In addition, all the technological factors will be brought to bear by the Japanese. In preparation for this, they have developed potent spot markets in the underlying—a necessary ingredient for success. In fact, their spot foreign exchange market is said to exceed that of New York and London combined, and trading in U.S. T-bonds in Japan is active.

These developments within the Japanese markets are particularly noteworthy, given steps taken by several exchanges to extend trading hours or modify the trading system to accommodate the Japanese. The new computerized trading system, Globex (for global exchange), allows for trading Chicago Mercantile Exchange (CME) contracts during CME closing hours (between 3:15 P.M. and 7:20 A.M.). There are only a silent screen and the sound of keyboards manipulated by able traders—no open outcry. Bids are entered on Eurodollar and currency futures through stations "connected to Reuters' global data transmission system" and are matched by computer. The system is not limited to CME contracts, and other exchanges may join in. Yet the Germans and the Japanese will be starting new exchanges in 1989/1990.

Globex may be the first step toward fully automated trading. The days of the floor trader may be numbered. His wizardry will have to be shown in front of a screen and not on a congested and sweaty trading floor.

The effects of Globex will not be felt by CME alone. The LIFFE (London), the MATIF (France), the SIMEX (Singapore), and other exchanges will be impacted as well. While the trading fees accrue to Globex, the commissions accrue to the broker placing the order. As different exchanges or investment houses from all over the world buy shares in Globex or a similar system, the need for adding exchanges would diminish. The next step would be a direct hookup between this system and the investor/trader, thus bypassing the broker.

This trend is not to be limited to options and futures exchanges. Electronic trading is already taking place in stocks and bonds and will continue to grow. The specialist may be placed on the endangered species list in the near future.

The proliferation of exchanges and trading mechanisms is nowhere near the proliferation of products traded on those exchanges. Their development continues in order to satisfy the insatiable desire of investors to find ever more effective ways to hedge every risk they are exposed to. One needs only look at the options and futures quotation pages in *The Wall Street Journal* in 1985 and compare them to those in, say, March 1989 to see how many new contracts have been introduced and how many have failed or survived.

New products will continue to be introduced in the 1990s and beyond. They may be variations on existing contracts or completely new concepts. An example of a new product is one introduced and withdrawn in 1989, the cash index participation (CIP) contract, first submitted for approval by the Philadelphia Stock Exchange, which was later to trade it. There are actually two contracts— one on the Dow Jones stocks (the Blue Chip CIP) and one on the S&P 500 (the S&P 500 CIP)—both of which *require* cash delivery. The new contract combines three features simultaneously:

- A common stock feature—indefinite life and trading at value (1/10th of the value of the S&P 500).
- A futures contract without underlying.
- An option contract because CIP allows for a quarterly cash-out. The holder (the long) can simply turn the contract in and receive cash for it instead of selling it in the open market.

Trading of CIP contracts did not begin as scheduled. The Chicago Board of Trade and the Chicago Mercantile Exchange filed a suit claiming that the product is a futures contract and that they should be the exchanges to trade it. Trading, however, did begin on the Philadelphia Stock Exchange in March 1989 but was suspended in September 1989.

The search for the perfect hedging tool or strategy will continue as people discover that at present there is no perfect hedge for all risks at all times and the system as a whole cannot be hedged. The increased volatility of most classes of financial instruments will add to the pressures.

The availability of a large set of options and futures contracts is a natural response to a real market need. Their acceptance and utilization, however, is still in the infancy stage. The volume of options and futures contracts will explode in the 1990s as more firms and individuals discover that these contracts are an essential ingredient in the process of portfolio management and as educational programs covering options and futures continue to proliferate. Very optimistic forecasts have been made for the German options exchange. In preparation, Commerzbank of Germany has been sponsoring seminars throughout Germany to educate bankers, investment bankers, and exporters/importers in options. The time lag between this and the developments in the United States is large indeed, but it will close very quickly. The Germans are eager to learn and to prove their competitiveness in the financial markets at every level in every financial product as they have done with their industrial products.

The intensity of competition in the financial markets and the incredible technology already in the hands of traders and investors will further increase the sensitivity of funds flows to interest rate differentials and will make the internationalization of portfolios a much easier and more desirable step. Technology will also make it possible to have "no stop" financial services, as James Tobin characterizes this new era. Armed with a personal computer, an investor will be able to pay his utility bill, find the latest quote on a stock or option, enter an order to buy or sell a security, and check on the latest football score.

Technological change can also further the institutionalization of the saving function. The ease with which one can deposit and withdraw funds from one fund and deposit in another and the increased emphasis on retirement comfort will increase the flow of savings funds to professionally managed pools. Banks have to offer competitive products to their clients as the latter's options multiply and their sophistication increases.

The bond markets will continue to integrate internationally, and new offerings with interesting and complex features will continue to come to the markets, utilizing even more flexible and creative underwriting and placement techniques. The warrant will become an even more popular feature of bonds. Trading around the clock will become more of a reality across many debt instruments, be they government or corporate. The issuance of corporate debt will be more of an international activity for an increasing number of corporations, as will the ownership of bonds for an increasing number of investors. "Bundled" bonds with options features to protect investors against certain risks will grow, as will the various techniques to unbundle them. The popularity of fixed- versus floating-rate issues will continue to depend on interest rate levels, expectations about interest rates, and the special circumstances of the issuer.

The Eurobond markets will continue to grow at high rates, overshadowing the growth of many domestic bond markets. The diversity in terms of issuers, types of issue, and currency composition will shift considerably. The currency composition will shift decidedly in favor of the yen and the ECU and away from the traditional dollar dominance. The developments on the LIFFE are very positive for the Eurobond market because the riskiness of the issues can be unloaded in the same geographic market.

The debt swap market will continue to shrink interest rate differentials across markets and in the process integrate the financial markets. Swaps, as professionals know, were a very effective tool for managing market and credit risk without altering balance sheet aggregates. They will grow, especially those swaps with option features.

This integration of the financial markets certainly has many good sides to it, but it has undesirable ones as well. The speed of adjustment to monetary policy changes will increase, causing exchange rates to overshoot. The independence of monetary policy at the national level will be diminished in the process. Also, the increased competition in the financial markets has led and will continue to lead to the systematic underpricing of risk. The fees on notes issuance facilities are, for example, half those of commercial paper—a very close substitute.

The equity markets will continue to become more international as a result of further international portfolio diversification and more liberal capital flow policies. The cross-listing of securities will grow considerably, as will the issuance of new shares on an international scale. The availability of stock index futures contracts on many foreign indexes will enhance the willingness of investors to buy foreign securities.

The linkages (correlation) across national markets will continue to grow with positive and negative effects. The lessons of the October 19 crash in this regard, when markets collapsed one after the other following the U.S. lead, will be very hard to forget.

The growth of mutual funds dedicated to international securities or to securities from a given country (e.g., the Korea Fund) will continue. Their attractiveness to investors will increase as more investors acquire geocentric investment perspectives.

Before concluding this section, we must consider major trends in Japan that are bound to influence the developments in its financial markets and banking system. Our discussion is based on a study by Alan Feldman of the IMF, which he presented at a London conference on Japanese financial growth held in October 1988. Feldman sees six forces for change:

• An aging Japanese population will have greater interest in longer-term investments. A larger role for women in Japanese firms (although in 1988 only 1 in 100 women workers was counted as management) and increased interest in improving their standard of living will translate into greater sensitivity to returns on their savings. This does not bode well for the PSS.

- Japanese banks and investment banks will have new opportunities as 1992 approaches and European firms begin to incorporate Japanese technology into their facilities.

- The nature of the current government debt structure and the continuing fiscal deficit will result in a higher supply of longer-term government bonds. The reliance on the PSS as a source of funds will have to decrease.

- The electronics age will increase opportunities in the market (e.g., make arbitrage easier and more accessible) and will lower transaction costs.

- The now dormant energy sector could re-emerge as a major financial concern, just as it did in 1973–1974.

- Borrowing is gaining more acceptance in Japan. "The growth of consumerism . . . may be of equal importance to the shift of political power in Japan toward urban areas."[2] There has been a marked increase in the use of debit and credit cards.

These forces, coupled with an unprecedented level of wealth for the Japanese people and an "overemployed" economy (each applicant has 1.14 jobs), will have profound effects on the Japanese financial markets.

The other financial markets discussed in this book will not see major shifts. The Australian markets may retrench a bit, and the dynamism of the Hong Kong market will depend on political factors—namely, how China will deal with Hong Kong in its struggle to become a major power and simultaneously to hold onto the Maoist ideology.

BANKING IN THE 1990s

The distinction between domestic and international banking will disappear. Banks will source money in the interbank market and invest funds internationally, either directly or indirectly. International events will influence monetary policy and interest rates and, consequently, the strategies and operations of all banks. Thus, all banking institutions are directly and/or indirectly influenced by international factors. Most banks have had to adopt a geocentric approach to their planning in order to assure their survival in an increasingly competitive world. This trend will continue and will reach the smaller firms.

The distinction between banks and investment banks will be much less pronounced in the 1990s. This change is actually independent of whether or not the Glass–Steagall Act is repealed. Banks will continue to securitize their assets and their liabilities, and investment banks will offer instruments that are functionally similar to those offered by banks. Banks will own investment banking facilities, perhaps with a limited product range, and will sell insurance and underwrite certain types of insurance. The trends in this direction are unmistakable. As banking operations evolve, they will be subjected to stricter supervision to compensate for any reduction in regulatory constraints. However, the frequency,

Exhibit 8.1
The U.S. Banking Industry, 1983–1987

	1983	1984	1985	1986	1987	1988*
Total Assets (billions)	$ 2,333	2,499	2,717	2,930	2,985	3,080
Nonperforming Loans $ (billions)	40.7	43.5	43.7	48.3	63.1	63.4
Bank Failures (number)	48	79	120	184	203	221
Net Income** $ (billions)	14.9	15.2	17.9	17.1	3.3	18.0

Source: Sheshunoff Information Services.

extent, and nature of the supervisory process will change. The coordination level among supervisory agencies and among regulatory agencies from different nations will also improve.

The banking sector will experience greater consolidation through mergers and acquisitions and through the streamlining of operations. This consolidation will be prodded on the domestic level by the disappearance of all restrictions on interstate branching. The five remaining holdout states will soon adjust to the realities in the marketplace. Technology will continue to act as a positive force in the expansion of banks on a national and international basis.

The changes anticipated in 1992 have already induced many American banks and investment banks to acquire financial institutions in Europe. This trend will continue.

Consolidation in the banking sector will also come as some banks fail to measure up to the competitive pressures. Exhibit 8.1 shows the glaring facts about the state of the U.S. banking industry. Nonperforming loans rose steadily between 1983 and 1988, as did bank failures. Industry profits fell dramatically in 1987 as banks took massive reserves against sovereign debt.

These industry problems will continue in the 1990s—with a silver lining, however. The sovereign debt crisis is still a menacing problem to commercial banks, and the final solution has yet to be offered. The policy pronouncement by Treasury Secretary Nicholas Brady in March 1989, following the riots in Venezuela, was fundamentally correct, but managed to increase confusion instead of allowing the banks to take a fresh step toward a radical solution to the problem.

Secretary Brady suggested a broad reduction in the $400 billion of debt outstanding. (A detailed program along these lines suggested by the author four years earlier fell on deaf ears at that time.[3]) The Brady program envisions three types of debt reduction transactions:

In one type, bank debt would be swapped for bonds of lower face value. In a second, bank debt would be traded for bonds of equal face value but with a lower interest rate. In the third, debt could be swapped for part-ownership of local businesses. To make these deals possible the proposal includes several major elements:

- Countries such as Mexico and Venezuela, which impose strong IMF-approved economic reforms and can show they are recapturing their citizens' private capital from abroad, would be entitled to use special measures to cut their debt burden.
- The first special measure would be the right to use some percentage, possibly 25%, of their normal loans from the IMF and World Bank to buy back bank debt or to guarantee bonds to be swapped for debt at a discount.
- The second special device would be "pools" of money in the IMF and the World Bank, drawn from existing resources, that these favored debtor countries could use as backing to effectively guarantee the banks that interest would be paid on loans for which interest rates or principal had been reduced.
- In addition, the favored countries would get Japanese loans to be used to replenish reserves, or to buy back debt or guarantee new discounted bonds.
- Banks would be asked to negotiate a joint waiver of standard clauses in their loans that impede debt reduction. They would then be asked to negotiate debt-reduction deals and, in effect, write down some portion of the old loans in return for getting a guarantee on the principal or interest of the bonds.[4]

These steps are very much in the right direction and will go a long way toward alleviating the problems. Their full implementation, however, requires considerable clarification, negotiation, and regulatory adjustment. The program, if accompanied by responsible new bank policies regarding loans to third world countries, will make for a healthier bank balance sheet in the 1990s.

As the hope for a solution to the sovereign debt crisis rises, new problems could emerge for banks, especially U.S. banks, as a result of their off-balance-sheet activities, and particularly their heavy commitments to a rather new phenomenon—leveraged buyouts (LBOs). Concerns over bank commitments to LBOs have been expressed by the Office of the Comptroller of the Currency and the chairman of the Federal Reserve Board. The problem lies in the size of the commitments as well as in the distribution of the commitments by industry: "about 40% of LBOs and other corporate restructuring are in so-called cyclical sensitive industries—over the past five years there were more than 1,500 such buyouts with values of more than $1 million, accounting for roughly 20% of all corporate restructuring."[5]

The stability of the U.S. banking industry will continue to be a source of concern in the 1990s. The level of concern will increase significantly should the economy soften. The pressures to innovate and to circumvent certain regulations may have helped some banks, but hurt others.

The developments in the United States are not much different from those in other countries. Consolidation through hostile takeovers is taking place in Australia. The Bank of Victoria, ANZ, Advance Bank, and other financial institutions have been involved in major acquisition deals in 1988 and 1989.

In Asia, bankers are more fee oriented than ever. Fee-based business is the logical answer to any slowdown in loan demand and to continuing pressures to reduce loan rates. The new strategy for Asia's bankers appears to focus on "Targeting equity products instead of debt instruments; treating some countries like investors rather than borrowers; and replacing the public sector strategy with a willingness to consider opportunities in the private sector."[6]

Whether these strategies will pay off or not is uncertain. What is certain, however, is that unless bankers continue to be (or become more) sensitive to their clients' needs they will undoubtedly lose market share.

We now take a close look at the prospective regulatory changes and the rationale for their occurrence.

The Changing Regulatory Environment in the 1990s

Regulation of financial institutions in the United States and other developed countries has been largely reactive. The changes that occurred therein do not speak for an inherently dynamic system or for a regulatory "master plan," with each new step (regulatory change) representing the movement of a dot on a chart. Having reviewed major regulatory changes in the leading financial centers, I am unable to recall one that was anticipatory in nature or that was not a copy of changes occurring in other markets. Regulators either lack the vision or do not believe that a proactive policy is necessary or desirable. In any case, the market seems always to be running ahead of regulators who are always trying to catch up. If this is the law of nature, then one should concentrate on the speed of adjustment in regulations instead of who leads or lags.

The regulation of any financial system imposes a cost on the system being regulated and on society as a whole. The latter cost is substantial. Consider only the cost of the Federal Reserve System. Therefore, all things being equal, a regulated company would have a higher total cost curve than would one that is totally unregulated. The avoidance of this "regulatory tax" has led to many innovations in the financial markets and to the huge expansion in off-balance-sheet activities by commercial banks. This cost must be compared to the benefits that accrue, for the most part, to the society at large. Regulation is therefore a tradeoff between efficiency on the one hand and fairness, safety, and integrity (of the system) on the other. Enlightened regulators have been speaking out clearly and wisely about the shape and character of a new regulatory structure. E. Gerald Corrigan, speaking in 1987, outlined a reasonable philosophy:

We simply cannot have a financial system in which a few participants seem to believe that standards of behavior start with the maximization of profits and end with the socialization of losses.

. . . The central question is not whether the banking and financial system should be subject to official supervisory oversight, but rather how we strike at the appropriate and reasonable balance between the dictates of competition and efficiency on the one hand and safety and integrity on the other.[7]

How the balance will be struck depends on many factors, including philosophical bias, the political power of certain interest groups, the true understanding of economic theory, and the evolution of the financial markets. It must be stressed that the economics for the others are much less predictable. The intent here is not to reproduce the discussion in Chapter 2, but rather to establish the necessary framework for our predictions with regard to regulatory changes.

Richard Dale offered four fundamental reasons for regulating the financial markets:

- Bank liabilities are "money" used as a main ingredient of monetary policy.
- The government may wish to channel the intermediated funds to specific projects or industries.
- Consumers must be protected.
- The financial system must be protected from bank runs, and the risks and costs of failure ought to be minimized.[8]

In a critical evaluation, James Brander[9] found Dale's propositions to be minimal justification for isolating banks for special regulatory treatment. Dale's last three reasons for bank regulation were dismissed on the grounds that the free market is the best allocator of resources and government projects simply drain funds from higher-valued projects, and that the mere presence of risk does not necessarily call for regulation. Risk diversification and the purchase of insurance are adequate methods for dealing with risk. But market failure, especially in the form of asymmetric information, does justify regulation.

Let us now consider the major features of bank regulation, their consistency with economic theory, and the necessary adjustments in light of economic rationality.

BANK REGULATION IN THE 1990s

Reserve Requirements

This regulation is an effective tax on bank deposits intended to "stabilize" the money creation process. Not all banking, however, is subject to reserve requirements. Offshore banking in Canada is not, and the roof did not cave in on the Canadian banking system. Brander argues as follows:

There is no basic reason why banks should be treated differently from other deposit taking firms. Macroeconomic control depends on total liquidity, not just on bank liabilities. In practice, liabilities of trust companies are "money" just as much as deposits are. As for "market failure" reasons for reserve requirements, such reasons have not been clearly demonstrated, but if they exist, it is hard to see why they should be different for other deposit taking institutions than for banks.[10]

Some of the regulatory alternatives that can occur in the 1990s with respect to reserve requirements are

- Eliminating reserves entirely
- Keeping reserves but paying interest on those reserves

- Dropping reserve requirements in favor of a borrowing limit (zero or some value related to bank size) from the Fed

This writer believes that the most likely scenario in the short run is the second because the system of reserve requirements is too well entrenched, whether economically justified or not.

James Tobin, Nobel laureate, argues for the appropriateness of reserve requirements:

While it is possible to operate a system with zero reserve ratios, that does not mean it is a good idea. For one thing, distributional equities are at stake. The taxpayers would lose the cheap placement of part of the national debt in required interest-free holdings. Moreover, a zero required reserve would mean that demands for federal funds would depend entirely on individual depositories' precautionary decisions to hold excess reserves and to borrow at the discount window. These depend on uncertainties that the central bank would find difficult to be forecast in aggregate; the more predictable demands for required reserves would be nonexistent.[11]

Capital Adequacy

Banking is one of the most heavily leveraged industries. Ninety-four percent of its assets are financed by debt.

Capital represents one of three major safety valves (lines of defense) for bank creditors (depositors). Regulation is thought to be the first line of defense— preventive medicine—bank profits being the second line and capital being the last line of defense. Capital is a cushion against losses, but it is also an important security blanket for depositors because it demonstrates to them the willingness of shareholders to put their funds at risk on a permanent basis.

Capital/asset ratios are used to control the growth of banks and the commitments they make to given borrowers. Consequently, they force one form of diversification (by the client), although overcommitment to one client is not impossible, as happened in the case of sovereign debt when the capital/asset limit per client (country) was very creatively interpreted.

At issue here is the definition of what constitutes adequate capital because no capital ratio is adequate if the decisions on the asset side are substandard or if a bank run hits the industry. The other issue is the definition of capital. Today, it includes perpetual bonds, perpetual floating rate notes (FRNs), and perpetual preferred stock. This most liberal of definitions is troubling indeed because it creates an equity "illusion" and increases the probability that creditors can force banks into liquidation if the banks are unable to meet their debt obligations.

Liberal as the definition of capital may be, banks have done all they can to circumvent capital requirements through off-balance-sheet activities. The new risk-based capital structure forces these off-balance-sheet items onto the balance sheet, using a conversion factor. What it does not do is force banks to classify existing on-balance-sheet items into various risk classes, each with a capital requirement, with the weighted average of capital requirements producing the desired capital ratio. The correlation structure between the various asset categories must be considered in the process. Unless this is required, and it ought to be, some banks will take unfair advantage of the deposit insurance system for which they pay a flat fee per dollar of deposit.

What should also be considered is some form of netting scheme in which the natural hedges that off-balance-sheet items provide for on-balance-sheet items is accounted for. This comprehensive view of bank activities should guide the bank examiners, and if available, it is likely that it would.

The extent to which regulators can hum this tune is limited, unfortunately. Banks with low P/E ratios and low price/book values will find it difficult to raise capital. Bank of America, like many others, had to sell its headquarters in order to improve its capital base. Also, a larger capital/asset ratio may cause banks to take undue risk on the assets to compensate for the added regulatory tax. The dynamic nature of this is also important because capital may be adequate under certain circumstances or at one point in time and totally inadequate under different circumstances or in a different time frame.

It is evident from the above that capital and deposit insurance could be traded in achieving "stability" of the banking system and that frequent and thorough supervision is essential for monitoring the more complex and comprehensive system recommended here.

The risk-adjusted capital base is one option for coping with balance sheet dynamics. Another is a variable FDIC premium. Both methods argue against uniform standards, and though the two options may be equivalent in theory, they are not in practice. The adjustment of the capital base may turn out to be much more difficult to realize than a realignment of the insurance premium. The latter has serious cash flow effects on a periodic basis, while the former occurs much less frequently.

The problem, however, is that either plan is likely to be applied to banks that are least able to withstand it, increasing in the process the probability that a "Hail Mary pass" will be thrown by bank management, with a considerable chance of bankrupting the bank. This is where supervision, and tough supervision at that, is paramount. Regulators should, and I believe will, shut down an institution before its equity capital becomes negative. A margin of error of one standard deviation from the mean should be applied in order to minimize the probability of shutting down an institution that has a good chance for recovery or that may not be insolvent to begin with. Another dimension to the problem is the political one—a form of agency problem. The closure of a bank in one's congressional district— with all its economic, social, and political repercussions—does not always sit well with political officeholders. The lessons from the S&L crisis were harsh and, hopefully, lasting. The 1990s will witness tougher regulators attempting to keep inept bank managers from reaching the pockets of taxpayers.

The economics of all the above are imbedded, once again, in the market failure area. Brander argued, however, that there is no prior reason "to believe that unregulated firms would choose levels of leverage that were too high from the public interest point of view." The market will ensure that such could occur at a cost too high to be acceptable. The other market failure deals with externalities where the bank management simply fails to consider the cost to creditors and debtors in driving the bank into bankruptcy. Brander finds economic theory on this issue insufficiently cogent to be fully convincing. We do feel, however, that the concerns are sufficiently serious to warrant capital requirements. It is best to err on the side of safety, especially when it comes to international banks, which are exposed to significantly higher risks than their domestic counterparts are. Among the risks are the following.

Foreign Exchange Risk

The losses in this area can be enormous. The Herstatt bank failed significantly as a result of foreign exchange speculations, Union Bank of Switzerland lost $150 million in its foreign exchange trading department, and Dai-ichi Kangyo lost $140 million between 1978 and 1982 in its Singapore branch as the foreign exchange trader trying to recover his losses sank further and further into trouble.

The Interbank Market Risk

This market can set a chain of events into motion that may be wholly unpredictable and uncontrollable. The weaker banks that rely more heavily on this market may be rationed out of it at a time when they most need it. Some banks source funds in this market in order to circumvent a lending restriction (e.g., a French bank may borrow from a U.S. bank in the interbank market in order to book a loan to a Russian entity which is off-limits to U.S. banks) or to make a loan for unproductive purposes (consumption loans).

Country Risk

The sovereign debt crisis brought this type of risk to the forefront of our concerns. Countries such as Argentina and Mexico had no resources to absorb the economic reversals, and this left the international banks totally exposed. Some borrowing by sovereign countries was corrupt, politically motivated, and void of economic justification.

We now look more closely at the payment system and the risks therein.

The Payment and Settlement System

The world payment and settlement system could be a source of problems in the 1990s. This system currently consists of the New York Clearing House CHIPS System and the Fed's Funds and Securities Transfer System (Fedwire).

CHIPS is a provisional payment system with a daily average volume of $450 billion. Payments through CHIPS are made during the course of a day. The final settlement takes place at the end of the day through the Federal Reserve Bank of New York.

The Fedwire clears about $250 billion in U.S. government securities and $400 billion in fund transfers among foreign and domestic banks. The Fed interposes itself between the payer and the receiver of funds by guaranteeing the finality of the transfer. The transfer of funds is affected through a computer network that can be tapped directly by banks and indirectly by their customers as determined by the affiliated banks themselves, and not the Fed, which is ultimately responsible for the system.

The Fed has been most accommodating and generous in its treatment of participating institutions. It charges nothing for its daylight overdraft or for its payment guarantee against funds flowing through the Fedwire. This could well change in the 1990s—and it should. The risk, if only from overreliance on complex technology, is real. The bulk of the transactions are concentrated in a few institutions, and the failure of any one could seriously jeopardize the viability of the system. Access, especially indirect access, to the system should be restricted and controlled by the Fed directly.

It must be noted that while Franklin Edwards may support the tightening of procedures, he does not see the problem as a "payments system risk," but rather as a part of the "general issue of financial institution soundness."[12] This is so in the Fedwire case. However, Professor Edwards does acknowledge the existence of systemic risk in the CHIPS system because it lacks the payment guarantee of the Federal Reserve. A chain reaction similar to a bank run is possible, although not very probable.

The Future of Glass–Steagall

The separation between banking and investment banking is becoming more fiction than fact, not only in the United States but also all over the world to varying degrees. The overlaps between banking and commerce and between banking and insurance are also becoming quite pronounced.

The distinction between banks and thrift institutions is vanishing as well. There is little, if any, economic rationale for maintaining the distinction between banks and savings and loans associations. No function performed by one cannot be performed by the other. If housing is an important policy objective, then banks may be required to hold a certain percentage of their portfolio in real estate mortgages and/or be given tax and other incentives to do so. Professor Tobin sees no reason for not merging these two institutions in the same manner that their insurers (FSLIC and FDIC) were merged recently under the S&L rescue plan of the Bush administration. In fact, many S&Ls have been acquiring bank licenses, and the trend will continue. Tobin has suggested that S&Ls "could place most of their mortgages into an investment affiliate without insured deposits and their insured deposits into a commercial banking affiliate."[13] The continuing hemorrhaging of deposits in the S&L industry and the public loss of confidence in the industry will hasten the day when the industry will be no more. Although few tears will be shed, this event may well be a news item in the 1990s.

The walls between banking and investment banking will continue to crumble. As Robert Parry observed, "the banks' cost advantages in executing intermediation functions are diminishing." These functions deal primarily with "evaluating a given borrower's creditworthiness and in taking on interest rate, liquidity and credit risks."[14] The erosion is due to securitization on both sides of the bank balance sheet, direct placement, the proliferation of credit rating agencies (personal and business), the increased information flow about every issue known to man as a consequence of huge laps in technology and decreasing access costs, and the emergence and expansion of derivative markets such as options and futures, which allow individuals and firms to lay off as much risk as they desire and to do so directly and quite inexpensively. Also at work is the desire of banks to provide a logical continuum to their activities. It does not seem fair or rational for U.S. banks to be permitted certain activities overseas, while being forbidden the same at home. Nor is it fair or logical to expect U.S. banks to be competitive internationally if they cannot offer the same type and level of service as any other bank in the field. Also, diversification requirements and the need to prevent disintermediation and to improve their performance and their ability to survive and prosper in a more competitive and dynamic economy necessitated the redefinition of the banking industry. Investment banking activities were a perfectly logical extension, and a lucrative one at that.

While nondepository firms are now able to offer virtually the full range of banking services—albeit, less efficiently than through outright ownership of commercial banks— banks are trying to broaden their nonbanking activities. To a certain extent, regulators are accommodating these pressures. Bank regulators have expanded permissible activities to include credit-related insurance, discount brokerage, (limited) securities underwriting, data processing, financial planning, and investment advisory services. Moreover, regulators now sanction bank holding companies' purchases of failing thrift institutions, thereby expanding the opportunities for those banking organizations.[15]

This trend will continue in the 1990s. It is most likely that banks will be able to offer a full range of investment banking services in the not too distant future. Indeed, some proposed legislation discussed below is calling precisely for this to occur.

The investment banks will be no less intrusive. They have been vigilant in protecting, albeit unsuccessfully, their turf and in trying to become banks in so many ways that circumvent existing restrictions. They will be able to go through the front door in the 1990s.

The three major stumbling blocks to the cross-fertilization of the two industries have been

- Self-dealing
- Undue access to the "safety net"
- Undue concentration of economic power

Self-dealing—allowing improper access to company assets by insiders and their relatives and friends (the "Bert Lance Effect")—could occur when one part of a bank holding company acquires undue access to the bank's financial assets. It is observed that Chase's commitment to its REIT was well under the arm's length requirement of fair dealing. Brander argues that self-dealing is not per se bad because it can allow for greater economies of scale and risk diversification. However, it can be an excellent vehicle for expropriating the wealth of minority shareholders in a less than wholly owned subsidiary which makes up the holding company. Self-dealing, unchecked, can also violate procedural fairness.

In addition, it creates market failure for the expectation of this problem will prevent minority shareholders from getting involved in the first place, so valuable economic transactions may be foregone. The basic source of inefficiency is asymmetric information.[16]

It is both desirable and possible to structure a banking system in which the banks are insulated from their subsidiaries involved in nonbanking activities. This is shown below.

The access to the "safety net," which effectively translates into a taxpayer guarantee for the banking sector, will be automatically extended to nonbanking activities. Consequently, every business entity will be provided guarantees of sorts (or a full guarantee) against bankruptcy. This case is particularly serious (from both capitalistic and efficiency perspectives) if banks are allowed to own commercial entities. There are several ways, however, to insulate banks from the commercial entities they own, and many of them are already in force. Transactions that favor an affiliate at the expense of the bank cannot be transferred to the safety net. Also, FDIC insurance does not cover the owner of the bank. Let us examine two cases of mixing banking with commerce, one of which was a total surprise to this writer.

General Motors Acceptance Corporation

General Motors Acceptance Corporation (GMAC) is a wholly owned subsidiary of General Motors. In 71 years of operation, it grew to be the largest financing company in the United States with assets of $99 billion at the end of 1988. It currently operates 236 offices nationwide and owns GMAC Mortgages with 71 offices nationwide and GMAC Capital Corp., a banking subsidiary in Utah. The latter offers CDs used mostly for funding GMAC activities. Its debt structure consists of $55 billion in short-term debt (a year or less) and $27 billion in long-term debt (over one year). Some of this debt was issued overseas. In 1988, GMAC had seven issues in the Eurobond market, raising a total of $700 million, and the borrowing schedule is becoming increasingly international. The bulk of its assets goes toward car financing, and its profits in 1988 amounted to $1.2 billion.

The ownership of GMAC has surely helped GMC sell cars, but there is no clear evidence that the public trust has been violated, despite the fact that several of GMAC's activities are banking-type activities.

First Nationwide Bank

This savings bank is a wholly owned subsidiary of Ford Motor Company and the second largest S&L in the nation after Home Savings of America. Ford Motor

Company acquired it in 1985, largely from National Steel Company which owned 80 percent of the bank. This savings bank operates in 15 states with 250 branches and assets equal to $26 billion. The interesting aspects of the Ford setup are that Ford simultaneously owns Ford Motor Credit Corporation—a $56 billion wholly owned subsidiary—and that two Ford executives sit on the board of directors of First Nationwide. Yet there is no documented evidence of abuse and self-dealing, and there is no public outcry for divestiture. Ford, First Nationwide, and the economy have not been hurt by this mixing of banking activity with commerce.

The problems, however, do not lie in isolated cases, but in a trend that can lead to undue concentration of economic power. West Germany allows the Crossover, but imposes strict ownership limits to prevent a few banking institutions from controlling the German economy. The ultimate level of concentration is a one-company nation or a nation where all the means of production are owned by the state. The consequences of this, however, are too well known from an economic efficiency point of view. This does not necessarily argue that any movement from the existing structure toward a more concentrated structure is necessarily anti-competitive. Bigger and better capitalized firms are healthier competitors, and as each decides to enter a new business area, it increases competition in the new area, even if the entry is through acquisition. The acquiring company may choose to commit more resources, or it may simply possess a better mousetrap. Tough antitrust laws will (should) take care of the rest.

The ideas on how to deal with unreasonable access to the safety net and with self-dealing abound. The work of Thomas Huertas is chosen here because it summarizes all the major proposals on insulating banks from their affiliates. Exhibit 8.2 summarizes the new provisions suggested for improving the "R-Factor" (insulation) between banks and their affiliates. The answer, on philo-sophical grounds at least, appears to be this: Do not prohibit an activity; rather, supervise keenly.

While many banking experts are largely convinced about the merit of cross-fertilization between banks and investment banks, they remain unconvinced as to the mixing of banking and commerce issues. If the summary of the 1987 Banking Symposium provided by Gordon H. Sellon, Jr., is an indication, then the road to acceptance of banking and commerce as a harmonious unit is rough indeed. Some people simply consider it a matter of faith. No solid argument (but much rhetoric) is offered as to why the separation ought to be maintained. The similar opposition that fought interstate branching all but withered away, and now some states are currently competing for banks from out of state to open branches in their jurisdiction.

The recent federal legislative initiatives to dismantle Glass–Steagall and to expand bank powers are quite liberal in terms of allowing banks access to every area of the U.S. economy. The psychological and philosophical hurdle of banks underwriting securities has been crossed. The battle is now over banking and commerce.

The Cranston–D'Amato bill (S. 1905) was the most liberal in this regard.

Exhibit 8.2
Supplemental Provisions Can Raise the "R-Factor" of Bank Insulation

	OCC	ABHC	Heller	ARCB	FDIC	R-Factor	Optimal
Anti-fraud[1]	X	X					X
Bear-down[2]				X			X
Stand-alone			X			P	
Arm's length			X			P	
Limit on daylight overdrafts					X	P	
Audit of affiliate transactions					X	P	
Back-stop				X		E	
Enforcement[3]							X

P - Covered by plenipotentiary provision[4]
E - Covered by extra-layer provision.[5]

[1] Affiliates are prohibited from stating or implying that their liabilities are obligations of an insured bank or implying that their obligations are covered by Federal Deposit Insurance.

[2] Bear Down: maintain adequate capital at all times. Owner of the bank will have to divert if the bank's capital falls below the minimum required level.

[3] This would grant the primary federal regulator of a bank controlled by a financial services holding company the authority to seek an immediate court injunction against any unsafe or unsound practice engaged in such a bank.

[4] Gives the primary federal regulator the authority to write rules and regulations regarding inter-affiliate transactions as to protect the safety and soundness of the bank.

[5] Would require banks controlled by financial services holding cos. to maintain supplemental capital.

Source: Thomas Huertas, "Redesigning Financial Regulation." Reprinted with permission of publisher, M. E. Sharpe, Inc. 80 Business Park Drive, Armonk, New York 10504 USA, from the January/February 1988 issue of *Challenge*.

Under this bill, banks would be allowed to offer all types of financial services and own (or be owned by) commercial firms.

Less liberal was the Wirth–Graham bill (S. 1891), which reflected proposals advanced by E. Gerald Corrigan, president of the Federal Reserve Bank of New York. The bill defined banks as "any institution with federally insured deposits." The bill also allowed for "commercial" holding companies (similar to those in Japan) in which financial and commercial firms can be included.

The Proxmire–Garn bill (S. 1886) had the strongest chance of passing the Congress. It was supported by the administration and the top administrators of the regulatory agencies. The most restrictive of the bills introduced in Congress, it would allow banks to become investment banks in a series of steps. Activities such as real estate, insurance, and commerce would remain prohibited.

These and similar bills introduced in the House of Representatives led to a series of intense debates and lobbying by various interest groups—but to no legislative action. Glass–Steagall remains on the books as of 1989. While there appears to be a consensus in the United States that Glass–Steagall should be repealed, there is no such consensus, unfortunately, on how extensive the reform should be. It is most interesting, however, that eight years of Reaganomics with a president so committed (openly at least) to the free market proposition did not produce a law that allows U.S. banks to take advantage of market dynamics in the same way their European counterparts, with whom they compete intensely in the international markets, have been able to do for years. The alignment of the administration behind Proxmire–Garn is puzzling, yet it may be understandable if it was thought that such a bill was the only one with a reasonable chance of making it through Congress. The clamor to change the banking laws in the United States has abated recently. The winds of change are still blowing—but they may die as a result of the recession predicted for the Bush presidency. The regulators will continue to resist full liberalization measures despite the fact that the technology for turning operating subsidiaries into passive investments is at hand. Perhaps regulators have less than full confidence in their ability to adequately supervise the institutions they are required to regulate by law.

The change, when and if it comes, would necessitate a significant realignment of regulatory responsibilities. This is long overdue. The crash of October 19, 1987, illustrated in rather dramatic fashion the dire need for streamlining regulatory responsibilities, especially in a moment of crisis.

The proposals for regulatory redesign are numerous. The leading ones, summarized in Exhibit 8.3, make obvious the fact that turf protection is paramount. The Fed wants more control, and the Comptroller of the Currency does all he can to see to it that the Fed's gain is not his loss.

The realignment favored by this writer is as follows:

- The Fed will focus on the conduct of monetary policy and exchange intervention policy, and act as a lender of last resort. Membership in the Federal Reserve System will be required of all banking institutions, defined as those accepting demand deposits.

- The Comptroller of the Currency will examine and supervise all banks. A system of information-sharing with the Fed must be established because the Fed needs access to the latest data in its bank-lending function. The frequency and the nature of bank examination will have to change. Technology should allow the Comptroller of the Currency to monitor those items on bank balance sheets that are most likely to get banks in trouble. One can conceive of the comptroller's office as the "management committee" that is internal to any banking institution. Banks will be able to conduct their business in a free environment, and the Comptroller's office will interfere only when certain limits are violated or when certain agreements or rules are breached.

- The Securities and Exchange Commission (SEC) will regulate all securities and their derived assets. There is no economic reason for the existence of the Commodity Futures

Exhibit 8.3
Summary of Proposals for Regulatory Redesign

	Corrigan	OCC[1]	ABHC[2]	Heller	ARCB[3]	FDIC[4]
Technique	BHC[5]	Bank Subs	FSHC[6]/BHC	Double Umbrella	FSHC	Repeal[7]
Consolidated official supervision	Yes (Fed)	Yes (OCC)	No	No	No	No
Permissible affiliates						
Financial	Yes	Yes	Yes	Yes	Yes	Yes
Nonfinancial	No	(?)	No	Yes	Yes	Yes
Insulation possible	No	Yes	Yes	Yes	Yes	Yes

[1] Office of the Controller of the Currency
[2] Association of Bank Holding Companies
[3] Association of Reserve City Bankers
[4] Federal Deposit Insurance Corporation
[5] Bank Holding Company
[6] Financial Services Holding Company
[7] Glass-Steagall Act and Bank Holding Company Act

Source: Thomas Huertas, "Redesigning Financial Regulation." Reprinted with permission of publisher, M. E. Sharpe, Inc. 80 Business Park Drive, Armonk, New York 10504 USA, from the January/February 1988 issue of *Challenge.*

Trading Commission. The latter's existing staff could man the section (bureau, as the Japanese would call it) in the SEC that would deal with futures contracts. This should markedly improve the ability of the SEC to react to major market developments. The arbitraging that takes place across the various markets makes it reasonable and necessary for one entity to oversee all sides of the transactions and not just the one side that it is currently authorized to supervise. This is a clear case where narrow specialization does not pay off.

- The FDIC will provide insurance to all deposit-accepting institutions. The maximum insurance will cover $50,000 in any one institution. Implicit insurance based on size (as in the Continental Illinois case) or any other criterion would be discontinued. An exemption in such a case would conflict with the Fed's responsibility as a lender of last resort. It should not. Banking institutions should be allowed to fail just like any other business entity.

Under this proposal, the FDIC will insure uncorrelated risk, while the Fed will be insuring correlated risk (risk across financial institutions). The government (the Fed) has a comparative advantage in providing insurance of this kind because it alone has the power to print money to meet major emergencies.

The above regulatory structure would allow for clarity of purpose and function, economies of scale in the regulatory process, and the elimination of waste resulting from duplication and unnecessary political bickering. This approach reflects national concerns and not the concerns of one regulator over another.

Changes, however small, take place in a context. The October 19, 1987, crash taught us that the discipline of market forces is not always effective. The more deregulated the market becomes, the fewer tools the Fed has to influence the direction of events. Changing the interest rates becomes the Fed's main policy instrument. The others will fade in importance and effectiveness or disappear altogether.

CONCLUSIONS AND RECOMMENDATIONS

Regulations exist because certain groups in society benefit from their existence at the expense of the rest of society. For example, interest rates ceilings make for cheaper funds for banks and lower returns to depositors. Few people in the banking industry are moved by altruistic reasons. The interest of the firm or industry they serve dominates their choices. That is why the process of regulatory reform is a painstaking one with potent political forces pulling in different directions. The victory by some is almost never permanent as the tides shift and new realities set in.

This book has been a journey through various regulations in different major markets. My hope is that the treatment of the major issues showed breadth and depth. No one can hope to deal with all the issues in a complete fashion in a single book. Many questions have been answered, but many more have been raised. The road of research on financial deregulation is rough indeed. My hope also is that the road has been smoothed a bit and that major problem areas, still unresolved, have been exposed for future research.

I trust that the reader will be very critical, but fair. I have pointed out through this book the difficulties in answering all the questions in a clear, definitive manner. The state of economic theory and/or the data does not allow for conclusive answers in some cases. That is why the answers range from absolute certainty to the "don't know." I trust that the next researcher will be able to be more conclusive.

The pressure to revert to protectionism is always present. Those of us who believe in free markets must continue to provide the needed quality research to make certain policy recommendations compelling, not only in the United States but also all over the world. The only certainty in the world today is that we all learn (or at least try to learn) from each other's mistakes. In this ever more interdependent world, we cannot hide the mistakes or the success—and we cannot hide their implements.

NOTES

1. Neil Osborn, "Running Scared in Windy City," *Euromoney* (February 1989): 38–45.

2. IMF Survey (March 6, 1989): 66.

3. See Sarkis J. Khoury, "Sovereign Debt: A Critical Look at the Causes and the Nature of the Problem," *South Carolina Essays in International Finance* (July 1985).

4. Johnnie L. Roberts, "Dun & Bradstreet Says Sales Growth in Credit Division Has Slowed," *Wall Street Journal*, 13 March 1989.

5. *Wall Street Journal*, 1 March 1989.

6. Roberts, "Dun & Bradstreet."

7. E. Gerald Corrigan, *Quarterly Review* (Federal Reserve Bank of New York) (Summer 1987): 203.

8. Richard Dale, *The Regulation of International Banking* (Englewood Cliffs, N.J.: Prentice-Hall, 1985).

9. James A. Brander, "Economic Foundations of Financial Regulation," Working Paper Series (Vancouver: University of British Columbia, 1989).

10. Ibid., 12.

11. James Tobin, "A Case for Preserving Regulatory Distinctions," *Challenge* 30, no. 5 (November–December 1987): 14.

12. Franklin R. Edwards, "Can Regulatory Reform Prevent the Impending Disaster in Financial Markets?" *Economic Review* 73, no. 1 (January 1988).

13. Tobin, "A Case for Preserving," 12.

14. Robert T. Parry, "Major Trends in the U.S. Financial System: Implications and Issues," (Federal Reserve Bank of San Francisco) (Spring 1987).

15. Ibid., 9.

16. Brander, "Economic Foundations," 19.

Select Bibliography

Adam, Niqal. "Echoes of 'Big Bang': Even the Crash Won't Discourage the De-regulators." *International Management* 43 (January 1988): 20.

"Adios, Glass–Steagall." *Financial World* (12 January 1988): 20.

Altman, E. I. "Discriminant Analysis and the Prediction of Corporate Bankruptcy." *Journal of Finance* (1968): 589–609.

"America's Investment Banks Fear for Their Future." *Economist* (5 December 1987): 78–79.

Andrews, Suzanne. "Does Glass–Steagall Matter Anymore?" *Institutional Investor* 21 (May 1987): 168.

Arvan, Alice. "Those Fabulous Japanese Banks." *Bankers Monthly* 105 (January 1988): 29.

"Bank Decontrol: Put Off Control? Here Is Why 'Confusion Abounds' in a Process That Vitally Affects All Business People." *Nation's Business* 73 (June 1985): 38.

"Banking Industry Thrives as Deregulation Takes Hold." *Barrons* 65 (30 December 1985): 38.

"Banks Are on the Brink of Breaking Loose." *Business Week* (7 March 1988): 99–100.

Barnard, Doug. "Deregulation: The Governmental Climate." *Credit* 12 (January–February 1986): 10.

Barrett, Matthew. "The Coming Crunch for Banks." *Euromoney* (April 1987): 88.

"Barriers Crumble," Special Survey from *Euromoney* (February 1988).

Bellanger, Serge. "Regulating International Banking." *Bankers Magazine* (November–December, 1977): 44–49.

———. "Going Global." *Bankers Magazine* (March–April, 1987): 64–69.

Bennett, Andrea. "Skirmishes on the Regulatory Front." *American Banker* 152 (8 September 1987): 11.

Benston, G. J. "Deposit Insurance and Bank Runs." *Economic Review* (Federal Reserve Bank of Atlanta) (1983): 17.

Bierwag, Gerald O. *Duration Analysis: Managing Interest Rate Risk*. Cambridge, Mass: Ballinger Press, 1987.

"Big Bang: U.S. Banks Hope the Shot Will Be Heard." *Fortune* (27 October 1986): 8.

Blum, Patrick. "Deregulation Went Too Far." *Banker* 136 (May 1986): 105.

Boreham, Gordon. "European Banking Developments." *Canadian Banker* 92 (February 1985): 83.

Bovenzi, John F., James A. Marino, and Frank E. McFadden. "Commercial Bank Failure Prediction Models." *Economic Review* (Federal Reserve Bank of Atlanta) (1983).

"Britain's Merchant Bankers Stir Their Cauldrons." *Economist* 299 (26 June 1986): 75.

British Columbia Ministry of Finance and Corporate Relations, *Credit Union Amendment Act* (Victoria: The Ministry, 1987).

Brostoff, Steven. "ACLI Debates Banking Deregulation." *National Underwriter Life & Health—Insurance Edition* (23 November 1985): 3.

———. "Senate Moves on Banking Legislation." *National Underwriter Life & Health— Financial Services Edition* (2 February 1987): 3.

———. "Prospects of Greenspan at Fed Raises New Deregulation Fears." *National Underwriter Life & Health—Financial Services Edition* (22 June 1987): 1.

———. "Study on the Prudence of Deregulation." *National Underwriter Life & Health—Financial Services Edition* (21 September 1987): 3.

———. "Industry Stiffens against Bank Deregulation Bills." *National Underwriter Life & Health—Financial Services Edition* (7 December 1987): 1.

Buell, Barbara. "Deregulation: A Two Way Street." *Business Week* (22 June 1987): 62.

Butcher, Willard C. "What Banks Want . . . (Entry into Securities Markets)." *New York Times,* 8 January 1988.

Byland, Terry. "U.S. Banks Respond to the Invasion." *Banker* 135 (March 1985): 99.

Calem, Paul. "How Deregulation Will Affect Deposit Markets." *American Banker* 150 (13 December 1985): 4.

Canner, Glenn, and Julia Springer. "Basic Banking." *Federal Reserve Bulletin* April 1987, 255.

Carron, Andrew S. *The Political Economy of Financial Regulation*. Washington, D.C.: Brookings Institution, 1983.

Celarier, Michelle. "Less Bull for Petit Ban." *United States Banker* 99 (January 1988): 88.

Chan, Yuk-Shee, and King-Tim Mak. "Depositors' Welfare, Deposit Insurance, and Deregulation." *Journal of Finance* 40 (July 1985): 959–74.

Clark, Lindley. "One Way to Help the Case for Bank Deregulation." *Wall Street Journal,* 3 September 1987.

Clarke, Robert. "Deregulation and the Lessons of History." *Bottomline* 3 (May 1986).

Climente, John. "A Case Study of Geographic Deregulation: The New Illinois Bank Holding Company Act." *Journal of Bank Research* 16 (August 1985): 150.

Climo, Beth. "Time Is Running Out on Deregulation Panel." *American Banker* 150 (18 October 1985): 4.

Cohen, David. "The Cost Argument for Expanded Banking Powers." *Bank Marketing* 17 (March 1985): 4.

"Compliance under Deregulation." *ABA Banking Journal* 79 (December 1987): 37.

Conover, C. T. "Conover Sees Deregulation from Both Sides Now: and Former Comptroller Still Favors Expanded Bank Powers." *American Banker* 150 (16 September 1985): 3.

Cooper, Kerry, and Donald R. Fraser. *Banking Deregulation and the New Competition in Financial Services.* Cambridge, Mass.: Ballinger Publishing Co., 1984.

Corrigan, Gerald. "Corrigan's Proposal to Reshape the Financial Services Industry." *American Banker* 152 (2 February 1987): 10.

Cosimano, Thomas F. "The Federal Funds Market under Bank Deregulation." *Journal of Money, Credit, and Banking* 19, no. 3 (August 1987): 326–39.

Cottell, Robert. "Slow Road to Interest Rate Deregulation." *Banker* 135 (January 1985): 81.

"The Crucible for Ideas." *United States Banker* 97 (February 1986): 20.

Crum, William C. "Banking in Insurance: A Guide to Chaos." *Bankers Magazine* (January–February 1986): 51–58.

"Deregulation." *Euromoney* (March 1988).

"Deregulation Express." *Banker* (January 1988).

"Deregulation Makes Its Impact." *Banker* (January 1986).

"Deregulation's Finale Could Hold Surprises; Lower Minimums and Tiered Rate Accounts Are Expected." *Savings Institutions* (July 1985): 104.

Diamond, Douglas, and Phillip H. Dybvig. "Bank Runs, Deposit Insurance, and Liquidity." *Journal of Political Economy* (1983): 401–19.

"Dismantling Barriers." *Banker* (June 1987).

"Don't Let Panic Stop Bank Deregulation." *Business Week* (1 April 1985): 110.

"Down and Under in Hong Kong." *Far Eastern Economic Review* (15 September 1988): 91.

"Down Tumble the Barriers." *Banker* (January 1987).

"Down Under." *Banker* (December 1987).

Duffy, John. "Are Banks Ready for French Revolution?" *American Banker* 152 (20 April 1986): 1.

———. "London Markets Dive on Anniversary of Big Bang." *American Banker* 152 (27 October 1987): 2.

The Economist, *Intelligence Unit Country Profile: Hong Kong, Macau.* Economist Publications, Ltd., 1986.

Edmister, Robert O. "Securities Industry Market Share Trends after Banking Deregulation." *Financial Analysts Journal* 42 (March–April 1986): 7–9.

———. "Bank Deregulation and Deposit Reform: Some Hard Questions for Congress." *Banking Law Journal* 104 (January–February 1987): 42–55.

Eichergreen, Barry, and Richard Portes. "The Anatomy of Financial Crises." In *Threats to International Financial Stability,* ed. Richard Portes and Alexander K. Swobada, 10–57. Cambridge: Cambridge University Press, 1987.

Eisenberg, Richard. "The De-Lovely, Deregulation World of Banking." *Money* 14 (September 1985): 70.

Erdevig, Eleanor H. "Small States Teach a Big Banking Lesson." *Chicago Fed Letter,* June 1988.

Estey, W. Z. *Report of the Inquiry into the Collapse of the CCB and Northland Bank.* Ottawa: Ministry of Supply and Services, 1986.

Evans, Richard. "Switzerland's Horn of Plenty or Icy Blast?" *Euromoney* (August 1986): 33.

"Federal Home Loan Bank Board." *Agenda for Reform,* 1983, Washington, D.C.

"Federal Interest Rate Deregulation Is Nonevent for West Virginia Thrifts." *American Banker* 151 (24 April 1986): 12.

"The Fed on Powers." *United States Banker* 98 (June 1987): 6.

"Fending Off the Foreigners." *Euromoney* (February 1988).

Fennell, Tom. "Regulating Deregulation." *Maclean's* 100 (October 1987): 36.

"The Financial Revolution Picks Up Steam." *Institutional Investor* (August 1986).

Fitch, Ed. "Banks Out to Break Regulatory Shackles." *Advertising Age* 58 (3 August 1987): 52.

Flannery, M. J., and J. Guttentag. "Problem Banks: Examination, Identification, and Supervision." In *State and Federal Regulation of Commercial Banks,* ed. Leonard Lapidus et al. Washington, D.C.: Federal Deposit Insurance Corp., 1980.

Forde, John. "Sell Deregulation to Congressmen, Comptroller Advises State Bankers." *American Banker* 152 (23 June 1987): 2.

Fraser, Donald R., and James W. Kolari. *The Future of Small Banks in a Deregulated Environment.* Cambridge, Mass.: Ballinger Publishing Co., 1982.

"Freeing American Banks: Congress Should Not Leave Deregulation to the Courts and Clever Lawyers." *Economist* 295 (22 June 1986).

Furlong, Fred, and Bharat Trehan. "Deposit Deregulation and Behavior of M1." *Federal Reserve Bank of San Francisco Weekly Letter,* 11 October 1985, 1–3.

Garsson, Robert. "Greenspan Urges Senators to Define Bank Powers." *American Banker* 152 (22 July 1987): 1.

——. "Previewing Fall Legislative Season: Opportunities and Risks for Banks: Will Proxmire Attack Glass–Steagall or Press for Limited Overhaul?" *American Banker* 152 (14 September 1987): 11.

Garsson, Robert, and Jay Rosenstein. "Give Banks New Powers." *American Banker* 152 (22 January 1987).

Garten, Helen A. "Banking on the Market: Relying on Depositors to Control Bank Risks." *Yale Journal on Regulation* 4 (1986): 129–72.

Gilbert, Gary. "The Future of Banking Deregulation." *Magazine of Bank Management* 62 (July 1988): 2.

Gillis, John. "The Self-Regulation Movement." *Financial Analysts Journal* 42 (May–June 1986): 16.

Gluver, David. "Australian Banks Living with Deregulation." *Banker* 135 (February 1985): 83.

Golembe, Carter H., and David S. Holland. *Federal Regulation of Banking.* Washington, D.C.: Golembe Associates, Inc., 1975.

"Good Terms, Yes, But Is This Love?" *Euromoney* (February 1988).

Greenspan, Alan. "The Case for Deregulation of the Banking Industry." *American Banker* 152 (4 June 1987): 15.

——. "Innovation and Regulation of Banks in the 1990's." Paper presented at American Bankers Association, Honolulu, 11 October 1988.

Gross, Laura. "Deregulation, Mergers, and Rise of Nonbank Banks Brings Heightened Competition to a Changing Industry." *American Banker* 152 (21 January 1987).

Hall, Sally. "A Self-Dealing Disappointment." *Canadian Consumer* 17 (March 1987): 50.

Hamlin, George W. "Why Small Banks Want Broader Securities Powers." *American Banker* (5 March 1987): 1–7.

Hane, George. "Nonbank Bank Debate." *Bottomline* 3 (April 1987): 7.
————. "Holding Companies: Politics and Economics." *Bottomline* 4 (September 1988):
     7.
"Has Australia's Luck Run Out?" *Banker* (January 1986).
Hatanaka, Saulu. "The Deregulated Japanese Banking System." *Business Japan* 32 (May
     1987): 30.
Heebner, Gilbert A. "Deregulation in Commercial Banking." *Business Economics* 20
     (July 1985): 15–20.
Henley, Jerrold. "Communities Need Banks to Have Securities Powers." *ABA Banking
     Journal* 80 (January 1988): 10.
"Holey Cow: Glass–Steagall Act." *Economist* 302 (10 January 1987): 64.
The Hong Kong and Shanghai Banking Corporation: Business Profile Series. 6th ed.
     Hong Kong and Shanghai Banking Corp., 1986.
"Hong Kong Banks: Wrong Tune." *Economist* 300, no. 7463, pp. 89–90.
"Hong Kong Tightens the Rules." *Asiaweek* 12, no. 11, pp. 42–43.
Hornik, Richard. "Shortening the Tether on Bankers: Congress Halts, at Least for Now,
     the March of Deregulation." *Time* (17 August 1987): 50.
Horowitz, Jed. "Wall Street Frets about 1987; Glass–Steagall Fight, Boesky Fallout
     Expected." *American Banker* 151 (4 December 1988): 1.
"How Banks Are Reacting to Final Reg Q Rate Changes." *ABA Banking Journal* 77
     (October 1985): 11.
"How to Beat Bank Deregulation." *Consumer Digest* 25 (September 1988): 8.
Hughes, Stephen. "A Place in the Sun." *Banker* 137 (November 1987): 24.
Hultman, Charles W. "The Regulatory and Supervisory Response to Changes in U.S.
     International Commercial Banking." *Issues in Bank Regulation* (Summer 1986):
     21–26.
"The Invasion That Fizzled." *Asiaweek* (3 June 1988): 48–49.
Jacobe, Dennis. "Money Market: Regulation Succeeds in Halting Rapid Growth." *Sav-
     ings Institutions* 106 (September 1985): 37.
Janklow, William J. "South Dakota and Financial Deregulation." *Bankers Magazine* 168
     (September–October 1986): 32.
Jao, Y. C. "Banking and Currency in Hong Kong: A Study of Postwar Financial Develop-
     ment." Macmillan Press Ltd., 1974, 244–64.
"Japanese Finance: The Impact of Deregulation." Special *Euromoney* Report (1986).
"Jap Markets Will Add Stock Index Futures." *Los Angeles Times* 31 August 1988.
"Jap's New Stock Index Futures Have Strong Start, But Uncertainty Remains." *Wall
     Street Journal,* 6 September 1988.
Jones, Culin. "Dismantling Barriers." *Banker* 137 (June 1987): 44.
Kane, E. J. *The Gathering Crisis in Federal Deposit Insurance.* Cambridge, Mass.: MIT
     Press, 1985.
Kanil, Shireen. "Waking Up." *Banker* 137 (December 1987): 45.
Keely, Michael C. "Bank Capital Regulation in the Early 1980's." *Federal Reserve Bank
     of San Francisco Weekly Letter,* 22 January 1988, 1–3.
Keenan, Michael. "The Scope of Deregulation in the Securities Industry." In *The De-
     regulation of the Banking and Securities Industries,* ed. Lawrence G. Goldberg
     and Lawrence J. White, 115–32. Lexington, Mass.: Lexington Books, 1979.
Kollar, Axel. "German Deregulation Strengthens DM Financial Market." *American
     Banker* 151 (5 June 1986): 15.

Kraus, James. "Serene Lazard Steps to the Fore as Deregulation Comes to France." *American Banker* 151 (6 March 1986): 2.

Kutler, Jeffrey. "The Era of Deregulations: Reshaping of the Legal Framework and Market Structures Had Many Beginnings." *American Banker Annual* (1986): 63.

LaGesst, "January 1 Deregulation Is a Wash for Consumers; Higher Fees, Tiered Rates Offset Liberalized Now and Super Now Account Regulations." *American Banker* 150 (31 December 1985).

Lake, David. "Japanese Official Sees Ways to Open Up Financial System." *American Banker* 150 (31 December 1985).

———. "Deregulated Big Banks in Japan Push to Manage Pension." *American Banker* (5 January 1988): 2.

Lebolt, Fred. "Step by Step to Reform." *Euromoney* (May 1987): 5518.

"Legislators Fumble the Ball after Black Monday." *Asian Business* (July 1988): 66.

Lemann, Nicholas. "Change in the Banks: Deregulation Has Brought New Interest Rates, New Financial Services, and New Problems to Institutions That Have Been Very Comfortable, and Very Stable, for Fifty Years." *Atlantic Monthly* 256 (August 1985): 60–68.

Lewis, M. K., and K. T. Davis. *Domestic and International Banking*. Cambridge, Mass.: MIT Press, 1987.

Litan, Robert E. "Taking the Dangers Out of Deregulation in Turbulent Times." *American Banker* 152 (20 January 1987).

———. "Which Way for Congress?" *Challenge* (November–December 1987): 36–43.

———. "Taking the Dangers Out of Bank Deregulation." *Brookings Review* 4 (Fall 1988): 3.

Lloyds Bank. "Hong Kong." In *Lloyds Bank Group Economic Report,* 13–14.

"Looking to the Futures as Protection." Supplement to *Euromoney* (April 1987).

Lord, Dennis. "Banking across State Lines: Deregulation and Interstate Buyouts Have Transformed the Industry's Map." *Fogua* 37 (Spring 1987): 10.

Lovett, William A. *Banking and Financial Institutions Law in a Nutshell*. St. Paul, Minn.: West Publishing Co., 1984.

Lusser, Markus. "Policy and Financial Innovation: Will There Be a Switch from Deregulation to Reregulation?" In *Threats to International Financial Stability,* ed. Richard Portes and Alexander K. Swobada, 257–62. Cambridge, England: Cambridge University Press, 1987.

McGhee, Neil. "Dispute over Deregulation Stymies Insures and Bankers." *National Underwriter Life & Health—Insurance Edition* (22 November 1986): 3.

McLaughlin, John. "Banking on Deregulation." *National Review* 39 (23 October 1987): 24.

Mahoney, Patrick, Alice P. White, Paul F. O'Brian, and Mary M. McLaughlin. "Staff Studies." *Federal Reserve Bulletin,* January 1987, 20.

Malarkey, John E. "A Regulator's View of the State of State Banking." *American Banker* 151 (21 August 1985).

Malik, Michael. "Something in Reserve." *Far Eastern Economic Review* (8 September 1988): 127.

Mandel, Michael. "You Can't Bank on Deregulation." *Dollars & Sense* (October 1987): 9–12.

Martin, Jurek. "A Cautious and Pragmatic Approach to Liberalization." *Banker* 135 (January 1985): 71.

Mathews, Gordon. "Marqer Expert Expects Hostile Bids to Multiply: Bank of New York's Adviser Says Deregulation Will Spur More Unsolicited Offers." *American Banker* 152 (7 October 1987): 2.

Melloan, George. "The FDIC's Arguments for Bank Deregulation." *Wall Street Journal*, 24 November 1987.

———. "The Efficiency Argument for Banking Reform." *Wall Street Journal*, 29 December 1987.

———. "Global Bank Deregulation Fans a New Debate." *Wall Street Journal*, 15 March 1988.

Merton, R. C. "The Valuation of FDIC Deposit Insurance Using Option Pricing Estimates." *Journal of Money, Credit, and Banking* (1977): 446–60.

Metzger, Robert. "Developing the Deregulated Branch." *Journal of Retail Banking* 7 (Summer 1985): 50.

Much, Marilyn. "Deregulation Fears: Study Reveals Merger Sentiments." *Industry Week* 226 (30 September 1985): 29.

Mullane, Donald. "Managing a Bank through Deregulation." *Review of Business* 7 (Fall 1985): 25.

Murphy, Patricia A. "The Leadership on the Hill." *United States Banker* 99 (January 1988): 20.

Nadler, Paul S. "Don't Blame Deregulation." *Bankers Monthly* (15 January 1985): 11–13.

———. "Regulation." *Bankers Monthly* 102 (15 August 1985): 4.

———. "Tricks for 85: Cashing-in on Deregulation." *American Banker* 150 (7 October 1985): 4.

———. "Deregulation Cuts Banks' Health Coverage Costs." *American Banker* 150 (25 November 1985): 4.

———. "Addressing Subtler Issues of Glass–Steagall Debate." *American Banker* (18 January 1988): 4.

Nash, Nathaniel C. "After 55 Years, Is It Time to Deregulate the Banks?" *New York Times*, 3 January 1988.

———. "Prospects of Action on Bank Legislation Funds." *New York Times*, 4 January 1988.

Navins, Louis. "Regulation: Putting the Genie Bank in the Bottle." *United States Banker* 36 (September 1985): 50.

Naylor, Bartlett. "Administration Lends Support to Reformers: Mayflower Group Unveils Deregulation Principles." *American Banker* 152 (21 January 1987).

"New Hong Kong Bank Law Will Tighten Supervision and Help Stability." *Business Asia* 18, no. 12, pp. 92–93.

"No More Milk and Honey." *Banker* (November 1987).

Norton, Robert E. "Unleashing Banks on Wall Street," *Fortune* (29 September 1986): 88.

———. "The Battle over Market Reform." *Fortune* (1 February 1988): 18–26.

"NY Fed Reportedly Will Name Yamaichi a Primary U.S. Bond Dealer." *Wall Street Journal*, 29 September 1988.

Okumara, Hirohiko. "Implications of Open and Competitive Financial Markets." *Banker* 135 (January 1985): 96.

O'Sullivan, Robert A. "Federal Reserve Bank Examination Procedures." Paper presented to Central Bankers Conference, 1987.

"A Place in the Sun." *Banker* (November 1987).

Pollak, Alex. "Banks Fight Hard on Home Front." *Asian Finance* (15 May 1988): 40–48.

Proxmire, William. "Sen. Predicts Future of Bank Deregulation." *National Underwriters Life & Health—Financial Services Edition* (14 December 1987): 1.

Putman, Barron H. "Financial Warning Systems and Financial Analysis in Bank Monitoring." *Economic Review* (Federal Reserve Bank of Atlanta) (1983).

Pyle, David. "Some Implications of Deposit Deregulation." *Federal Reserve Bank of San Francisco Weekly Letter,* 10 February 1984, 1–3.

Rafferty, Kevin. "The Financial Revolution Picks Up Steam." *Institutional Investor* 20 (August 1986): 243.

Rapping, Leonard, and Lawrence Fulley. "Specialization, Deregulation and the Interest Rate." *American Economic Review* (May 1985): 108.

"A Rationale for Continued Deregulation of the Banking Industry." *American Banker* 151 (26 February 1986): 8.

"Regulator." Supplement to *Euromoney* (April 1987).

Rehm, Barbara. "General Accounting Office Report Questions Benefits Resulting from Bank Deregulation." *American Banker* 152 (13 July 1987): 1.

Rodowski, Robert, and Eric H. Sorensen. "Deregulation in Investment Banking: Shelf Registration, Structure, and Performance." *Financial Management* 14 (Spring 1985): 5.

Roll, Richard. "The International Crash of October, 1987." UCLA, 1988. Typescript.

Rose, Peter S. "The Impact of Financial Services Deregulation: The Hypotheses and the Evidence from 240 U.S. Metropolitan Banking Markets." *Quarterly Journal of Business and Economics* 26 (Spring 1987): 55.

Rose, Sanford. "Random Thoughts." *American Banker* 152 (1 September 1987): 1.

Rosenstein, Jay. "Proxmire's Promises Are Fading." *American Banker* 152 (2 March 1987): 10.

―――. "Proxmire Postpones Banking Bill Vote as Hopes for Expanded Powers Fade." *American Banker* 152 (5 March 1987): 1.

Sato, Milsu. "Banking Deregulation: Today and Tomorrow." *American Banker* 140 (September 1985): 12.

Savage, Donald T. "Interstate Banking Developments." *Federal Reserve Bulletin,* February 1987, 79–91.

Seidman, L. William. "The Future of U.S. Bank Supervision." *Issues in Bank Regulation* (Spring 1987): 16–23.

―――. "Glass–Steagall Restricts Banking More Than It Helps." *American Banker* 152 (26 August 1987): 4.

Selquin, George, and Lawrence H. White. "The Evolution of a Free Banking System." *Economic Inquiry* 25 (July 1987): 439.

Shale, Tony. "Surviving the Big Bang." *Euromoney* (April 1986): 89.

Simon, Bernard. "Canada Shakes the Four Pillars." *Banker* 137 (February 1987): 24.

Sinkey, J. F., Jr. *Problem and Failed Institutions in the Commercial Banking Industry.* Greenwich, Conn.: JAI Press, 1979.

Skully, Michael T. "Financial Institutions and Markets in the Southwest Pacific." 1–90. Macmillan, 1985.

―――. "Australian Banking: Its Regulation and Internationalization." Paper presented at Pacific Asian Management Institute, University of Hawaii, Honolulu, 1988.

―――. "Australian Futures Market." Paper presented at Pacific Asian Management Institute, University of Hawaii, Honolulu, 1988.

———. "Australian Securities Market." Paper presented at Pacific Asian Management Institute, University of Hawaii, Honolulu, 1988.

Spong, Kenneth. *Banking Regulation: Its Purposes, Implementation, and Effects.* 2d ed. Kansas City, Mo.: Federal Reserve Bank of Kansas City, 1985.

Srodes, James. "The Ax Wielders: The Politics of Killing Glass–Steagall." *Financial World* (12 January 1988): 28.

Stoakes, Christopher. "Big Banks and the Law of the Agency: Conflicts of Interest Could Delay Financial Deregulation in the U.K." *Euromoney* (December 1985): 41.

Sudo, Philip. "Small Banks Add to Chorus against Glass–Steagall." *American Banker* 152 (2 March 1987): 3.

Sutcliff, Robert J. "Regulation and Banking: Benefits of Competition in Lending." *Credit & Financial Management* 87 (June 1985): 14.

Tidwell, Drew V. "Effective Compliance Management: How to Stay Out of Trouble; Coping with the Regulation of Deregulation." *Bankers Magazine* 170 (September–October 1987): 29.

Tierry, Jacques. "Deregulation: Fashion or Progress?" *American Banker* 151 (23 May 1968): 15.

Tillier, Alan. "French Banking: A Year of Dramatic Change." *American Banker* 151 (28 November 1986): 5.

Timberlake, Richard H., Jr. "Legislative Construction of the Monetary Control Act of 1980." *AEA Papers and Proceedings* (May 1985): 97–102.

Tiwari, Kashi Nath. "The Money Supply Process under Deregulation." *Financial Review* 21 (February 1988): 111.

Triqaux, Robert. "Reagan Report Urges More Bank Deregulation." *American Banker* 150 (7 February 1985): 3.

———. "How Do Banks Spell Relief?" *American Banker* 151 (31 March 1986).

———. "Should Banks Be in the Securities Business?" *American Banker* 152 (2 February 1987): 13.

Tuccillo, John A. "Deregulation and Thrift Strategies." *Business Economics* (July 1985): 21–26.

"Two Foreign Firms Added as Dealers in U.S. Securities." *Wall Street Journal*, 30 September 1988.

Udell, G. F. "Technology and Bank Monitoring." In *Technology and the Regulation of Financial Markets,* ed. A. Saunders and L. J. White. New York: D. C. Heath, 1986.

Volcker, Paul A. Statement before the Subcommittee on Financial Institutions Supervision, Committee on Banking, Finance, and Urban Affairs, U.S. House of Representatives, 7 May 1986.

Wall, Larry D. "Has Bank Holding Companies' Diversification Affected Their Risk of Failure?" *Journal of Economics and Business* 39 (November 1987): 313.

Wallich, Henry. "Whither American Banking Reform?" *Challenge* 28 (September–October 1985): 43.

West, R. C. "A Factor-Analytic Approach to Bank Condition." *Journal of Banking and Finance* (1985): 253–66.

"Will the Bankers Follow the Beer?" *Euromoney* (August 1988): 53–67.

Winkler, Matthew. "Ruder Says Banks Should Be Allowed to Compete in the Securities Business." *Wall Street Journal*, 3 December 1987.

"Wither the Banks?" *Euromoney* (August 1988): 69–70.

Wong, Jesse. "Hong Kong Takes Control of Small Bank to Stem Spate of Withdrawals."
    Asian Wall Street Journal Weekly, 15 September 1986.

Wooden, James. "Structural Changes in U.S. Banking." *Bankers Magazine* 168 (May–
    June 1985).

Work, Clemens P. "Is Bigger Better in Banking?" *U.S. News & World Report* (12
    October 1987): 52.

"World Welcomes Watchdog." *Euromoney* (June 1986): 76–94.

Wylle, Charlmers. "It Can't Be Just a Dash Here, a Dollar There. The Recipe for Banking
    Reform Has to Be Crafted Carefully." *Bottomline* (May 1986): 23.

Yeager, Leland. "Deregulation and Monetary Reform." *American Economic Review* 75
    (May 1985): 103.

Yonemura, Tsukasa. "Midway in Financial Deregulation Where 'Maru-vu' Is the Ulti-
    mate Factor." *American Banker* 151 (11 December 1986): 11.

Zweid, Phillip. "If the Ax Falls on Glass–Steagall, Here's . . . What's Next." *Financial
    World* (12 January 1988): 21.

Index

About the Author

SARKIS J. KHOURY is a Professor of Finance at the University of California, Riverside. He is the author of thirteen monographs and books, including *The Valuation and Investment Merits of Diamonds,* also from Quorum, as well as numerous articles dealing with international finance, banking, and investment.